ENGLAND'S ASHES

The ECB would like to thank all of the England players and management for making the summer of 2009 a memorable one for cricket in England and Wales.

Also by The England Cricket Team
with Peter Hayter

Ashes Victory (2005)

ENGLAND'S
ASHES

*The exclusive and official story
of the npower Ashes Series 2009*

WITH PETER HAYTER

This edition first published in Great Britain in 2009 by
Orion Books
an imprint of the Orion Publishing Group Ltd
Orion House, 5 Upper St Martin's Lane,
London WC2H 9EA
An Hachette UK Company

1 3 5 7 9 10 8 6 4 2

A CIP catalogue record for this book is available
from the British Library.

ISBN: 978 1 4091 1496 3 (hardback)

Printed and bound in the UK by CPI Mackays, Chatham ME5 8TD

The publishers would like to thank Getty Images for providing
photographs and for permission to reproduce copyright material.

The Orion Publishing Group's policy is to use papers that are natural, renewable and
recyclable and made from wood grown in sustainable forests. The logging and manu-
facturing processes are expected to
conform to the environmental regulations of the country of origin.

Every effort has been made to fulfil requirements with regard to
reproducing copyright material. The author and publisher will be
glad to rectify any omissions at the earliest opportunity.

www.orionbooks.co.uk

Contents

Introduction: interview with Andy Flower,
Team Director   1

First Test, Cardiff   17

Second Test, Lord's   71

Third Test, Edgbaston   123

Fourth Test, Headingley   161

Fifth Test, The Oval   189

The Ashes Series 2009 Statistical Record   241

Introduction

At the turn of the year, the England cricket team went through a major internal upheaval, the outcome of which was the appointment of a new captain, Andrew Strauss, to replace Kevin Pietersen, and a new director of cricket, Andy Flower, being promoted from assistant to replace Peter Moores.

After the tumult of the winter's tour to India – brutally disrupted by the terrorist attack in Mumbai – the relationship between Pietersen and Moores had broken down, and, when England were bowled out by the West Indies for 51 in the second innings of the first Test in Jamaica, the team faced an uncertain short-term future. At that stage, the prospect of the summer visit by Ricky Ponting's Australians appeared daunting.

Flower admits that when he was first approached and asked to consider standing for Moores' job, he was extremely cautious about applying.

On the evening of 23 August 2009, as dusk fell over south London, Flower found himself sitting on the outfield at The Oval with members of his management team, reflecting on the fact that they had all been part of a performance that enabled England and their supporters to experience once again what Ashes victory had felt like in 2005, and help erase the bitter taste left by a 5–0 defeat Down Under in the winter of 2006–07.

Once the champagne had been washed out, Flower sat with Peter Hayter to discuss how he, and they, had got there.

PETER HAYTER: Can I take you back to the final evening at The Oval, and this nice image I have of you guys out on the square – you, the management, watching those foxes running across the pitch? It must seem like a lifetime ago, but do you remember what thoughts were in your mind at that stage?

ANDY FLOWER: Well, I can't remember who suggested getting out there for a beer – I think we took some champagne with us actually – but it was one of the management group and we all just thought we'd get away from the noise in the changing-room and go and have a quiet moment and reflect on what had just happened. I can't remember whether there were stars or not, but we just sat on the covers and talked about the series and enjoyed each other's company.

I'd quaffed quite a lot of champagne by then. I don't remember many particulars, but it was more a feeling of satisfaction really, of not just a job well done, but of overcoming a challenge, overcoming a hurdle, because beating Australia in a five-match Test series is just a great achievement.

PH: Can I take you back to the start of the year? Obviously, there was a lot of confusion and chaos with Peter Moores going and Kevin Pietersen being removed as captain, and, when you were approached by the ECB and asked to consider the job full time, the feeling was that you were a little bit cautious about the idea, first of all.

FLOWER: Definitely. I genuinely thought long and hard about whether to take the interim coach's position, firstly because I wasn't sure if I wanted to step into Peter Moores' shoes in those circumstances. I respect the guy a lot, and he's taught me a lot and I didn't feel very comfortable about it. So I spoke to the people closest to me and initially decided that I would take the interim coach's position, and I also spoke to Peter. I said, 'Listen, this is what I'm contemplating. Does this sound wrong to you that I would then take over as interim coach?' And he said, 'No. Go for it. I'm always going to give you full support, so go for it.'

I probably expected him to say that because he's that type of bloke, but I also needed to hear it. And then, actually, in the West Indies, I took the interim coach's position with a very clear thought in my mind that I would do this job as well as I could for the two months we were in the West Indies and try to get things back on track, heal a few wounds. It was also important to win.

Obviously the other topic was, am I going to apply for the main job, the permanent one? I wanted to see how things panned out first, both with the management and with the players, because there'd been such upheaval. I wanted to see how things were gelling, and whether I thought it could work with me being in charge. So as I was doing the coach's job, I was evaluating that kind of thing as well.

PH: Events in Jamaica – the 51 all out and the defeat – can't have encouraged you to think this is a job I *must* have?

FLOWER: We were devastated by that result, but what it did was it allowed us to get into a room together in Antigua and discuss various topics properly and honestly. I chaired the meeting and the players opened up. There were only a few management people in there, or coaches, should I say, so it wasn't the usual big squad meeting, and players opened up and were very honest. Well, as honest as they get sometimes.

Generally, it's sometimes important to acknowledge frailties or weaknesses because once you've acknowledged them you can then address them and do something about them, and I think some of our players were honest enough to do that.

That enabled us to make a new start both as individuals and as a team. It allowed us to draw a line, certainly, under the 51 all out, but also some of the other crap that had gone on. We moved on and we made a new start.

I can't remember exactly when I decided to apply, but it was

3

getting very close to the closing date for applications and Hugh Morris [managing director of England Cricket] was on that tour, and he was enquiring as to whether I'd go for the job. By that time I had thought, Look, I can make a difference here; I might not get this opportunity again and I want to go for it.

PH: I presume by that stage you also felt you had a reasonable working relationship with Strauss? How important was that in your thinking?

FLOWER: It was very important because I realised that he and I could work together from probably the first time I met him, which was even before I took the interim coach's job. Before I decided to take it I got the train down to London to meet with Strauss, and chucked a few ideas around to get a feel for whether we could work together. Even from that first meeting I thought we could. The fact that I saw a future where the two of us could create a strong bond, a unified leadership, I thought that, yes, things could work here.

PH: And when you were interviewed, did they say, by the way, you haven't got to do much this year, just win the Ashes? How was that discussed and how was that thought of?

FLOWER: The ECB goals are very clearly stated and the Ashes is one of them, and another is a ranking of number one in the world. So I knew how important the Ashes was to the English public, the English cricketing public and our employers. There was no ambiguity about that. In the interview, no, it wasn't mentioned in such stark terms, but it was quite a rigorous interview. It lasted close to two hours, at the Landmark Hotel in London, and they delved into my motivation and character.

Hugh Morris was there and Gordon Lord. Angus Fraser was on the interview panel along with Dennis Amiss.

PH: So they offered you the job and now, clearly, you have certain things on the agenda. You've got a West Indies Test and a one-day series coming up in May, you've got the World Twenty20 in June, but you've also got Australia as well. How did you set about planning your Ashes campaign?

FLOWER: Well, I spoke a lot to our players to glean information about their experience and their knowledge of Australia, and obviously to include them in the future planning, but most of my conversations on this topic were with Strauss. We also got information from a few other sources: ex-coaches who had been involved in Ashes series and, obviously, you know about [former Australia coach] John Buchanan's brief involvement before the series started.

I don't really want to go into much detail. What I would say, though, is that I've got a lot of respect for John Buchanan. He's a very experienced and knowledgeable coach, and during the couple of times that I met him before the Ashes started he imparted information that was relevant and important. But never during that time did he act in a . . . it sounds a silly word to use . . . a treacherous manner.

He can always hold his head up in front of the Aussies and say that, but equally, you know, he's a professional coach and he was good to talk to about coaching and playing and general excellence. And I'd love to get some exposure to him in the future as well.

There was a dossier compiled on the Australian players by our batting coach Dene Hills, who had also been working with Australia until recently. He provided a detailed assessment of their strengths and weaknesses, but again, I'd like to say that at no time did he delve into any real personal stuff that would compromise his loyalty to Australia, as someone who'd been in their camp. It was very much restricted to a professional summation of strengths and weaknesses that any cricket coach might give. Obviously he had a better knowledge of those things than most.

PH: Anything of a Langer nature in that stuff?

FLOWER: It was more cricket-relevant than mere . . . than character assessments . . . although character assessments were in there

5

and possible weaknesses were highlighted.

PH: OK. So let me know the thoughts behind the battlefield trip to Ypres prior to the start of the Ashes series – what was the value of that?

FLOWER: The idea had first been mooted by Hugh Morris and Peter Moores when Peter was in charge, and not necessarily specifically with the Australia series in mind, but more to do with our growth generally as a group. Hugh reminded me of the original idea and said, 'Do you think there's any scope for using this?' I liked the idea straight away, and we started planning towards it.

I thought it was a good time to do it, although I knew there might be a backlash in the media for something they might see as a PR exercise, but that was the last thing I wanted it to be seen as by our players. I wanted it to be something meaningful.

You ask why we did it. I thought it was a great opportunity for our group to see something different. I believe that cricketers are a cosseted bunch, that they can live in this comfortable little world. The more we can experience life outside of this cosseted world, the better we'll be as a group of blokes, so that was basically it.

PH: Was it an idea of putting what they were doing into a wider context?

FLOWER: Yes, it was. As I said, I think we're generally spoilt as professional cricketers, and in no way were we trying to make direct parallels with what we do and life-and-death situations, but I thought that, yes, putting what we do into context would be healthy.

I also thought there are some lessons we can take from the military in terms of team-building and, on that basis, we invited four men from various branches of the army and air force, and a military historian along as well. We had some interesting conversations casually with these men, and also an interesting briefing from all of them on various aspects of what it meant to be in a 'team'.

PH: Of course, there was the situation with Andrew Flintoff and his poor timekeeping. What was your reading of all that?

FLOWER: Yeah, that was . . . look, it was unfortunate. Certainly a storm in a teacup, I reckon, but just an unwanted complication on what was a really good trip. It took a little of the gloss off it.

We came back from Ypres and went straight into the warm-up game against Warwickshire at Edgbaston in early July, and instead of us merely concentrating on cricketing matters, there was that in the background. Look, Fred was sorry for what happened and genuinely so, and it wasn't the end of the world. But equally, we do have some team rules and standards that we want the guys to stick to and he knew he hadn't quite stuck to those.

The media reaction was very aggressive. I was surprised by the almost . . . there was this desire in the media to see something happen and to see some retribution, but Strauss and I both thought, Listen, he's made a little mistake here, but it's not the end of the world and you don't drop people from a Test match for that type of error unless it's constantly repeated.

Certainly, since I have been coach and since Strauss had been captain, that was the first sort of misdemeanour, if you like, and we had said when we came in that the slate was clean, we were starting afresh and we had to back that up with our actions. So there's no way it would have been right to mete out some serious sentence on Fred for such a small matter.

PH: Obviously, Andy, the bigger picture was always going to be the Ashes, but you did have the World Twenty20 as well going on and, of course, the West Indies series. The defeat against Holland wouldn't have done a great deal for your sense of optimism, would it?

FLOWER: Yeah, that was quite a shock. We're so inconsistent in all of our cricket and that, combined with a form of the game that is quite difficult to predict, made for some ridiculous results.

Losing to Holland, but beating India and Pakistan, just shows how inconsistent we can be. It shows what we're capable of on both fronts. Unfortunately, it highlights our inconsistency and that is an area we have to address.

PH: And, of course, going into the Ashes series, that's something you're aware of. What can you do as a coach? Is there anything you can actually do to improve that, or are you just hoping for the best?

FLOWER: I don't think there's anything you can do about those types of inconsistencies in the really short term. I think they arise from – this is my personal opinion – I think those inconsistencies arise from not having drilled your basics well enough, because if the team has the basic underlying principles, if you like, to batting or bowling, and to team work, then you will have your ups and downs, there's no doubt about that, but there will be more consistency. I don't think we've nailed down our basics well enough, to be honest.

PH: And, presumably, if you do that, the graph goes up steadily. You'll win some and lose some, but the direction the graph goes is steadily up rather than a mountain range.

FLOWER: That's right, and you will pretty much eliminate things like your 51 all out or your losing to Holland, so those will become fewer and further between. That is an area we are focusing on right now.

PH: OK, now before the start of the series, in terms of selection, the major development was Bopara coming in at number three. Obviously he got the runs against the West Indies, but what were your thoughts about him going in first wicket down in such a high-profile series? Presumably you thought he could cope?

FLOWER: Look, we knew that this was a slightly risky move because, ideally, you'd want to bring in a player like Bopara probably at about five or even six in Test cricket. However, if you look at the alternatives available, there was Michael Vaughan, who was palpably out of form, Ian Bell, who we'd dropped recently in the West Indies and it was too early to bring him back, and in fact some might argue that he was brought back even too early when we did recently, so I thought we were stuck a little for alternatives. I trusted Ravi because I know him quite well from Essex. I like his confidence, and I also think he's got a very high ceiling in terms of his skill and talent.

So I thought it was a worthwhile gamble to take. He got his runs against the West Indies, and I thought he looked the part and he certainly showed that he was physically capable of playing quick bowling, but we were not yet sure about how he would cope with a sustained, accurate attack. But for me, the gamble was worth taking and I thought he handled it magnificently.

PH: Going into the first Test in Cardiff, can you recall your last message to the team before the game?

FLOWER: We knew they might have a vulnerability in the spin, and if we could deliver two spinners to their one and have pitches that were helpful to spin, we thought that was an area we could exploit. As in a last message, we were very much concentrating on our skills, and we'd made a decision about how to handle any potential distractions; we weren't replying to, or reacting to, any comments coming from the Australians. Things in the media – we didn't want to read the media. We wanted to stay away from it. We kept newspapers out of the changing-room.

So we minimised distractions, basically, and concentrated on our skills. We broke down our focus into looking at one session at a time and winning those sessions.

PH: Now, obviously, a key element of your plans were two of your major players, Flintoff and Pietersen, and by the end of the first Test there were doubts about both in terms of their fitness. What was your understanding of how they would be, physically, during the series?

FLOWER: It was a worry. To be honest, I thought Flintoff would play the first Test and that might be it for him. I didn't think his knee would handle two Tests in a row. So I had sort of prepared myself for the fact that he would play in the first Test and that would be it.

Pietersen I wasn't actually that worried about. I thought he'd muddle through the Test series. So, obviously, I got both of those completely wrong.

PH: Yes. Don't become a doctor when you quit, by the way.

FLOWER: No. With Pietersen, I could see that he was obviously being distracted by his Achilles problem. Kevin wasn't happy with the way he performed in Cardiff. He knew he'd been distracted, and he knew he probably didn't give as much to the team as he could have. He was concerned about the forthcoming Tests and whether he'd be fit enough to play a full part in them. I still thought he would muddle through and handle the pain, so he was picked for Lord's on that basis, but he struggled again at Lord's.

Flintoff was determined to play the whole series, and good on him for that, but he obviously has a terrible history of injuries and then, knowing the sort of pounding his knee and ankle would take when he inevitably bowled his allocation of overs, I just didn't think he could play two Tests in a row.

PH: And you say you were planning for life without him – what did those plans involve?

FLOWER: Well, mainly it involved the two-spinner attack, but after the first Test we re-evaluated that. They played the spin very well at Cardiff, and we weren't all that sure of Monty's form and confidence and, therefore, we had to change tack quite drastically as soon as we saw what was happening at Cardiff.

PH: So if Fred hadn't played at Lord's, what would your attack have been there? Onions for Fred, and what else would you have done?

FLOWER: To be honest, I can't recall exactly what our contingency plans were. I think there was a healthy debate between Strauss and me about whether to go with either five bowlers or six bowlers.

PH: Right. You picked Graham Onions, and I presume Harmison would also have come into your thinking if Fred was the guy to go. Would there have been discussions about a like-for-like replacement, a bang-it-in bowler, if Fred wasn't around?

FLOWER: Yeah, Harmison was always in our bowling discussions. We know what he's capable of. If we're talking about five fast bowlers in a squad, he's always in that discussion.

PH: So in fact, although Fred announcing his retirement prior to Lord's was something of a distraction, you would have just been delighted that he was able to play in the second Test?

FLOWER: Yes. I thought that was a bonus for us. I didn't think he'd make it, and my views were probably the same during that Lord's Test. I thought, There's no way he's going to make the third one.

As it happened, his bowling at Lord's was amazing. I've heard a few quotes about 'the best spell of fast bowling I've ever seen' from various commentators, and it was. Throughout that Test match he bowled superbly – accurately and with enough movement to trouble people. It was a truly great performance, I thought, because even when he wasn't taking wickets he was creating doubt in their minds.

PH: And actually you could see that it was painful as well, apart from anything else. So it was a great bowling performance from a bloke sound of wind and limb, but for a guy with only one good leg, it was extraordinary.

FLOWER: It was extraordinary, and anyone who saw it will remember it for those reasons, both for the quality and, obviously, for the fact that there's this big, heavy bloke pounding down on something that's painful, and repeating it often.

Afterwards, in the dressing-room, I talked to each player in turn and highlighted their contribution to our victory. I can't remember exactly what I said to Strauss, but it would have been something about the strength of his leadership, certainly with the bat in the first innings, but also for his strength when others might have felt doubt. He was strong and he was there for the team to lean on, if you like.

PH: Tell me about Leeds. What happened there?

FLOWER: I felt a little uneasy coming into the Leeds game, to be honest, for a couple of reasons. One of them might have been my history there with England. We'd beaten the West Indies there soundly a couple of years ago, and then we'd lost quite badly to South Africa there last year, so that was part of it.

But I also thought that our players might have been distracted by the sight of the finishing line and the constant chat in the media about Headingley being the opportunity to take the Ashes. They were just round the corner, and there was the cup – get your hands on it boys.

Just from listening to the players, I picked up some of this in their chatter, and I always think you're getting ahead of yourself if you're thinking that way because it takes an incredible amount of energy, strength and skill to win a Test match or a first-class match. If you're talking about crossing that finishing line before you've contemplated all the heartache and hard work that it takes to win matches, I think that's a dangerous place to be.

My sense was that we thought if a couple of people play brilliantly, we'd snatch victory at Headingley and everyone would be heroes. Then we had the slight distraction with Flintoff not being fit enough to play, and Matt Prior going down and having to plan in a hurried fashion to get another keeper up. Then Strauss being involved in those last-minute plans when really he should have been getting his head around facing the first ball from Hilfenhaus. And I'm not convinced that we made the right decision on the toss either, but who knows if it would have made any difference or not, but with that uncertainty, with Stuart Broad batting at seven, you know, we might have been better off bowling first in those conditions.

PH: You had a meeting at the hotel, didn't you, on the evening of the last day of the match, and people said it was an extremely productive meeting in as much as it allowed you to put Headingley to bed. What are your recollections of the meeting?

FLOWER: Well, first we had to decide what we were going to do after such a dire performance because we were disappearing back to our homes. Some guys were going to go and play a little more cricket for their counties, some were having that week off and taking a break before the Oval Test, so I thought it was dangerous to disappear around the country without getting closure on the Headingley game. So we arranged a room back at the hotel and we got back into that room and sat down, and there were probably a few similarities to the Antigua meeting. The players were honest and we discussed some of the lessons we'd learnt, and determined that next time we returned there we would not make the same mistakes again.

Anyway, we did get closure after that meeting. Everyone disappeared and resolved to get their heads right for the Oval game, and that's what we did.

PH: Was there any possibility in your mind that somebody like Ramprakash or Trescothick or Key would come into your thinking for The Oval?

FLOWER: Well, Key was a possibility because he'd started getting into some form. He had a bad start to the year and then he had quite a good end to it, but Jonathan Trott had displayed the sort of qualities we were looking for and he was bang in form as well. Look, regarding Ramprakash and Trescothick, I know the sort of media speculation that week was amazing to behold but we, as the decision-makers on selection, have a responsibility to English cricket. I respect those guys a lot, but I don't think picking one of them would have been a responsible decision.

PH: Prior to The Oval, did you say anything to the guys before the match to try to take the pressure off? Obviously the hype was building up. What sort of mood did you feel the players were in prior to the start of that match?

FLOWER: It was quite important to get the mood right for the start of the match. We knew there might be a hangover from the Headingley defeat. We knew the Aussies were cock-a-hoop. We knew people were talking about momentum and the fact that it had shifted so hugely in favour of the Australians, but we also knew we had come back from adversity a number of times in the last six months, and that if we played well we could put them under pressure. We had beaten them at Lord's. We knew they didn't have an invincible side – obviously a very good side, but a side we could beat. These were facts. So we were determined to make sure we went back to our pre-series principles, we revisited those because nothing had really changed. We decided that possible distractions like Headingley, like the selection discussions that had been going in the media in the last week, like the possibility of winning the Ashes or losing the Ashes, these distractions had to be dealt with and handled well by the players.

We also knew that to concentrate on our skills was the most important thing we could do. Yes, there would be pressures involved, the normal sporting pressures, and we had to execute those skills under pressure.

PH: Did you think you'd got enough in the first innings – 332? What were your thoughts about that?

FLOWER: I thought we were light on runs, to be honest. I thought we had made the same mistakes we had made throughout the series, of people getting in but not getting really big scores. I thought we were quite a lot of runs light.

And I was concerned about the first innings and whether they would get a lead that was going to be clearly match-defining. So when we saw the ball take a puff of dust that second morning, obviously I thought, OK, that's given us a little more hope here.

And then Broad just bowled fantastically. Talk about a match-defining innings, that was a series-defining spell.

People talk about what was important in the series, well, we bowled them out cheaply in three first innings. So if people wonder whether we deserved to win the series, on that basis we did.

After the first two Tests people were calling for Broad to be dropped. I think he might have got a bit sloppy with his preparation and Ottis Gibson [the bowling coach] took him in hand thereafter, and they focused on the very simple principle of accuracy. From that moment on he started looking like a more dangerous bowler.

His spells at Edgbaston were better than they were in the first two Tests. That kept him in the side for the fourth Test, where he got 6 in an innings at Headingley, which in turn enabled us to trust him for the last Test. Then he came good in the last Test.

PH: A little bit about Strauss now. Obviously you and he found in each other people that you could work with from the time you took over the job, but all captains have to deal with the business of having to look after their own game as well as being captain, and he seemed to be able to do that consistently. Were you able to help him with that at all?

FLOWER: I don't think he needed much help with it. I think he needed a few reminders along the way about the importance of doing exactly that. I remember John Buchanan saying to him – and I remember watching Strauss's face when John said it – that one of his challenges over the next couple of months was to make sure he was leading with the bat in hand.

It was just a one-liner from Buchanan, but it certainly woke Strauss up to the fact that he had to perform this role and compartmentalise the others. In the end he did that very well. He's a strong man, and part of that strength is being able to say, Right, I've got to concentrate on this role now, and being able to do that.

PH: OK, Andy. Key moments, things that you felt were critical or maybe changed the course of events, and maybe some final memories from the last day?

FLOWER: Obviously Collingwood, Panesar, Anderson batting in Cardiff and some of the smaller contributions around that. Flintoff batted for a long time out of character. You know, there were various contributions to the fact that we could hold on. One of the things I mused on after that Cardiff Test was all the many hours put into Panesar's and Anderson's batting. These guys are not great batsmen, but they and their coaches have put countless hours into their batting and that's the reason why, so they can do something like that. So the Cardiff Test was obviously huge. Flintoff and Strauss at Lord's. Swann's contributions throughout the series – or certainly in the two wins – and his extrovert nature when we needed a lift. I thought Trott's selection and his consequent runs under pressure, the way he handled himself in that last Test, was significant, as was sticking with Broad through the series and him backing that judgement up in the last Test to provide the defining spell.

PH: Sure, and how did you feel that last afternoon, the last half-hour or so when you knew you were going to win . . . Even for you, never one to count his chickens, that last period would have been enjoyable?

FLOWER: Yeah, look, it was great. What I really loved watching was the team take those wickets, and seeing how they celebrated the wickets and what it meant to them. I also liked watching their celebration on the podium and then the fact that they could walk around that stadium in front of the whole crowd who had stayed for the award ceremony, and thank the English public for their support and also celebrate with their families, almost like you'd involve the families after a club match.

But also while I was watching that afternoon I had certain thoughts about the future as well, and what we've got to do because yes, we've won the Ashes and we've beaten Australia, it's a very fine achievment and it's very satisfying for everyone involved. But it is only one series, and we want more than that.

First Test, Cardiff: 8–12 July

Glamorgan County Cricket Club, and their friends at the Welsh Tourist and England and Wales Cricket Boards, had left nothing to chance. From around midnight on the eve of the first Test match ever to be played there, anyone drifting within 50 miles of Cardiff by car, train, plane, bike or on foot would have had to hold very hard indeed to resist the force pulling them inexorably towards the city centre. Everywhere you looked the signs pointed to Sophia Gardens and the brand spanking new, and very blue, Swalec stadium within, their message, though expressed differently through various slogans, the same. It read, in Welsh and in English, 'This way to the 2009 Ashes.'

The hype, while perhaps not as manic as in 2005, had been just as intense, so much so that while captain Andrew Strauss, returning to the side after having sat out the World Twenty20 and now anticipating his first Ashes Test in charge, was more than happy with his side's preparation, at the back of his mind he also feared a negative response.

'I think we arrived at Cardiff, if anything, slightly overdone,' Strauss recalls.

'There weren't really any issues of selection. We knew we wanted to play two spinners because we believed the pitch would take turn.

'The only thing we were not in control of was the hype. It increased gradually at first, then, in those last couple of days, it really made us all aware of what an Ashes series is, once again. Going into that first day, while we were aware that feelings were going to be different to the feelings you'd have for a normal series; it still takes you a bit by surprise.

'In a way the atmosphere was quite similar to the first day at Lord's four years earlier. But, to a certain extent, we were all stepping into the unknown; we weren't quite sure how the wicket was going to play, it was a new venue – and when you combine that with the anthems and ceremony prior to the start of play, it just built up the anticipation.

'Certainly in the period immediately prior to the start of the match, I was as nervous as I'd been on a cricket field.'

Senior batsman Paul Collingwood, Strauss, Andrew Flintoff and Kevin Pietersen were the four survivors from the side that drew the last Test of the 2005 series at The Oval to secure Ashes victory. The Durham man had been drafted in to add to the batting strength after Simon Jones's injury at Trent Bridge, and as such earned a mouthful from Shane Warne during the 2006–07 series for his pains. 'You got an MBE last time, right?' Warne taunted him. 'What, for scoring seven and ten at The Oval?'

Whatever relief he may have felt that Warne's absence from the field would give his ears a rest, Collingwood also believed he and his team-mates were overeager. 'We allowed the pressure to get to us, and if you do that you struggle to enjoy the situation. We were desperate to get the first punch in and be ultra-positive and, maybe, the adrenalin was flowing too freely.'

> '**Certainly in the period immediately prior to the start of the match, I was as nervous as I'd been on a cricket field**'
>
> *Andrew Strauss*

England's tactical plan was straightforward. Pick two spinners in a five-man attack – for the first time in a home Ashes Test since 1993 – bat first, make a sizeable total and put the Australian batsmen under increasing pressure on a deteriorating track through a combination of Graeme Swann and Monty Panesar. But it could only work if England batted first and to bat first, they had to win the toss of a coin, specially minted by Test sponsors npower for the occasion. No fifty-pence piece, this: it had neither 'head' nor 'tail', but a batsman on one side and the word 'npower' on the other.

Strauss recalls: 'It was a toss we desperately wanted to win. In fact, as we were lining up, I said to our mascot, "If you believe strongly enough we're going to win the toss, we will win it."'

Sahibaa Ali, a 15-year-old kidney patient awaiting a transplant, told the England captain: 'I will.'

'Ricky Ponting and I had agreed beforehand that, as the batsman had a head on him, his side would be "heads",' Strauss explains.

'So I tossed, he called "heads" and he called wrong. The coin came straight down flat, no landing on its side, rolling or anything.'

Intriguingly, television pictures showed Strauss, Sky's Mike Atherton, Sahibaa and ICC match referee Jeff Crowe all intently following the coin's parabola, with Ponting, baggy green cap pulled on tight, staring down at the landing area. It was unclear whether his eyes were open or shut.

Strauss told Atherton: 'We're going to have a bat. Monty and Graeme are in. We think it might spin at the back end, but we've still got to set the match up well.' Ponting explained that, in the absence of the injured Brett Lee, he would be relying on the three-man pace attack of Mitchell Johnson, Ben Hilfenhaus and Peter Siddle that had served Australia so well in the recent Test victory over South Africa, so no place for Stuart Clark, Australia's most prolific bowler in the 5–0 home win two years earlier with 26 wickets. Indeed, the selection of Hilfenhaus meant they went into the series with an attack that had not bowled a single ball in Ashes cricket between them. Nathan Hauritz, treated roughly by county batsmen in the warm-up matches, would provide their spin option.

Speaking the weekend before the biggest match of his captaincy so far, Strauss responded to questions regarding his assessment of the current Australian side by saying: 'When you look at the Australians of two years ago, their side possessed some of the legends of the game, certainly of our generation, and probably in the case of Warne and McGrath, of all time.

'That's a huge loss for any side to bear. The Australian system always produces good players, but in terms of experience those guys had, as well as their wicket-taking deliveries, their ability to score runs, their presence on the park, at the moment their replacements don't have that aura about them.'

Strauss would have been further buoyed that the man regarded universally as his trump card, not to mention the one marked 'Get Out of Jail Free', was at last fully fit for action. Furthermore, Andrew Flintoff was also ready.

'With very few exceptions, any sportsman who says they don't have a fear of failure is a liar,' says Flintoff. 'I care if I don't perform, not just for myself, but because I feel I am letting other people down as well. What's more, I've never been very good at hiding my emotions.

'Looking back at what happened in the first Test four years earlier, and even in Australia the last time, I let all those feelings get on top of me. I just wasn't myself at Lord's back in 2005. It was my first Ashes Test, the hype had been building up for so long and the magnitude of the occasion got to me. I was worrying about what everyone was thinking of me, of what everyone expected of me. Everyone was saying, "To win the Ashes we need Fred to do this, we need Fred to do that," and I let myself get sucked in.

'Normally I get a few butterflies, but this was different. I became insular, introverted. When we bowled and I got the wicket of Adam Gilchrist, something very weird happened inside me. I looked at the photos afterwards and I just didn't recognise myself. I saw this look of pure aggression on my face, with my eyes popping. It was almost like I was possessed. It was scary.

'Then, when I was waiting to bat, I just sat in my chair in silence.

That's not me. Normally I'm buzzing about, out on the balcony clapping every run.

'I was reaching for everything, clutching. I was thinking to myself, I've got to get into the game here. I've got to score runs. I've got to take wickets. I've got to take catches. And I was acutely aware of comments from the crowd. I was focusing on all the wrong things. I was so tense and, as the match went on and our good start turned into a defeat, I just felt myself getting smaller and smaller.

'It wasn't until afterwards I realised I had put so much pressure on myself that I hadn't given myself a hope of performing naturally and, therefore, at my best. I sorted it out after that, and from the second Test onwards, at Edgbaston, things improved.

'Though we were all nervous, this time the energy was all positive. My attitude was, after all I've been through, including those times back in 2007 when I really feared I may have to quit and find something else to do with my life, if I didn't go out there and make sure I tried to enjoy playing in an Ashes series, what would be the point?'

And if it did all come right in the weeks ahead?

'There's no doubt about it,' he insists. 'While I don't think the feelings we had in 2005 could ever be replicated, Trafalgar Square and all that, because of what I'd gone through since then, if I could play a major part in us winning this time, I felt that would be more of an achievement and something I'd have even more pride about.

'We had a new team on this occasion, and while there was no Shane Warne or Glenn McGrath or Matthew Hayden, Justin Langer or Adam Gilchrist, Australia are still Australia and the Ashes are still the Ashes. It's what I've kept going for.'

After the toss there was still the small matter of around a thousand national anthems to get through, made more bearable for the eager players by the prospect of their being sung by the delectable Katherine Jenkins – in a fiery Welsh red dress that caused such consternation in the BBC *Test Match Special* box that Jonathan Agnew was forced to go for a long lie-down – and, of course, 'Jerusalem', sung by 'England's Tenor' Sean Ruane, with the same gusto he gave it all round Trafalgar Square that glorious September afternoon in 2005.

Thus Test cricket came to Cardiff, its 100th home, accompanied by the Welsh Guards, a range of celebrity warblers and a giant red carpet laid out in the Cross of St George, all quite a contrast, one would assume, to the more humble beginnings at Sheffield's Bramall lane, the last 'new' Ashes venue, way back in 1902.

And finally, the beginning.

CARDIFF, DAY ONE: ENGLAND 336 FOR 7

Such had been the dramatic effect of the opening few deliveries of the two previous Ashes series that the first ball of 2009 was a hotly anticipated event in itself. Steve Harmison will remember roughing up Justin Langer at Lord's in 2005 for as long as he lives, and his double wide in Brisbane in 2006 for longer than he cares to. So the opening action came, when it finally did after what seemed like several lifetimes, as something of an anti-climax.

The stage was set, the outfield a lush green, the house full – 16,000 – and Australia's new pace sensation Mitchell Johnson, ball in hand, ready to tear into England captain Strauss and Alastair Cook, who were about to embark on their 55th opening partnership for England, more than any other pairing.

Safe to say that, at least in comparison with recent history, this opening over was memorable for being unmemorable. The first couple of deliveries were comfortably allowed to pass outside the off stump and both openers were off the mark by its end. But at least now the talking had stopped, a feeling shared by Cook in particular.

Cook says: 'From my point of view, the build-up was so long. I didn't play for England after the Test series against the West Indies, just for Essex, and then you get the trailer on Sky Sports News and you see it's 83 days to go to the Ashes and you think, Yeah, that's bloody miles away, and then, subconsciously, it must have an effect. I think maybe a few people at home would have noticed that, a few days before meeting up, I might have gone a bit quiet. Once I'd got into batting I was better, but overall I don't think I handled the pressure very well. To be honest, I didn't particularly enjoy it. It just seemed like such hard work.'

Harder for him, when, from nowhere, at 21 for 0, he fell to Michael Hussey's brilliant flying catch in the gully off Hilfenhaus.

Next over, Ashes debutant Ravi Bopara, on 0, misjudged the low bounce of a ball from Siddle that followed him until it hit him in the throat. He wore another in the bowler's next over when, still not off the mark, an inside edge thudded into his thigh. Bopara had entered this series on the back of three consecutive Test hundreds against the West Indies, but this was an examination of a far greater magnitude. England's new number 3 got off the mark with a snick past the stumps for four. Nevertheless, although he mixed some sublime strokes with others more likely to make English hearts skip a beat for different reasons, he and Strauss looked set to build a sizeable partnership.

Then, one-and-a-half hours into the series, with England on a comfortable-sounding 63 for 1, Johnson sent down the 20th, and arguably the best, over of the entire match. The Queenslander's formidable displays in South Africa earlier in the year meant he had arrived on British shores with some reputation to live up to. This burst suggested he was more than capable of doing so.

The third delivery, a yorker, snaked under Strauss's bat and rapped the England captain around the ankle, but umpire Billy Doctrove adjudged the ball to be missing leg stump. Bopara was then hit on the shoulder by the next delivery, before enjoying a narrow escape of his own, induced by a slower ball which was uncertainly lifted over mid-off for three. When Johnson produced a 92.6mph thunderbolt short ball next up, Strauss had nowhere to go and the ball ballooned to first slip. England were 67 for 2.

By lunch, the over after Bopara had fallen after failing to spot a second – 79mph – slower ball from Johnson and spooning it to Phillip Hughes at point, they were struggling at 97 for 3.

Strauss recalls: 'To be three down at lunch was not a great effort. I got done partly because the ball didn't bounce as much as I thought it would and partly because really it was the last ball I was expecting them to bowl, to be honest. I thought he was trying to bowl full and straight at me.

'When Ravi came out to bat I said to him, "There's no demons in the pitch. Just enjoy it." But it's an Ashes series, there's nowhere to hide, so any kind of nerves you have or any weakness you show might be exposed at some stage and, to me, he looked a little bit more nervous than I'd seen him before. It's a shame he got out when he did, because I think he was just starting to play his game.'

Bopara, whose 35 on his Ashes debut contained six fours, saw things a tad differently. 'People commented that I looked nervous,' he said, 'that maybe I played so many shots and scored at such a rate because I was too pumped and "searching" too hard. I certainly didn't feel too nervous. Nor do I believe the atmosphere affected me at all, despite the massive build-up and all the hype, which seemed to have been going on for a year.

'In reality, once you are out there playing you are aware of very little else but what is going on around you. The biggest noise I heard came from tapping my bat on the ground.

'When that second ball from Peter Siddle nipped back at me and thumped into my throat, it actually woke me up a bit, which was just what I needed.

'And I played so many strokes because that was the way I saw the bowling. There were a lot of indifferent deliveries; none of their guys really settled into a length or a channel, bowling either really full or short, and that gave me several scoring opportunities.

'What did surprise me was the quality of Mitchell Johnson's slower ball, which did me not once but twice. We knew he had it in his armoury, but I had never actually come across it before and from where I was standing there was no discernible change of pace or action, just a suggestion of him cutting his fingers across the seam as he released the ball. I got away with the first one, just, but the second one caused a horrible slow death. At least the ball was in the air long enough for me to remind myself that if he bowled it again I needed to make sure I've got all of the ball before going through with the shot.'

Two generations of Australians grew up believing that the word 'Englandmiddleordercollapse' was one of the longest in the dictionary. Pietersen and Paul Collingwood, whose last act before lunch was to demonstrate just how slow the Cardiff pitch was when his attempted pull to deep backward square ended up dribbling through midwicket off the toe of the bat, spent the break endeavouring to close their minds to any such notion.

England were desperate for a partnership, and the time had come for all-out aggression to be replaced by calm accumulation. The pair delivered, matching each other run for run and shot for shot, albeit in their completely different styles. Already England's most productive fourth-wicket pair in Tests, they also became the most successful against Australia in an afternoon session during which they doubled England's lunch score, crucially, with no further loss of wickets.

> 'What did surprise me was the quality of Mitchell Johnson's slower ball, which did me not once but twice'
>
> *Ravi Bopara*

Collingwood reflected: 'At the point we came together the innings could have gone either way. Had we been bowled out for 290-ish all the momentum would have been with Australia. We just concentrated on consolidation.'

For Pietersen, Collingwood was the ideal partner for the job ahead: 'We complement each other,' said Pietersen. 'Our difference in height and styles means bowlers have to vary their lengths when we are batting together, and that gives us so many scoring options. Our goal was simple; to bat for as long as we could.'

Australia had clearly been planning for Pietersen; they had nominated him in advance as the key to England's batting and, little by little, had stepped up the psychological pressure by reminding anyone prepared to listen of a couple of the batsman's nicknames. 'The Ego' was the favourite of Pietersen's former Hampshire team-mate and Ashes opponent Shane Warne, while many of their number particularly liked 'FIGJAM' or 'Flip I'm Good, Just Ask Me' – or thereabouts.

Ricky Ponting made no effort to hide how they believed his bowlers would get Pietersen out (overlooking the customary 'Red Bull' run to get off the mark, of course). They bowled full and straight, looking to exploit his tendency to play across the line with a big backlift, no doubt having spotted his susceptibility against such deliveries from West Indies pace pair Jerome Taylor and Fidel Edwards during the countries' two series in 2009.

Pietersen held firm, though many in the crowd were surprised he did not use his feet to the off-spinner Hauritz as various county players had done. As yet the real reason he did not was unknown to everyone but him, though the more eagle-eyed among England's supporters had started to see things which made them hope their eyes were deceiving them.

All England supporters knew 'KP' had come into the series carrying a huge burden of expectation as the wicket Australia prized above all others. What most didn't know was that he was also

ABOVE: England fans show their support during the first day of the 2009 Ashes series at the SWALEC Stadium in Cardiff after the Welsh authorities defended their right to host the opening test on 8 July 2009.

RIGHT: Kevin Pietersen's first-innings dismissal brought howls of criticism . . .

. . . but senior batsmen Collingwood, Pietersen, Strauss and Flintoff score 200 between them in the first innings at Sophia Gardens.

ABOVE: A glimmer of hope on the third day in Cardiff as Broad bowls Michael Clarke for 83. BELOW: Monty Panesar and James Anderson congratulate each other as their heroic last stand secures a draw for England in the first Test.

A cloudy start to the second Test at Lord's.

England captain Strauss celebrates his century on the first day at the home of cricket – his first Ashes Test match as captain at Lord's. He goes on to score 161, laying a strong platform for his side.

England's opening pair Strauss and Cook reached 50 after just 49 minutes, and went on to make 196 for the first wicket.

RIGHT: Bowlers Broad, Anderson and Swann, all celebrate taking wickets – three, four and four respectively.

BELOW: Freddie in action. 'When Fred bowls like this, when he is in this mood and when his body can stand it there is simply no question about it – he is the best bowler in the world,' Kevin Pietersen.

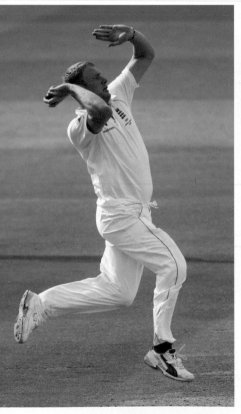

England triumph and congratulate Freddie on his accession to the honours board, taking five wickets for 92 at Lord's.

carrying the knowledge that the injuries to his Achilles tendon and his back that both he and the ECB medical staff believed had been successfully managed could flare up again at any time.

In the event it took a matter of a few deliveries for the worst possible news to dawn on England's gun batsman. There was no single, specific moment of truth, no split second when he over-reached or slipped or got hit, but he was already in considerable pain before he had reached double figures, and soon what started as the suggestion of a limp became a certainty. All of which told him he was in real trouble.

'I had never been so edgy before a series for the simple reason that with the Achilles the way it was there was a chance I wasn't going to be able to deliver my best. Everything had been about managing the injuries to make sure I was fit for the Ashes, physically and mentally. I'd had painkilling injections, cortisone and pills and overall my rehab had gone really well. For the two weeks before Cardiff I had been absolutely fine.

'Then, on day one of the biggest series of all, it just flared up again. Maybe it was the pressure, the intensity of what we were doing and then the release of starting the series. All I knew for certain was the pain, which grew and grew. Finally, every time I took a step it felt like someone was stabbing my Achilles with a long, thick needle.

'Batting became hard work, knowing that I wasn't going to be able to run at Hauritz. I wasn't going to be able to dominate the bowling. I wasn't going to be able to play my game. It was so disappointing.'

Yet, though by now clearly hampered, Pietersen's partnership with Collingwood was slowly but surely pulling England clear of danger. Pietersen became the fifth-fastest England batsman to reach 1,000 Ashes runs – including a 21-over spell without a boundary. Although he did not call for acting physio Steve McCaig, it was obvious to all in the England dressing-room that the injury was worse than England had dared to dread. In the circumstances, it was a minor miracle Pietersen was able to play at least some of his trademark shots. But there was more pain coming his way, this time in the ear region.

The partnership that held England together ended at 228 for 4 when Collingwood edged Hilfenhaus to Brad Haddin, who went for the ball in front of first slip and held on with both hands.

Then, at 241 in the 71st over, Pietersen reached wide outside off stump – and wider and wider as the bowler saw him coming – to paddle Hauritz over his shoulder into the vacant area behind square leg. In the end he did well to reach the ball; less well to deflect it onto his helmet and, according to his critics, the resulting ballooned catch to Simon Katich at short leg was worthy of all available barrels.

Geoff Boycott was at the forefront of the barrage of criticism. 'Pietersen is like a spoilt child, the family favourite who can get away with anything because he is the golden boy,' fumed the Yorkshireman. 'Until someone takes the trouble to discipline him, he will keep making the same stupid mistakes over and over again.'

Unsurprisingly, Pietersen and his team-mates took a different view. According to Strauss: 'I just never understand when people criticise him for playing shots like that. If you look at it rationally, even though it was a wide shot with no fielder at 45 degrees on the legside, it's very, very hard to get out for that ball. A top edge would usually just sail over his head and then you get two runs for it, so the odds were massively in his favour. To be honest with you, I think a lot of the criticism that KP's received recently has been far over the top and I think there's a malicious intent there since the captaincy issue, which has made life difficult for him. I think some people have been very keen to knock him down, and I thought this was another occasion.'

Collingwood said: 'We're all fantastic balcony players, aren't we? Sitting there saying, "What the hell did he play that for? He was going so well!" KP brings you that X factor and can play those ridiculous innings under extreme pressure, just like he did in 2005, because of the approach that he has, and you've got to allow that to breathe and accept he will make mistakes along the way. He goes for shots that other people won't go for. It's not a major issue.'

Pietersen recalls: 'It's really simple. Hauritz chucked it wider deliberately because he knew I was going to sweep, so fair play to him. But the shot was on. I'd been doing it the whole day. I swept probably 10, 15 runs down and spinners absolutely hate it when you sweep them off a good length. I did it loads to Warne in 2006–07 and he hated it.

'Maybe, in hindsight, if that ball was bowled to me again, I'd just leave it alone. So that makes it sound like it was a shot I probably shouldn't have played, but when you bat and you bat for such a long time – I'd faced 150 balls – you play shots occasionally which sometimes you get away with, sometimes you don't get away with. If that hadn't clipped my helmet it would have gone down to fine leg for one run, I would have been on 70 and I could have got a big score. I didn't think it was a risky shot at all.'

For England, the rest of the session reminded onlookers of two things: that Matt Prior was, by a margin, the best batsman of the wicketkeepers available in the country and that Andrew Flintoff rarely looks as good as he does against the Australians. Prior was the silkiest batsmen of the three to pass 50 on the opening day, while Flintoff rekindled memories of his batting in the 2005 series with booming back-foot boundaries either side of the wicket. It was a sight for sore eyes.

Former skipper Nasser Hussain called the England all-rounder's 37: 'The best innings I have seen from Andrew Flintoff for four years. If he goes about every innings like that for the rest of the series then he will score lots of runs and at a speed which gives England time to get wickets.'

'Maybe, in hindsight, if that ball was bowled to me again, I'd just leave it alone. So that makes it sound like it was a shot I probably shouldn't have played, but when you bat and you bat for such a long time – I'd faced 150 balls – you play shots occasionally which sometimes you get away with, sometimes you don't get away with . . . I didn't think it was a risky shot at all'

Kevin Pietersen

As well as registering a heartfelt apology for his poor timekeeping on England's battlefield trip to Belgium, Flintoff had vowed to produce a performance with bat as well as ball to render his misdemeanour a distant memory. And he was sure he was fully fit after all the ankle problems that had dogged him since before he had stirred the nation in 2005, he was ready to take out four years of frustration, of rehab, of constant uncertainty over whether he would be able to perform at his best again and of the fear that his best days were behind him, and take out his dismay at what had happened Down Under in 2006–07, with bat as well as with ball. And he was sure the recent work he had done with former England coach Peter Moores at Lancashire was about to pay off.

'With my bowling, I'm not bothered where my arms and legs go,' says Flintoff. ' I just concentrate on trying to get the ball down the other end as quick as possible, and I realised I had to take that mentality to my batting. So, instead of trying to play perfect shots, I'd gone back to "see the ball, hit the ball". And it feels so natural again. I did feel there was something special round the corner.'

Yet, although runs flowed against the second new ball, in time-honoured fashion, Australia soon hit back, with Peter Siddle bowling both Flintoff and Prior in his final two overs.

The full weight of what was about to be dumped on Pietersen would not occur until the papers arrived the following morning. For now, he had other things to occupy his thoughts, starting with a trip to hospital.

'It's a sinking feeling when you've done all the rehab, you know what you want to be able to do and then suddenly your body says no. Mentally that really really hurt me. My wife Jess and I went to the local hospital. Our team doctor Nick Peirce was with me and I knew I just had to get something done. I sort of hobbled into the hospital and they injected me with an epidural.'

Strauss ended the first day of the series with mixed feelings. The total (336 for 7) was not disastrous, and Fred's batting had given cause for real optimism that he wasn't far off his best form. But the fitness of his star batsman was a worry and, just as concerning, apart from Pietersen's partnership with Collingwood, his side's batting had been just a touch frenetic.

'Maybe we had been over-aggressive,' Strauss admitted. 'We had stressed that, as a team, we had to be really up for the fight and stand up to Australia and go at them. But if you keep a dog on a leash for too long and then let him go, he flies off and runs everywhere, and maybe the way we ended up playing reflected that.

'One of the things we were quite keen to stress in the build-up was that when we get the opportunity to get on top of them we've got to take it, but we've also got to play a situation well. So that doesn't mean blind aggression all the time. Maybe, I think, we got that a little bit wrong on that first day.

'I certainly had a feeling that whatever it was, 336 for 7 wasn't necessarily a great effort on that wicket.'

CARDIFF, DAY TWO: ENGLAND 435; AUSTRALIA 249 FOR 1

Reading between the lines was not necessary on the morning of the second day of the first Test. The papers, radio, television and all the world's websites agreed. Depending on your personal taste, Pietersen's shot was ill-timed, arrogant, reckless, mad, or all of the above.

Swann recalls: 'The press went to town, but we never looked at it and went, "Ah, Kev, what have you done?" It was just a wicket that's fallen. It didn't seem like the huge deal the press made of it the next day, but maybe that was because we'd lost seven wickets and seemed to have lost the initiative a little bit. Maybe the press reaction was more about, "Right, we need a scapegoat, and who better than KP?"'

Pietersen admits the coverage didn't help his sense of well-being. 'You've got to try your hardest to brush it aside. This year has been really tough for me. What happened at the start of 2009 through to this moment, this has been the toughest year, mentally, I've ever experienced.

'Some of the comments that come your way are made with good intentions, some people will have a go just for the sake of it and, to some, I can't do right for doing wrong. So I've actually told a lot of my family and friends that if there's anything critical in the papers and stuff, please don't text me about it. I'd rather not know.'

What hurt Pietersen more was the knowledge that all his hopes of playing a full, unhampered part in trying to regain the Ashes were close to being dashed after one day's play.

I was really down in the dumps, so much so that during the match I sat in the corner of the dressing-room like a silent little child.'

Dr Nick Peirce, whose medical team had made sure Pietersen and Flintoff were ready for action at Cardiff, recaps: 'Kevin's case was complicated in as much as he had two problems. He had a lower-back problem and he had an Achilles problem. He had some physio throughout the West Indies tour, but by the time he got back to England his back was pretty much back to normal, and then he had a back flare during the World Twenty20. The reason he missed the Holland game was not because of his Achilles, but because he suddenly developed acute sciatic-like discomfort down his leg, and he ended up having a form of epidural to calm the nerve down. The pain went away and he was able to play through the rest of the World Twenty20 with no problems. But that day in Cardiff, when his Achilles suddenly flared again, he was finding it difficult to contribute as much as he would like in the field and, of course, running between the wickets was more and more uncomfortable. We were aware that it was having a negative effect in a number of ways. He was having to find his runs in different ways. In retrospect, I don't think we can say there was one particular key moment, we just know his Achilles wasn't up to the intensity of what he was asking it to do.

'If you keep a dog on a leash for too long then let him go, he flies off and runs everywhere, and maybe the way that we ended up playing reflected that'

Andrew Strauss on England's first-day batting

'He was taking regular painkillers and analgesia to try to push him through, and we managed it with a number of different strapping techniques, but every time he planted his foot, stretched it one way or another, there was just a very sharp nerve pain. He made it through the Test match and, of course, he was happy with the draw and everything else, but he was aware that he wasn't right.'

'The next day there was some improvement,' Pietersen recalls. 'I asked Strauss if I could field in the gully, and I was just trying to stay out there for as long as I could, but, from then on, I just wasn't myself. I wasn't up for a fight at all.'

On the field, England's mood improved quickly. As Strauss knew, the overnight score was serviceable, but possibly below par, and England needed all the runs they could muster to put Australia under pressure, no matter how they came. And how they came . . .

The decision to send out James Anderson as nightwatchman on the first evening had been met with derision, given that he was protecting numbers 9 and 10, but Swann played like a senior pro as England created havoc in little over one hour. Rarely can an Australia captain have witnessed his first-choice attack being put to the sword so mercilessly by two England tail-enders. No wonder Ricky Ponting was giving it the full teapot as England played with a freedom that reduced the Australians to a rabble.

Swann arrived at the crease following Stuart Broad's demise with the hosts 355 for 8, and his ninth-wicket alliance with Anderson, of 68 runs in just nine overs, included three consecutive boundaries off Nathan Hauritz, the last from a reverse sweep that clearly got Kevin Pietersen's seal of approval on the balcony.

Swann quite liked it, too: 'In the morning Andy Flower had said to me and Broady, you've got a very important role now, saying you're both positive players, we could really get the momentum back here. I didn't have a set plan that I was going to go out and tee-off. I just went out thinking in the same sort of vein as I did against the West Indies at Lord's; if it's anywhere near to me to have a drive at, I'm not going to pussyfoot into it, I'm going to throw my hands at it and if it's short I'm going to have a flap at it. And I remember, probably only my fifth or sixth ball . . . I remember flipping Johnson over midwicket off the front foot, and it was complete instinct. I just saw the ball and hit it and it went for three on the big boundaries. As I reached the far end I thought to myself, What made me do that? But then I thought it was going to be one of those days. If I can do that, I can play any shot!

'I remember I tried to block one that went through the slips for four along the ground, and then I drove one through point and Johnson just looked at me and said, "How f***ing lucky are you, mate?" And I smiled and thought, Well, hopefully very lucky because I'm about to have a go at you. And then I was up to 20 and then, before I knew it, Hauritz came on and obviously straight away I was thinking, right, short straight boundaries, I'm going to have a go. I hit one wide of long-on, the next ball hit it straight back over his head and by that point the Barmy Army were cheering and screaming and you could sense the Aussies getting a little bit ragged.

'As for the reverse sweep, a year or so ago my coach at Notts, Mick Newell, banned the shot because so many people were getting out trying it. Being a shade anti-authoritarian I argued the point that if I practised it and played it well enough, and it's one of my shots against spinners, you can't possibly ban it. And he said, No, no, you're never allowed to play it. So from then on, every time I batted against a spinner, and almost in the worst situations possible, nine down, saving the game, I'd play this reverse sweep. I got away with it so often that in the end he buckled and said, "OK, play your reverse sweep, but if you ever get out to it again, you'll have me to deal with."'

'As Hauritz was running up to bowl, I just thought I'll get the reverse sweep out. The next thing I knew I'd gone round and smacked it and it went for four again. I was determined to enjoy it, and once I get going I haven't really got a brake, it's just foot to the floor until the engine blows up.'

Swann's lofted drive off Hilfenhaus, pitching millimetres from the rope in front of the River Taff End sightscreen, was possibly the shot of the innings, which ended at 435 after 106.5 overs, leaving

England with a chance to get into the Australians before lunch on day two. Sadly for them, England's bowlers once again failed to curb their enthusiasm.

Middlesex had been castigated for granting Australia's new batting star Phillip Hughes a two-month contract at the start of the 2009 summer that many saw as a glorified net for the Ashes. Those that had bowled to him during a rich run glut spoke of an ungainly, yet uncompromising, technique.

Steve Harmison had done his bit to redress the balance with two snorting short balls to claim his scalp in Australia's contest with England Lions at Worcester the previous week, yet, in truth, England now bowled poorly at the left-hander, offering him too much width and bowling too much short stuff.

Stuart Broad accepts England got their plans wrong, though he dismisses nerves as a factor: 'What I'd done in practice for the first two days, when I was warming up, was that I was actually putting myself in that position and thinking, right, this is game time and this is the way I'm going to try and bowl the first ball of my first spell. So when I got there, I felt like I'd done it four or five times anyway and didn't feel particularly nervous.

'As Hauritz was running up to bowl, I just thought I'll get the reverse sweep out. The next thing I knew I'd gone round and smacked it and it went for four again. I was determined to enjoy it, and once I get going I haven't really got a brake, it's just foot to the floor until the engine blows up'

Graeme Swann

'The plan was to try and go very heavy at them. In hindsight, the pace of the wicket probably didn't allow us to do that. We should have adjusted to the wicket a bit quicker, but I don't think I was a hundred per cent prepared for how straight we had to bowl at Hughes. As the series progressed, it became clear that you were better off being down the legside [to him] than a foot outside off stump.'

With his opening attack of Broad and Anderson blunted, Strauss gave Swann a chance to ride the momentum his batting had created. That didn't work either.

According to Swann: 'Straussy threw me the ball for a couple of overs before lunch and I just couldn't grip the thing. It was new, but I also had a big cut on my finger. I had tried putting superglue on it, but I couldn't really feel the ball properly in my hand. So the first couple of balls didn't come out as well as I wanted and, unfortunately for me, that was the way it went for the rest of the innings.'

In the event, it took the intervention of you-know-who to lift both England's spirits and the crowd's mood.

One of the unmistakable sounds of 2005 was that which preceded a spell of bowling by Freddie. All over England, from Lord's to The Oval, the energy behind the roar that greeted the sight of him peeling off his sweater or simply being handed the ball could have powered a small market town for a month. Now it was the turn of the Welsh to give their version of the Freddie roar.

'One of the great things about having Fred on the field is how the crowd respond to him. It doesn't matter whether you've played fifty Ashes Tests or none, opposing batsmen can simply be spooked,' says Strauss.

Hughes, playing in his first, was about to understand the phenomenon. Each of Flintoff's opening six deliveries were thunderbolts timed at speeds in excess of 90mph, and his angle from around the wicket cramped Hughes for room. The second ball left

Hughes ducking and on his knees. To the beat of 'Freddie, Freddie, Freddie', Australia's bright young thing was being led a merry dance. In his next over, England's talismanic all-rounder just failed to hold onto a caught-and-bowled chance offered by Simon Katich's drive. Flintoff opened his bowling account for the 2009 Ashes with two consecutive maidens of power, purpose and intensity and, in the circumstances, the Australian openers did well to survive as long as they did. Finally, however, half an hour after lunch, in Flintoff's fourth over of the session, and 15th of the innings, Hughes succumbed to one that nipped back to take the inside edge, well caught by Matt Prior to reduce Australia to 60 for 1.

Ricky Ponting's painful memories of defeat in 2005 had been one of the motivating forces driving his team to a whitewash in the 2006–07 series. His demeanour as he approached the crease and while he occupied it suggested that even though that revenge had been sweet, it was not complete.

Although he survived a raucous leg before shout off Stuart Broad from his first ball, after being struck borderline off stump, his feet were soon moving like a lightweight boxer back and forth across his skipping rope. By tea he had 44 and was on the way to becoming only the fourth man in history – behind Sachin Tendulkar, Brian Lara and Allan Border – to pass 11,000 Test runs. At the other end, Katich was unrecognisable from the young batsman who had been bamboozled by reverse swing in the last series in England.

But though focusing intently on his own business, he noticed that when his skipper reached his fifty from 71 balls just after tea, his bare acknowledgement of the fact indicated that a half-century did not even come close to what he had in mind. 'You can tell by the way he is going about his business,' said Katich. 'He doesn't have to say much. Those of us who went through what we did four years ago know how much it hurt.'

The quality of the surface had already been put into context as Australia's second-wicket duo began the final session on 142, and the nearest England came to stopping the first two hundreds of the series came at 154 for 1 when Swann appeared to have Katich plumb in front on 56, only for umpire Billy Doctrove to disagree. The pair ended the day in the best possible fashion, with Katich celebrating his first Ashes hundred three overs before the close and Ponting – after dwelling for a couple of moments in the nervous 90s with an uppish drive and an on-off single or two – scampering through to his eighth and, staggeringly, his 38th three-figure score in Test cricket, during the final over of the day.

Worse for England, far worse as it turned out, was that Flintoff was starting to feel some discomfort in his right knee. At 179 for 1 Ponting had rocked back to cut Swann through the covers. Flintoff was cheered every stride of his wholehearted chase to the line and the noise reached a crescendo when he dived full length to pull the ball back from the rope by inches. The heaviness of his fall caused a flicker of concern, but it disappeared just as quickly when he rose, ran back, picked the ball up and threw it in, after gesturing that he could have done with someone backing him up to collect it and do some of the work for him.

Unbeknown to Fred, his team-mates or a single soul in the ground, the consequences of this moment would be huge.

According to Nick Peirce: 'Fred came into that first Test at Cardiff completely fit and clear. He had torn a meniscus in his right knee while out in the IPL on 21 April; he came back and had an operation on the 27th, and we had a six- to eight-week timescale for his rehab to prepare him for the Ashes because we didn't want to push the internal architecture of the knee joint, the wear and tear aspect, too far. The operation was done by Andy Williams, the country's leading knee surgeon, and we really couldn't have had better care for him. We named him in the World Twenty20 squad on a technicality, though the idea that he was going to be fit for it was a possibility.

'He played two four-day games for Lancashire, then for England against Warwickshire and we really had no issues with him at all. He's been absolutely fine. His knee was good. There was no swelling. He was strong. He was doing lots of training. He was training twice a day, three times a day, supervised through Lancashire by his long-term friend and physio, Dave Roberts.

'So by the time he got to Cardiff he was in good form, in a good shape mentally and physically for the cricket – he was absolutely ready to go. Then we feel that there was a moment on the boundary when he dived to pull the ball back in and then picked it up and threw it in, when he landed on his left leg and then braked with his right leg, it hyperextended it and he sustained another injury to that knee.

'At the time, he didn't really notice it in the same way as he had done with the meniscus, and it was probably the fact that he then carried on and bowled another 30-odd overs that could have caused the swelling and discomfort around the knee. What he had was a lot of soft-tissue swelling.

'We didn't know it at the time, but we think that was the incident that set it off.'

CARDIFF, DAY THREE: AUSTRALIA 479 FOR 5

In the recent past, due to the presence of a Victorian nicknamed 'Hollywood' (i.e. Shane Warne), the idea of England planning to turn an Ashes Test into a trial by spin would have been followed by the arrival of men carrying some calming medication. At the International Cricket Council's annual awards ceremony the previous September, ECB chairman Giles Clarke had playfully goaded Ponting: 'It will be different this time, Ricky. No Shane Warne.' But so untroubled had Ponting been so far by Swann and Panesar, that by the start of the third day England were already counting down the overs before they could put plan B into operation, namely reverting to the fast men with the new ball.

Swann is brutally frank: 'I'd been struggling since ball one. Bowling full tosses wasn't in my strategy at all and, as time wore on, I don't think anyone would have been happy with the way Monty and I bowled.

'There was a lot of talk before the game about how the spinners were going to win this match, which created a bit of extra pressure. I think some people got very excited when it turned for a one-day game two-and-a-half months before, which seemed a bit premature. Then again, they tended to ignore the stats that showed, in first-class cricket until that point, that spinners had only taken something like 10 per cent or 6 per cent of the wickets.

'If there's no pace in the wicket, it can turn all you like, but a batsman knows if he doesn't want to play shots, he doesn't get out.'

Monty concurs: 'There wasn't much pace or bounce, and it just made it very difficult to create opportunities. And I think, because of that, it just made it harder for everyone. It was a matter of trying to stay in the game.'

England had been encouraged by events in Broad's first over of the day to believe that the pitch might yet start to misbehave enough for their first-innings total to be decisive, with one delivery to Katich tearing a chunk right off the top of the surface. But the England captain spent the rest of the day, and much of the next, rueing just how deceptive appearances can be.

By the time Strauss threw the ball to Jimmy Anderson for the first use of the new cherry, Australia had progressed to 281 for 1. Ponting's response was to pull the second delivery emphatically for four before cover-driving another boundary. When, with his first ball back, to his smirking embarrassment and, maybe to the relief of his biggest mate, Steve Harmison, Flintoff fired one wide off first slip from his opening delivery at the other end, Strauss may well have been trying to recall what plan C was.

Suddenly swing arrived, enough, at least, for Anderson to beat Katich's half-forward push with a ball that thudded into his pads to end his 325-minute stay at 299 for 2, and he then had the out-of-sorts Michael Hussey caught behind driving to leave Australia on 325 for 3.

Ponting's insatiable appetite took him to his 13th score of 150 in Test cricket shortly before lunch, but England still believed that, with a lead of 100-plus, if they could just get past the Aussie skipper quickly, victory might still be within their reach.

Now desperate for his bowlers to maintain pressure, Strauss may already have been preparing a suitable response when Panesar appeared to drag a ball down wide of off stump of the variety that Ponting had been putting away clinically for more than six hours. But photographs of what happened next indicated Ponting's eyes had simply grown too big for his stomach. The effort of trying to smash the ball so hard he would kill it merely served to throw the batsman off balance, his right hand punching through the shot so hard that, but the time the ball had cannoned into the middle and off stumps from the bottom edge, it had flown clear of the handle.

Three wickets had gone down for 32 runs in 10 overs. England, 104 ahead, sensed a chance. But once the effects of the new ball had worn off, vice-captain Michael Clarke and Marcus North simply shut the door in their faces. One by one Strauss employed all possible permutations as Australia's fifth-wicket pair went about their business. And by the time Australia had reduced the deficit to a mere eight runs, his thinking had even extended to a bowling style employed by Paul Collingwood that had older members of the audience wallowing in nostalgia.

For generations all Glamorgan supporters were brought up in the certain knowledge that England selectors have been unable to see beyond the Severn Bridge. How else could any sane cricket-watcher explain the fact that both their opening bat, Alan Jones, and Don Shepherd, their legendary purveyor of cutters or medium-fast spinners, had been so studiously overlooked? Yet here, unless they were dreaming, was Shepherd's ghost in the Durham man's form.

Sadly for the rheumy-eyed Glamorgan supporters, and for England, the chief result of the experiment at this stage was the sight of the second ball exploding out of the rough wide of North's off stump and sailing for four byes, followed by the third.

Prior wasn't too thrilled either, recalls Collingwood: 'It wasn't all that amusing for Matt because he had no firm idea where he should stand. He wanted to stand up to the stumps, but when I told him I wanted him to stand about four yards behind he told me where to get off. "Shut up, I'm not standing in clubland."

And while hardly anyone took too much notice of Flintoff's temporary absence from the field after lunch, just one look at his face gave Panesar something else to ponder.

'When Freddie came to the ground in the morning, I kind of felt, is he fully fit? Is he OK? Is something up?' Panesar recalls. 'And then maybe I got a better idea, because there were some signals I picked up on. Maybe the pace wasn't as high, and I think he had kind of a worried look after the first day. I got the feeling that maybe something was not quite right here.'

With Australia comfortably positioned at 458 for 4 at tea, and already in front, Strauss must have feared what was to come through the rest of the contest. The Australians might have lost their platinum-plated attack, but the baggy green machine still churned out run-getters.

England's bowlers had endured a miserable winter in 2008–09, during which they had failed to get 20 wickets in a match in every one of their six Tests. Now even ten seemed an awfully long way away when rain stopped play with Australia cruising on 463 for 4, a dozen minutes into the evening session. The previous Test in England between the sides at The Oval four years earlier had featured home supporters twirling umbrellas, urging the rain to aid the cause. Rain did fall, but the pre-series agreement to employ floodlights wherever possible in a bid to eradicate lengthy periods lost to weather meant the players returned for half a dozen overs later in the session. It was the first time artificial light had been used in a Test match in Britain and, as such, meant Clarke became the first victim in such conditions when he made a mess of a short ball from Broad that he could have dodged and gloved down the legside.

England's bowlers could not be faulted for their effort, but even if the tone of the headline on the back page of the next day's *Sun* was a tad cruel – 'Roothless versus Toothless' – a close-of-play score of 479 for 5, a lead of 34 with five wickets intact, meant they would have found it hard to argue with its sentiments.

CARDIFF, DAY FOUR: AUSTRALIA 674 FOR 6 DECLARED; ENGLAND 20 FOR 2

With the weather grim on the morning of day four and the forecasters predicting even worse to come, Strauss admits England arrived at the ground with their head in the grey clouds.

'I think we got duped by the weather forecast a little bit,' he admits. 'Whether it was at the back of our minds or whatever, we assumed we would only be playing for about an hour or so on the day, which is a very bad mindset to get into. In the event, they batted on for almost two sessions and then, even when we went into bat, we were assuming the rain was just about to come. It did, but by the time it did we'd lost two wickets.'

Australia's batsmen had two things on their minds – more runs and a chance to try and bowl England out for victory on the final day.

Marcus North, a man who has passed through more English counties than Sir Ian Botham managed on his charity walk from John O'Groats to Land's End, developed another partnership with

Brad Haddin. Resuming on 54 in his third Test, and a controversial choice, North picked length and width with precision, leaving any balls he did not have to play, and scuttling pulls and his favoured drives over the turf for a dozen boundaries, managing to pierce a seven-man offside field with calm precision.

Strauss's seamers were ground down, slowly initially, and faster after Flintoff took the third new ball in the 164th over of the innings with on Australia 559 for 5.

Worryingly for coach Flower and bowling coach Ottis Gibson, looking on from the balcony, this was the third time in five Tests they had qualified for the third new ball. Australia responded with all-out attack, and this time not even Flintoff could stem the tide. Indeed, when the all-rounder stiffly gave chase to a push from North for two that took him to 96 and the score to 571 for 5, Panesar's fears from the previous evening shivered all round the outfield.

According to Strauss: 'Fred always said he was OK every time I spoke to him, but, possibly, yeah, there were a couple of times towards the back end when he just didn't look to have his normal zip. It's always a tough one with Fred because it's hard to get the ball out of his hands.'

North, the first compass point to play Test cricket according to new *Test Match Special* scorer Malcolm Ashton, reached three figures with two further twos in a row from James Anderson, finishing with a push behind point that ended in a spectacular, albeit needless, slide into the crease. It was his most manic moment of an innings spanning five hours, which was worth 101 at lunch. 'Leading into that I was so nervous I couldn't breathe,' North later admitted. 'The emotions had taken over a bit.' At the age of 29, he admitted his apprenticeship had been long but worthwhile. 'It certainly hasn't felt easy. Test cricket is an intensity like no other,' he said.

With Australia on 577 for 5 at lunch, 142 ahead, it wasn't only the England supporters who were struggling to retain the will to live. Up in the media centre one scribe was putting the finishing touches to his selection of a team with Welsh names: openers Morgan Richie, Morgan Everyone; strokeplayer Dai Laffyn; blocker Dai Wondering; and paceman Rhys Lightning.

Swann concedes: 'Apart from a couple of full tosses, I didn't actually pitch too short or too full. It was just one of those games where if you were slightly off, you didn't look like getting a wicket. That was what worried me more than anything, how blunt I felt. I didn't feel like taking wickets.'

According to Panesar: 'There were times when I thought the rough should help me, but I struggled with my lines. The rough was on line between a fifth and sixth stump, whereas normally it's at fourth stump, and I really had to get it out there. I felt that if I got it out there, then maybe I was in the game. But when I did, and it turned, the pitch was so slow they had time to adjust.'

Pietersen was growing increasingly concerned about his painful Achilles and the implications beyond Cardiff. One particularly wild throw to Prior betrayed his mounting frustration.

The keeper, meanwhile, had long since realised that overt attempts to keep spirits up were almost certainly a waste of his time and energy: 'In that situation, when you are in the field for so long it is hard work, because one by one you can almost feel the guys getting quieter and quieter and you've got to try and find a way of keeping everyone going, keeping the buzz going, keeping yourself going.

'We hung in, but it is tricky, and the other thing is, in a situation like that I've had issues in the past of people saying I'm a loudmouth, so what are you meant to do? Are you meant to disappear and not say anything, not crack a joke or anything like that?

'I'll be honest, there wasn't a lot of banter. It was all very serious and kind of like, Come on lads! Keep going! But behind the words we were all thinking, ****ing hell, how long are we going to be out here? Because at one stage I thought we were going to be fielding for three days.'

'I'll be honest, there wasn't a lot of banter. It was all very serious and kind of like, Come on lads! Keep going! But behind the words we were all thinking, ****ing hell, how long are we going to be out here?'

Matt Prior on Australia's three days at the crease

Swann says: 'You keep plugging on, but the fielders had given up by that point. They were just letting it bounce two yards in front of them and under-arming it back in. You think, even my mates, the fielders, have given up on trying to get me a wicket, what's the point?'

At 597 for 5, Swann joined Flintoff and Anderson, who had earlier 'celebrated' the landmark with a weary handshake, as England's bowling centurions. Then Haddin, who had used his feet to became a walking wagon-wheel of boundaries after lunch, slog-swept Swann for six over the midwicket fence to propel Australia past 600, and take his sixth-wicket partnership with North to 150. In the next over, from Panesar, Australia posted the tenth-highest Ashes score in history after a ball spun out of the rough to hit first slip Collingwood on the head via Prior's knee for two byes, then Haddin's slash dropped safely between the infield and outfield. For England it was that good.

On the eve of the series Ponting had predicted that his fledgling team could produce something special on this trip. Now, when Haddin tucked Collingwood to deep square leg for a single, his century from 138 balls meant they had made history as the first Australian team to contain four centurions in a single Ashes innings; Katich, Ponting, North and Haddin providing a lesson in will and persistence that put England's failure to develop any one of their ten double-figured scores into centuries to shame.

Once his lavish celebration had died down, Haddin pushed the accelerator flat to the floor in the manner, if not the style, of his predecessor Adam Gilchrist, even blasting Collingwood for a flat six to bring up Australia's highest score against England since 1934, surpassing the 659 for 8 declared they made in Sydney in December 1946.

Possibly a tad after the horse had bolted, it was about this time that Swann felt he started to bowl well. 'It just never felt as nice coming out of my hands until, perversely, right at the end of their innings. The last few overs, when Haddin and North were batting, and with everyone on the boundary, and me just trying not to go for fours then, suddenly, out of nowhere, it felt perfect in my hand again. That was important for me, because if it had carried on feeling like crap all game, then I'd have been a nervous wreck going to Lord's. I don't like bowling at Lord's anyway, despite the West Indies game, and I would have been thinking that if I can't feel the ball properly and I'm not sure where it's going, then I'm not going to play much of a part in this series.'

When Haddin eventually holed out to deep midwicket and the longest boundary on the ground, Australia had advanced to 674 for 6 – the fifth-highest score by either of the two sides in the history of Ashes tussles. The even 200 shared by North and Haddin represented the highest-ever sixth-wicket stand by an Australian pair in England. With the threat of rain hovering in the air, however, Ponting sensed this was the moment to pull out.

England were presented with the task of scoring 239 simply to make their opponents bat again and, as the floodlights cranked into operation, with their weary top order on a hiding to nothing, visibility questionable, two days after the umpires had let Australia come off for bad light in similar circumstances, Strauss may have wondered why they had to go out to bat at all. With conditions juicy for the bowlers, it proved a declaration timed to perfection.

First Johnson removed Cook, trapped lbw playing around his front pad. Then, with the lights now in full bloom, Ben Hilfenhaus enjoyed a more fortuitous decision when Ravi Bopara was also deemed leg before to a ball that television technology suggested would have comfortably cleared the stumps.

England were 20 for 2 at tea when the rain swept in and prevented another ball being bowled. Even with light rain predicted for Cardiff the following day, the Australians none-theless fancied their chances of claiming the required eight wickets on a wearing fifth-day Sophia Gardens track to go 1–0 up in the series.

Collingwood offered a rallying cry ahead of England's attempts to keep the scores level: 'We have to get the brain into gear for what we have to do. The batsmen have got to take responsibility. We've got three sessions to bat, and you have got to see them through as an individual and not leave it to anyone else. Tomorrow is about putting your hand up and being the man to see the three sessions through.'

In the Sky commentary box, former skipper Bob Willis delivered the following verdict: 'Predictions of England winning 3–0 or 3–1 are now up in smoke. The people who made them can be led off to cloud cuckoo land.'

CARDIFF, DAY FIVE: ENGLAND 252 FOR 9; MATCH DRAWN

Tension sucked most of the air out of the stadium as 16,000 people shuffled into the stands to witness England's attempt to save the match. Even before play had begun, a heated confrontation between Kevin Pietersen and Mitchell Johnson betrayed a similarly fraught mood among the players.

As both teams went through their final preparations, Pietersen, battling to focus on the job ahead and against the feeling that his injury would almost hamper his attempts to carry it out, struck a pull-shot in the direction of the Australians.

Johnson kicked the ball away, then marched across to the England batsman with several of his countrymen in tow and with anger in his eyes. Pietersen, also accompanied by team-mates, responded by advancing on the Australians. For a moment it looked as though a Wild West shoot-out was on the cards but, thankfully, a serious confrontation was averted when Stuart Clark, the Australian 12th man, ushered Johnson away. 'It was a case of a few guys on the ground taking each others' space,' reflected Australia captain Ricky Ponting afterwards. 'It started to get messy, there were a few words, but there was Test cricket to play.'

Probably not a moment too soon, it began.

Australia had the last laugh with Pietersen when, from the fourth ball of the fourth over of the morning, he left a delivery from Hilfenhaus, bowling from the Taff End. In the previous over he had edged a ball from Johnson that hadn't quite carried to second slip. This time he left one that started straight and stayed straight and flattened his off stump. Some observers also wondered whether all the criticism that had been thrown at England's premier batsman over the manner of his dismissal on day one might have had a subconscious effect.

Strauss, watching from the other end, concedes they might have had a point. 'I thought it was always going to be difficult for him on day five, anyway,' he said, 'because what was required is so against what his game's about. Maybe that's why he did what he did.

'Was it in his mind, after what had happened, that he had to be defensive? I think it was. Was that because of the stick he'd got? I don't know.'

It was 11.18am. England were 31 for 3. Pietersen was gone and, within little more than an hour, Strauss and Prior had gone with him, both victims of Nathan Hauritz, the man many originally derided as a wasted pick.

From the fifth ball of the 17th over, Strauss rocked back and smashed a short ball from the off-spinner hard through the covers for four and allowed himself a sigh of relief at this respite from the mounting pressure. He could hardly believe his luck when Hauritz's next delivery was another buffet-ball. He certainly couldn't believe what happened next.

'That cut shot was almost the only one I was going to allow myself to play off Hauritz. I'd hit the previous ball for four and this one was even worse, short and wide and lovely and, to my dying day, I will never know how I didn't clatter that one as well. Maybe I tried to hit it too hard and I ended up nicking it. It was doubly frustrating because I'd batted for 45 minutes or so and was feeling pretty comfortable.'

It was 11.44am. England were 46 for 4 and in deep trouble.

The night before that final day, England's number 6, Matt Prior, had urged himself into the mindset of England's saviour. 'I'd said to myself: "Right, tomorrow's a big day, someone's going to have to be a hero tomorrow – can you be the man?" And I felt so good going into the day. I had batted well in the first innings, and when I was batting now I didn't feel in any trouble at all.

'The mistake I made was I got too far ahead. I stopped worrying about what I was actually doing and started thinking, Right, let's get to lunch and then tea. As a result, I didn't just concentrate on what was happening now. Suddenly one turns, bites and you're out. I was gutted.

'I felt I had let the team down, to be very honest. The rest of the day was murder.'

It was 12.25pm. England were 70 for 5. On the dressing-room balcony, even Strauss feared the worst. 'By the time we were five down, it looked like the game was gone,' he admits.

Following his audacious hitting in the first innings, coming in at this point of crisis gave Andrew Flintoff the chance to show that he was also prepared and able to defend if necessary. At this stage, although 35 overs and two full days in the field had obviously taken its toll, no one would have guessed that he was already close to a dramatic decision regarding his long-term future in the game. Reports emanating from Australia over the weekend had suggested that Queensland were keen on offering him a temporary winter haven for their 2009–10 Twenty20 campaign – although that did not seem to add up with England's scheduled Test tour of South Africa over the corresponding Christmas period. Discussing a separate issue on BBC's *Test Match Special*, Geoff Boycott had predicted Flintoff would not play Tests beyond the current series. But Boycott being Boycott, most listeners considered the comment no more or less significant than his usual strongly expressed opinion.

For now Flintoff knuckled down to share a 50-run stand with Paul Collingwood, interrupted by a lunch interval during which, Strauss admits, the mood in the dressing-room was, at best, resigned. England had edged to 102 for 5 and cut the deficit to 137 runs, but two full sessions still yawned in front of them like a bottomless pit.

'You always hope for miracles, and Freddie was still there,' says Strauss. 'But I think, in our heart of hearts, we all thought the game was gone.'

Not that Collingwood required any more motivation for the task at hand, but from early in his innings his focus was sharpened further when Aussie skipper Ponting thought it appropriate to remind him of one of the worst experiences of his career.

Defeat in the second Ashes Test in Adelaide on the 2006–07 tour had, by his own admission, 'ripped the guts' out of him. Trailing 1–0 after the first Test in Brisbane, England responded with a first innings of 551 for 6 declared in the city of churches, with

Collingwood making an epic 206 in a record stand of 310 for the fourth wicket with Pietersen. But when, after Australia made 513, the time came to bat again and secure the draw, too many England batsmen got stuck, including the Durham man, who was left unbeaten on 22 in their second-innings collapse to 129 all out, which allowed Ponting's side to take a psychologically crushing 2–0 lead.

'You always hope for miracles, and Freddie was still there. But I think, in our heart of hearts, we all thought the game was gone'

Andrew Strauss on the dressing-room at lunch, the final day

According to Collingwood: 'My memories of batting on that last day in Adelaide are all pretty grim. I had Shane Warne at one end, who was not exactly easy to score off when the ball was ragging so much and, against the seamers, it was reverse-swinging massively both ways. I couldn't actually line a ball up to get my back lift any higher than playing French cricket because I didn't know which way the hell the thing was going. I was literally surviving, but my biggest regret in that second innings is that I didn't just try to hit a few more runs as we were going along. Afterwards I couldn't get it out of my mind that if I could have done that then Australia wouldn't have had the opportunity to go for the win.

'Batting on the last day in Cardiff, merely to survive, that thought was in the back of my mind. Then, helpfully, Ricky raised the issue a couple of times in my earshot when we were out in the middle, saying stuff like, "It's just like Adelaide again, boys, it's just like Adelaide," and, "What are you getting your team into this time?"

'But actually, it was exactly what I needed. I thought to myself, OK Ricky, let's see who's saying what at the end of the day.'

Collingwood's plan was simple. Indeed, he'd spent much of the previous evening running over it again and again.

'The night before I had dinner with Ottis Gibson, our bowling coach and my former Durham team-mate, and I said to him: "If I get a bit of luck tomorrow, you'll see the ultimate Stonewall Collingwood." And all through the innings the phrase kept running through my mind.

'My plan was to bat the day. It wasn't about batting in ten-over chunks or going in stages, it was literally to bat all day.

'The pace I batted at did not bother me one iota. I remember, after lunch, I faced 35 balls, apparently, without scoring and I wasn't bothered. I just loved watching every ball roll back off the bat and shouting at the top of my voice, Noooo! I loved it.'

As the afternoon session wore on, Collingwood's ability to stay focused was tested almost every ball, but three incidents in the space of a few minutes, just after drinks signalled the midway point of the final day, stretched it to its limit.

First, in the over after the break, Flintoff's patience finally

'I remember, after lunch, I faced 35 balls, apparently, without scoring and I wasn't bothered. I just loved watching every ball roll back off the bat and shouting at the top of my voice, Nooo! I loved it.'

Paul Collingwood scores 20 off 34 overs

seemed to crack as he steered a drive off Johnson to Ponting at second slip to end his 71-ball stay. Flintoff paused for a moment before departing, checking with Ponting that the ball had carried. A nod from the Australian captain confirmed the catch was good and no more needed to be said.

It was 2.35pm. England were 127 for 6 and the best part of 50 overs were still to be bowled.

Moments later, Johnson's next ball slammed into the pads of new batsman Stuart Broad. Collingwood winced, all but convinced the seventh-wicket stand was over before it had even begun.

Broad claims he was never in doubt. 'As soon as it hit me I thought the ball was sliding down the legside. Johnson had a bit of a moan and apparently TV showed it was hitting leg stump, so he was probably entitled, but there you go.'

And as if all that were not enough to jangle taut nerves, at the end of the over, two protesters intent on drawing attention to an airline's alleged maltreatment of its employees raced onto the pitch and, though they failed to unravel their banner, one did manage to demolish the stumps at the striker's end and cause a five-minute hold-up.

'I remember everything being eerily quiet for a while,' says Broad. 'Colly and I were just blocking it for ages.

'I might have imagined it but, as time passed, I did think I noticed a few heads dropping a degree or two. Then things hotted up again when I had a little run-in with Peter Siddle.

'He bowled me a length ball, I played it defensively and it ran down towards the third-man boundary. I was running towards the other end but checking back to see if the ball was definitely going over the line. I wasn't looking at Siddle at all, he was obviously frustrated that I'd managed to nick a four, and he just lowered his shoulder and barged me.

'I was standing there asking him, "What was all that about?" and he was just staring back at me, so, as I walked back, I accidentally brushed shoulders with him again. And then for the next 15 minutes I got an absolute barrage from everyone around me.

'I don't know whether they hadn't seen Siddle barge me because they were looking down towards third man, or whether they'd just seen me go at him, so they thought I'd instigated it, but they gave me heaps, saying things like, "So you think you're a tough guy," and all that sort of stuff. It made me very determined just to keep blocking it, really. I didn't need psyching up that day, but it certainly made me very determined not to get out.'

Indeed Broad, watched by his sister Gemma, England's new statistician, dad Chris and grandfather Ken, aged 91, succeeded for 69 minutes before he was struck plumb in front by Haurtiz.

As he walked off television pictures appeared to show Broad scowling at umpire Aleem Dar, prompting Mike Atherton on commentary to declare: 'England need to take a good look at themselves in the game, not the umpires.'

Chris Broad, now an ICC match referee, but once a feisty Ashes-winning left-handed England opener not averse to showing his displeasure at decisions he didn't agree with, took note.

Broad Jr explains: 'Dad wasn't happy. He said to me that on the television it looked like I was staring at the umpire. And I said, "No, I was looking at Colly saying, I've had a shocker.'

'Colly had said to me, "Keep playing straight, keep playing straight," and then I went on the back foot and I tried to hit the ball through square leg. So I was looking at him, thinking, "****", and he was like, "Oh, no, what have you done?" The camera angles may have suggested something else, but what they saw was actually me showing my disappointment to my partner that I hadn't stuck to our gameplan.'

It was 3.46pm. With 25 minutes to go before tea, England were 159 for 7.

But if the Australians thought they could brush aside new batsman Swann with the short ball, he was utterly determined to prove them wrong, no matter how much pain it caused him.

'They set a field with a short leg, leg gully, deep square and a fine leg, so all my options were gone really,' he recalls. 'I thought, I can't possibly hook, so I'll just try to get underneath the short ball, and every time Siddle seemingly banged it in I just went to duck; the lack of bounce in the pitch meant it was bouncing nowhere near as high as I thought and clattering into me. Three times in an over he did it; one on the arm and a couple on the glove.

'It was obviously quite funny for everyone else watching, but when I went off at tea I just said to Andy, "I need some ideas here, because my instinct is to try and get underneath it, but it's not bouncing high enough and I keep getting whacked." And Fred just came over and said, "Why not just stand there and bloody hit it!" So after tea I went out and I did just that.'

As the teams emerged after tea for the 15th and final session of the contest, the equation had been simplified: Australia required three wickets to win, and England needed 70 runs to make their opponents bat again.

England knew they could alter the outlook completely if they could get into the lead because a break between innings would lop off three overs from those remaining in the day's original 98-over allocation.

Swann continued to be bold. Collingwood recalls: 'The closer we were getting to the target of making them bat again, Swann played more and more shots to calm himself down.' But after he had struck four boundaries in an attractive 31, he was bowled attempting a pull off Hilfenhaus.

'That was ridiculous,' he says. 'I had been telling myself all along, don't play cross-bat shots – just don't. Even then, Colly didn't look like getting out, and with Jimmy going in I didn't think we'd lose another wicket. I genuinely thought we were going to save this game.'

It was 5.30pm. England were 221 for 8 with more than an hour still to bat. Swann was almost certainly in the minority.

Yet, by the time Aleem Dar signalled the match had entered its final 60 minutes, with a minimum of 15 overs to be bowled, even Strauss had allowed himself to dream. 'Suddenly,' he says, 'it just started to look like, Hold on, they're not looking like they're going to take a wicket here, and that offered a glimmer of hope.'

And, just as suddenly, that hope was gone again. With the deficit now down to just six runs, after 244 deliveries spread over five and a half hours, Collingwood attempted to cut a ball from Siddle over gully only for his former Durham colleague Mike Hussey to cling on, agonisingly, at the second attempt.

Collingwood was so distraught that it seemed for an instant he might have to be physically removed from the field of play, by force if necessary.

'The horrible part of getting out was the reason I got out. I could have batted all day. I do honestly believe that. But we spoke about it in the dressing-room during tea, that once Jimmy came in I would have to start farming the strike, which is pretty difficult to do when they're bringing all the field in for the last couple of balls of every over.

'Obviously if we went past their score it would have been a double whammy; they would have needed to bat again, and that would have meant more overs out of the game, so with that in mind, I started to go for balls that I was originally leaving well alone. And by thinking about things like that I let myself slip out of my bubble of concentration. I lost my rhythm a bit.

'I didn't actually go for the ball that got me out until the last second. It was a half-hearted shot with no conviction, and as soon as I'd hit it I was saying, Please don't catch it.

'For a moment, when Hussey parried it, I thought I'd got away with it, but when he caught it, it was like the whole world had crashed. Literally, I don't know how I didn't go down on my knees, just thinking, That cannot have happened. But in that moment I was a hundred per cent convinced I'd cost England the Test match.'

Collingwood may have been much maligned, by Shane Warne in particular, for being awarded the MBE in 2005 despite playing just one match, but he had justified those letters after his name in South Wales. Magnificent Batting Effort.

Yet he was surprised by the subdued response when he returned to the dressing-room, until he realised the reason behind it.

'Nobody said, Well batted. Nobody said anything, actually. I'd been out there for hours trying my nuts off and I came back to absolute silence. It was unbelievable. I was quietly taking my kit off, by myself, thinking I must have messed up big time because even the boys aren't saying anything.'

Then the comforting truth dawned on him.

For some time, overseen by Cook from inside the dressing-room shouting at any transgressor to sit down, shut up or keep their place, his team-mates inside and out on the balcony had been engaged in the usual series of superstitious exercises understood by cricketers worldwide since time immemorial as imperative in order to keep the cricketing gods onside.

Broad, by now absolutely desperate to answer the call of nature he had first heard when his county team-mate Swann walked out to bat 45 minutes earlier, recalls: 'That's cricket superstition. If you're doing well, you're not allowed to move. So we had two or three of us dying to go to the toilet, but as soon as anyone even showed to move, Cookie would be straight onto us, saying, Sit down mate.

'It's one of those things that if you do decide to bite the bullet and go for it, and Monty or Jimmy were to get out, then it's all your fault.

'When Colly came back in, it was weird because no one said a word. He'd played an absolutely awesome innings, batted for six hours or so, and, because we had this superstition that we couldn't move, everyone was either on the balcony or in the shower room just sat on the floor. When Colly walked in it was just pure silence. There was a bit of dejection, though.'

It wasn't only Broad's bladder that was suffering. His fingernails were taking a right bashing, too. 'I'd tried to distract myself with this little routine,' he explains. 'I'd watch a ball, take a deep breath, then chew one of my fingernails for a little bit, the second on my right hand. Then I'd cup my hands together in front of my face, like when you're a kid trying to make the sound of an owl hooting, and just blow into them until the next ball was bowled. Then I'd repeat the sequence over and over again.

'I'd started doing it when Swann went in. I suddenly realised I'd done it for an over and we'd done OK, and I thought if I stop now he might get out, so I'll just keep doing it. I didn't used to be super-stitious. I am now.'

Ter-whit-ter-whoo.

It was 6.03pm. England were 233 for 9 and Monty Panesar was walking out to join Jimmy Anderson with a minimum of 63 balls to face. Collingwood was not the only one fearing the game was up.

According to Strauss: 'I'd spoken earlier in the day to Andy Flower about how long we could reasonably expect Monty to bat for. We agreed. Two overs. Maybe.'

Pietersen, on the balcony, had started asking how many runs people would settle for to try and defend from one over. Ten? Twelve? As the players watched their number 11 walk out to bat, there were no takers. Cometh the hour, however, cometh the Monty.

'I had thought to myself, the night before, What if that situation does arise?' says Panesar. 'What if I've got to bat to save it [the game] and I thought, no, I don't think that'll happen. I think the others will see it off.

'At lunch, when we were five wickets down, I thought it was game over. I thought we were going to get bowled out before tea.

'But then, as the day unfolded, it was just getting closer and closer and I'm thinking, Bloody hell, I could be going in for 10 overs to save this Test match.'

And now, he was.

Anderson met him on his arrival, uttered a pointed 'good luck' and tried to hide the feeling inside that 'this was going to be tricky now'.

'No one had said much in the dressing-room, though I did sense the feeling that it would be a miracle if I got through this. I think everyone in England was saying, 1–0 Australia. But Jimmy said to me: "Just watch the ball."'

Panesar took his guard and waited. One ball might be all it took. One unplayable delivery. One mistake. One heartbeat.

Siddle ran in and, in the instant Panesar's bat moved towards a good-length ball, must have thought he had England's number 11 there and then. But the ball missed the blade by a whisker and Panesar, who had decided to count down every ball, counted 'one'.

'To be honest,' he recalls, 'in that moment I thought it was all over. I'm not sure how the ball missed the bat or the stumps, but I settled down after that. Paul Collingwood was my batting buddy, and a lot of what we had worked on over the past nine months came together. One of the best things he taught me was to switch off between deliveries, to make sure I relax and then focus again, taking time out, making sure my shoulders were relaxed and my breathing was right. I didn't really think about surviving until the end, just the next ball.

'And we all know Jimmy is a fighter. As time passed and the ball came and went, if you know you have a guy at the other end who's up for it, you find some more fight as well.'

> 'I'd spoken earlier in the day to Andy Flower about how long we could reasonably expect Monty to bat for. We agreed. Two overs. Maybe'
>
> *Andrew Strauss*

61

Anderson recalls: 'Right from the start of the day we all understood how hard it was going to be to survive. And I'm not sure if we thought, deep down, that we could actually do it.

'There were two things I was concentrating on: one was watching the ball and the other was taking as long as possible between deliveries. That meant walking as far as I could to square leg without taking the mickey and just maybe patting down the wicket or something as well, from time to time. That did two things: it took up some more seconds and distracted me from what was actually going on.

'And we kept talking to each other in between overs and in between balls. I kept shouting down to him after he played a good shot or left one well, and I think just everything that was going on in the middle took our minds off the actual situation of the game.

'Mind you, it did seem as though this match was never going to end.'

Back in the dressing-room, a few of their team-mates knew the feeling.

Swann couldn't look. He had taken himself off to watch the German Grand Prix on television. Matt Prior busied himself by bouncing a tennis ball, over and over and over again.

'When Colly got out,' Prior says, 'to be honest with you, you're sort of putting the game to bed. I got up, went into the changing-rooms and I found a tennis ball. I was just walking around bouncing this tennis ball; I couldn't go outside, the changing-room was just nerves. That's what I did for the rest of the day.'

While Panesar and Anderson battled to retain their cool in the middle, the dressing-room was, by now, in a state of some confusion. The issue was the actual, correct time the game was due to end.

Initial thoughts that England merely needed to bat out 15 overs in the final hour were rudely interrupted by the realisation that Australia would almost certainly bowl more than the minimum in the time available. Finally, it was agreed that the end of the match would arrive at 6.50pm, come what may. But with the statutory ten-minute break between innings should Australia have to bat again, it would mean that if England were still batting when the clock went past 6.40pm, they would have achieved the 'Great Escape'.

The problem for Strauss was that the two people who most needed to know – Anderson and Panesar – were blissfully unaware of what was required.

'It was a bizarre situation,' Strauss says. 'Until about 20 minutes to go, we thought we were just playing the overs. It was only then that Phil Neale, our ops manager, said that actually we've got to play to time. So we had to work out exactly when that time was and then let Jimmy and Monty know.

'There was nothing malicious in terms of time-wasting. We sent the message out to Jimmy, but the 12th man, Bilal Shafayat, actually did spill water on Jimmy's glove. Jimmy wanted another pair, so Bilal had to go back with another pair.

'From the balcony we weren't sure if Jimmy also said he wanted the physio as well, so we sent on Steve McCaig, just in case.

'If we'd been intentionally trying to waste time, we would have done it a lot earlier and gone a lot further. The fact of the matter was that it was very important that Jimmy knew exactly what the situation was. In those situations, there's a lot of running around trying to make sure we're absolutely clear on it.'

When Anderson waved the physio away, Ricky Ponting was not amused. Nor was he, one suspects, by the fact that McCaig, deputising for Kirk Russell who was on paternity leave, is a true gold-and-green Aussie.

When McCaig returned to the dressing-room, he was crestfallen. Swann explains: 'Ricky gave Steve a right ear-bashing, and the poor guy was gutted. "Ah, mate" Steve said. "That bloke is my hero."'

The battle to survive made for excruciating, but compulsive, viewing for every home supporter in the ground or those glued to the radio, television or internet. Every act of resistance was greeted with sighs, gasps and cheers. Nor was it any different on the England dressing-room balcony.

'I was on the edge of my seat,' explained Strauss. 'As a batsman, to have to watch numbers 10 and 11 do your job for you is not a place you want to be, really. I always felt one of the main dangers was Monty running himself, or Jimmy, out.'

One television shot of the England skipper hardly able to watch through clenched fingers proved the point and, in truth, Panesar did his best to fulfil his captain's prophecy a couple of times. But when Anderson jabbed down on consecutive Siddle deliveries, which both squirted to third man for four, England were in credit. At that point, there were a minimum of seven overs remaining, although any changeover for a new innings would reduce that to four.

> 'If we'd been intentionally trying to waste time, we would have done it a lot earlier and gone a lot further'
>
> *Andrew Strauss*

Ponting now leant on his 'Punter' nickname and gambled by pairing part-time off-spinner Marcus North and Hauritz together. The theory was that two slow men would get more balls down the other end in the time available and, therefore, offer more wicket-taking opportunities.

According to Anderson, however, North's introduction, at the start of the 102nd over, was the moment he actually believed he and his partner could actually pull it off.

'I thought, Brilliant. We can do this now,' he said.

North's effort safely negotiated, with the pavilion clock showing 6.39pm, Ponting passed the ball to Hauritz for one last crack. On the balcony, Strauss & co. were sure the match had come down to this: if Australia took the final wicket before 6.40pm, they would have one over to bat and 13 runs to get plus any scored in the meantime; if they failed to take a wicket, England would be safe.

When asked about the tension he felt during that final over, Anderson recalls: 'Not much, really. I saw each ball, blocked each ball and when that last one squirted off Haddin's pads and Monty called for a run, I ran.'

But, if the match was over, why weren't they punching the air?

Anderson and Panesar came together in the middle of the pitch, umpire Aleem Dar, presumably waiting for England to declare to bring the match to its close, waited and waited, and Anderson was now thinking they might yet have one more over to face. Finally, and very graciously in the circumstances, Ponting decided the time had come to put everyone out of their agony.

'I really wasn't certain what was going on,' Anderson admits. 'I think I'd just been talking to Aleem about how long to go, saying, "Surely that's got to be the last over." And then Monty and I had a chat about doing brilliantly, just keep going, same sort of thing. And then, as I turned round to go and walk back to the other end, I saw Ricky coming towards me from extra cover. He held out his hand and said, "Well, played mate," and that was that. An incredible feeling.'

A split second passed before the crowd realised it too, and then it erupted in an explosion of noise and relief.

Panesar remembers: 'The noise was unbelievable. I remember thinking, I can't hear my voice. I can't hear Jimmy. It was ridiculous. Massive.'

In the dressing-room, finally, Swann stopped watching the television, Broad made for the loo, Prior stopped bouncing that bloody tennis ball and Cook stopped policing the balcony. But while their hearts may have been screaming something else, the players all made sure they kept their reactions within bounds.

'We didn't want to celebrate,' Pietersen recalls. 'We just said, No, we're not happy with a draw. We're not happy at all. We haven't played well. We're lucky to have come out of this.'

Swann agrees: 'What a lovely feeling. But we were very conscious of not showing too much emotion at the end, because I truly believe that if you celebrate wildly, it's a real sign that you're clinging on by the skin of your teeth and you're happy with that.'

According to Collingwood: 'As soon as Jimmy and Monty had gone into the dressing-room, they were swallowed up by the rest of us, but from a team's point of view, we didn't want to be seen to be celebrating a draw in view of everybody. We were obviously delighted, but we were also realistic in that we played sh**e and got away with it. Simple as that.

'There was a real sense of joy, though. I looked around and everybody had a little smile on their face. Monty was so pumped up. He was sitting there, nodding his head up and down like Churchill the dog. It was just brilliant.'

Panesar says: 'I was trying to take it all in, what we'd done and what it meant, but I actually didn't realise how nerve-racking that whole period of play had been until I came home and I was watching it on Sky Sports. And I thought, Oh my God, how did we get through that?'

Strauss says: 'I had mixed emotions. We all gave them a big hug, and I think we were all really proud of what they'd done, but we realised, for the majority of the Test, we'd been under the cosh. The reality was that we underachieved there and it's our job to overachieve.

'Crucially, though, for the first time in a while, we hadn't lost the opening Test match in an Ashes series, and we could move on to Lord's with some momentum.'

The Australian reaction, understandably, was somewhat less sanguine, as Ponting indicated when asked about alleged time-wasting tactics.

'I don't think it was required. He changed [the gloves] the over before and I don't think they'd be too sweaty in one over,' Ponting said. 'I'm not sure what the physio was doing out there. I didn't see anyone call for the physio to come out. As far as I'm concerned, it was pretty ordinary, really. But they can play whatever way they want to play. We came to play by the rules and the spirit of the game. It's up to them to do what they want to do.' Although the Australians declined to take the matter further, Ponting inferred that 'others might have a look at it'.

Strauss responded: 'If Ricky is upset, that's a shame. Our intentions were good. We weren't deliberately trying to waste a huge amount of time. Those weren't our tactics. Those two were playing very well out in the middle, and the reality of the situation is that Australia didn't take the final wicket and we got away with a draw.'

> 'We were obviously delighted, but we were also realistic in that we played sh**e and got away with it'
>
> *Paul Collingwood*

Down Under, Strauss found himself on the receiving end from Malcom Conn in *The Australian*. 'Andrew Strauss is either a weak leader or he has no idea about the spirit of cricket,' wrote Conn. 'Either way, the decision to send an acting 12th man and physiotherapist onto the field to deliberately waste time in the dying minutes of the tensely drawn first Test is disgraceful. It is clearly against the spirit of cricket and borders on cheating.'

But Strauss had the last word, and gave it to Collingwood: 'He just brought his character into the performance today,' said Strauss. 'He is a tenacious little redhead, that is what he is, and that's how he plays. He never takes a backward step, and he fights. It's the only way he knows.'

First Test, Cardiff, Wales

8, 9, 10, 11, 12 July 2009

Result: Match Drawn
Toss: England, who chose to bat
Series: 5-match series level 0–0
Umpires: Aleem Dar (Pakistan) and BR Doctrove (West Indies)
Match referee: JJ Crowe (New Zealand)
Player of the match: RT Ponting (Australia)

England 1st innings		R	M	B	4s	6s
AJ Strauss*	c Clarke b Johnson	30	90	60	4	0
AN Cook	c Hussey b Hilfenhaus	10	31	25	0	0
RS Bopara	c Hughes b Johnson	35	76	52	6	0
KP Pietersen	c Katich b Hauritz	69	196	141	4	0
PD Collingwood	c †Haddin b Hilfenhaus	64	150	145	6	0
MJ Prior†	b Siddle	56	99	62	6	0
A Flintoff	b Siddle	37	66	51	6	0
JM Anderson	c Hussey b Hauritz	26	69	40	2	0
SCJ Broad	b Johnson	19	22	20	4	0
GP Swann	not out	47	54	40	6	0
MS Panesar	c Ponting b Hauritz	4	15	17	0	0
Extras	(b 13, lb 11, w 2, nb 12)	38				
Total	(all out; 106.5 overs; 442 mins) 435 (4.07 runs per over)					

Fall of wickets 1–21 (Cook, 7.6 ov), 2–67 (Strauss, 19.6 ov), 3–90 (Bopara, 24.4 ov), 4–228 (Collingwood, 65.3 ov), 5–241 (Pietersen, 70.5 ov), 6–327 (Flintoff, 86.4 ov), 7–329 (Prior, 88.3 ov), 8–355 (Broad, 93.5 ov), 9–423 (Anderson, 102.4 ov), 10–435 (Panesar, 106.5 ov)

Bowling	O	M	R	W	Econ	
MG Johnson	22	2	87	3	3.95	
BW Hilfenhaus	27	5	77	2	2.85	(4nb, 1w)
PM Siddle	27	3	121	2	4.48	(5nb, 1w)
NM Hauritz	23.5	1	95	3	3.98	(3nb)
MJ Clarke	5	0	20	0	4.00	
SM Katich	2	0	11	0	5.50	

Australia 1st innings		R	M	B	4s	6s
PJ Hughes	c †Prior b Flintoff	36	61	54	5	0
SM Katich	lbw b Anderson	122	325	261	12	0
RT Ponting*	b Panesar	150	313	224	14	1
MEK Hussey	c †Prior b Anderson	3	24	16	0	0
MJ Clarke	c †Prior b Broad	83	176	145	9	1
MJ North	not out	125	357	242	13	0
BJ Haddin†	c Bopara b Collingwood	121	200	151	11	3
Extras	(b 9, lb 14, w 4, nb 7)	34				
Total	(6 wickets dec;					
	181 overs; 724 mins)	674 (3.72 runs per over)				

Did not bat MG Johnson, NM Hauritz, BW Hilfenhaus, PM Siddle
Fall of wickets 1–60 (Hughes, 14.6 ov), 2–299 (Katich, 84.6 ov), 3–325 (Hussey, 90.1 ov), 4–331 (Ponting, 94.5 ov), 5–474 (Clarke, 136.5 ov), 6–674 (Haddin, 180.6 ov)

Bowling	O	M	R	W	Econ	
JM Anderson	32	6	110	2	3.43	(1w)
SCJ Broad	32	6	129	1	4.03	(2w)
GP Swann	38	8	131	0	3.44	
A Flintoff	35	3	128	1	3.65	(7nb, 1w)
MS Panesar	35	4	115	1	3.28	
PD Collingwood	9	0	38	1	4.22	

England 2nd innings		R	M	B	4s	6s
AJ Strauss*	c †Haddin b Hauritz	17	78	54	1	0
AN Cook	lbw b Johnson	6	17	12	1	0
RS Bopara	lbw b Hilfenhaus	1	4	3	0	0
KP Pietersen	b Hilfenhaus	8	20	24	0	0
PD Collingwood	c Hussey b Siddle	74	344	245	6	0
MJ Prior†	c Clarke b Hauritz	14	37	32	1	0
A Flintoff	c Ponting b Johnson	26	89	71	3	0
SCJ Broad	lbw b Hauritz	14	61	47	1	0
GP Swann	lbw b Hilfenhaus	31	73	63	4	0
JM Anderson	not out	21	69	53	3	0
MS Panesar	not out	7	37	35	1	0
Extras	(b 9, lb 9, w 4, nb 11)	33				
Total	(9 wickets; 105 overs;					
	414 mins)	252 (2.40 runs per over)				

Fall of wickets 1–13 (Cook, 4.3 ov), 2–17 (Bopara, 5.3 ov), 3–31 (Pietersen, 10.4 ov), 4–46 (Strauss, 16.6 ov), 5–70 (Prior, 26.3 ov), 6–127 (Flintoff, 49.4 ov), 7–159 (Broad, 66.4 ov), 8–221 (Swann, 86.1 ov), 9–233 (Collingwood, 93.3 ov)

Bowling	O	M	R	W	Econ	
MG Johnson	22	4	44	2	2.00	(1nb, 4w)
BW Hilfenhaus	15	3	47	3	3.13	(4nb)
PM Siddle	18	2	51	1	2.83	(2nb)
NM Hauritz	37	12	63	3	1.70	(2nb)
MJ Clarke	3	0	8	0	2.66	
MJ North	7	4	14	0	2.00	
SM Katich	3	0	7	0	2.33	

Close of play
8 Jul day 1 – England 1st innings 336/7 (JM Anderson 2*, SCJ Broad 4*, 90 ov)
9 Jul day 2 – Australia 1st innings 249/1 (SM Katich 104*, RT Ponting 100*, 71 ov)
10 Jul day 3 – Australia 1st innings 479/5 (MJ North 54*, BJ Haddin 4*, 139 ov)
11 Jul day 4 – England 2nd innings 20/2 (AJ Strauss 6*, KP Pietersen 3*, 7 ov)
12 Jul day 5 – England 2nd innings 252/9 (105 ov) – end of match

Second Test, Lord's: 16–20 July

Andrew Strauss may have been buoyed by the dramatic and magnificent rearguard action of Anderson and Panesar on the final day of the first Test at Cardiff, but he had plenty to digest as he drove back to London the following morning and to his home ground, Lord's, the venue of the second Test; not least that his best batsman Kevin Pietersen and his talismanic all-rounder Andrew Flintoff were both struggling badly with injury.

The soreness in Flintoff's right knee had worsened progressively during the remainder of the match at Cardiff. Now, with only three days before the second Test was due to start on Thursday 16 July, his next appointment was with leading knee specialist Andy Williams in London.

Dr Nick Peirce explains. 'There was a fair amount of pressure to ensure that Flintoff could get through the second Test. It's a difficult balance. You don't want to mask an injury, so we didn't, because that can cause problems later on, but we wanted to explore all possibilities of getting him fit to play.'

That meant injections, cortisone divided into two doses and given into the soft tissues at the back of the knee as two injections; and a further injection given into the knee of a lubricant, Ostenil. This is an artificial synovial fluid that occurs as a natural lubricant in the joint, essentially oiling the knee. The drug is made from a highly purified form of bacteria, originally found in the guts of horses. When this information became public, one commentator joked, 'They think he'll be OK to play, but they'll have to feed him a mixture of hay and oats and put a blanket on him at the end of every spell. He's going to be a bit toey whenever those police horses go by, and on Sunday he's 7/4 favourite for the 4.25 at Kempton Park.'

Not that Flintoff was amused in the slightest. Indeed, he later described the day he spent with Williams, whose last needle injected a homoeopathic substance, as one of the least enjoyable of his career. And it was in these moments that the all-rounder finalised a decision about his cricket future that he had been considering for some time.

Rumours had already been circulating that Flintoff was about to confront a choice over whether he should continue to play in all forms of the game or merely some of them. One or two observers speculated that he might be ready to give up on international cricket altogether to allow him to cash in on the Twenty20 dollar, but the 31-year-old Lancastrian, who had always stressed how much it meant to him to play for the 'Three Lions', was determined that, if he was going to have to modify his contribution to England's effort, he did not want to curtail it completely. With this in mind, and still suffering not only from the fatigue he and his team-mates had felt in Cardiff, but also the growing soreness in his damaged knee, and mindful of the prospect of another crowded schedule of international cricket up to the end of the summer and beyond, he decided enough was enough. Once these Ashes were over, Flintoff would retire from Test cricket.

> '**It was a decision I made for the sake of my body and my sanity**'
>
> *Andrew Flintoff on his decision to retire from Test cricket*

'It was a decision I made some time before, and I made it for the sake of my body and my sanity,' he said. 'There's a limit to how much you can put your body through, and a limit to how much you can put yourself through emotionally and psychologically if most of the time when you should be enjoying your Test career, you're actually going through rehab and recovery.

'One or two papers had been speculating, so when I came away from seeing the specialist I decided the time was right to bring an end to all of that. I must admit I did feel a strong sense of relief that it was all going to be out in the open soon.'

Flintoff informed Strauss of his intention later that day. Though not totally unexpected, the news added to a growing list of issues occupying the England captain's thoughts as he approached the biggest match of his career.

'I knew what was in Fred's mind regarding the decision he may have to make about his future,' said Strauss, 'but I wasn't aware he was going to finalise it quite so soon. It was something we all pretty much expected him to be doing. There had certainly been rumours circulating that this was his intention come the end of the series, but the immediate issue was to work our way through what it meant as far as the team was concerned.

'What myself, the coach and Fred as well had to decide were the pros and cons of Fred making the announcement before the Test; whether, if he announced his decision here and now, it might actually be a distraction. Would it cause a big media interest? Of course. Would it distract us from our cricket? We were pretty sure it wouldn't. Finally, we felt the only person who might be distracted by it all would be Fred, as the other players would be fine. In fact we thought that making the decision public may provide a bit of relief for him and mean that he could just go out and enjoy his final four games. All things considered, we decided he should go ahead and make the news public as soon as everyone was ready.'

The announcement of England's squad for the second Test that day at 2pm had already caused the cricketing press to prick up its ears as it contained the following quote from national selector Geoff Miller: 'We have added Stephen Harmison to our squad . . .

as Andrew Flintoff injured his right knee at Cardiff and will undergo a precautionary scan later today.'

The sports desks of the national papers were moved to red alert on the Tuesday morning when the *Sun* ran a back-page story strongly predicting that Flintoff was about to announce his retirement from Test cricket from the end of the series.

The first many of the players knew of what was about to take place that day, however, was when they arrived at the ground for practice, or, in the case of Harmison and Alastair Cook, when they were travelling with Flintoff in Harmison's Volkswagen Touareg, en route.

Cook recalls: 'Fred told us on the journey from the hotel what he was going to do. He said he was going to make the announcement that morning, just to end all the speculation. He was amazed that information had already leaked out to one paper, and he said he wanted to go public so that people would stop writing about the ifs and maybes. He just wanted to get it all out in the open and move on. He was very straightforward about it in the car. He spelled it out, saying: "Well, this is how it's going to happen," in such a matter-of-fact way that it didn't sound as momentous as it might have done. To be honest, the news didn't exactly come as a shock. We all knew in the back of our minds that he couldn't keep putting himself through it.'

According to Anderson: 'The way Fred told us, just before practice, didn't allow for much sentiment. He said: 'I don't want this to detract from the series or practice or anything, but you might be asked about it later, so this is what I'm going to do. And that was that.'

Even though Pietersen had enough on his own plate, he felt for his team-mate. 'I know, I've been in the dressing-room with Flintoff for five years and I see how many injections he has had and how many scans. I've seen how many ice packs he's strapped onto his body. It's tough when somebody has to make a career decision like that because of injury; not because he doesn't want to play any more, but because his body won't let him. We all felt for him.'

Broad remembers: 'I'd heard nothing beforehand. We had a dinner on the Monday night in the Long Room, and I sat at a table with of a few of the press guys and there was actually a bit of a discussion concerning whether Fred might do this or that . . . and, to be honest, I didn't have a clue. I said, "Oh, I imagine he'll see out the series and see how he goes." Then, the next day, hearing him say it, his reasoning was very logical. Every Test he plays he's sore.

'I've not been in Fred's position where he's done two years' solid rehab. I can't imagine how frustrating that would be because when I've been injured for a week and I've not played, I'm already narky. So to have two years of it, I can only guess at how frustrating that must be. Also, to me, Freddie's one of those players who deserves a proper send-off, to have a chance to quit while he can still do himself justice on the field.'

In due course, Flintoff's decision was confirmed by the ECB in the following media release:

'England and Lancashire all-rounder, Andrew Flintoff, has today announced his retirement from Test cricket following the conclusion of his involvement in the current npower Ashes Test series.

Flintoff will continue to make himself available for selection for one-day internationals and international Twenty20 fixtures. After making his Test debut for England against South Africa in 1998, the 31-year-old has gone on to play 75 Tests for his country. Flintoff said: 'My body has told me it's time to stop. Since 2005, I've had two years where I've done nothing but rehab from one injury or another. It's been something I've been thinking about for a while, and I think this last problem I've had with my knee has confirmed to me that the time is now right.'

With Flintoff's long-term future addressed, it was now down to the medical team to concentrate on the immediate issue of getting him fit to play an Ashes Test within 48 hours, if humanly – or even superhumanly – possible.

According to Nick Peirce: 'This was a chance for him to have his moment in the sun, a chance to help him put some things right regarding what had happened in the 2006–07 series.

'All sorts of factors come into your decision-making as to how far you as a medical team are prepared to go to allow someone to play in these circumstances. Ultimately the question is, "Is he risking something dangerous?"'

'Fred himself was absolutely determined to play. He had lost a bit of confidence in his knee because he had sharp discomfort in it when bowling at Cardiff. We had a scan on the Monday night to check whether anything had significantly changed and to try and reassure him it was safe for him to play.

'Ideally, what we wanted him to do was to bowl a five- or six-over spell on the Tuesday and see how it recovered, and then to bowl him again on the Wednesday to see how the knee would react day to day. He batted on the Tuesday, that was no problem, but he didn't bowl until the Wednesday, the day before the Test match, when he bowled five overs at good intensity. He felt confident and didn't have a reaction, but we still waited until Thursday morning, at which point he made the decision to go for it.

'There was a risk but, on balance, it was a risk that was more likely to pay off than not. But Fred wouldn't have had it any other way.'

As if that wasn't enough for Strauss to deal with, he also had the issue of Kevin Pietersen's worsening Achilles problem. Pietersen admitted he had not been at the races at Cardiff. In fact, so down in the dumps had he been throughout the first Test that, at the end of the match, he spoke to Andy Flower and indicated that if this was as good as he was going to be maybe he shouldn't play at Lord's.

'Normally I'm quite a jovial guy in the dressing-room,' says Pietersen. 'People are abusing me. I'm abusing them. Just having a real good banter. But in Cardiff I moped around and I was not a good influence. Afterwards, I sat down with Andy Flower, the doctors and the medics and just said, "Guys, if that's how I'm going to be – just standing there and not being able to deliver – I can't play, because it doesn't do anything for the dressing-room."'

Strauss listened to Pietersen, as did Flower, but the England captain knew that if his number 4 could be persuaded out of his current mindset, and if the medics said it was safe for him to play, he could still be a key figure at Lord's.

'Fred was one issue,' said Strauss. 'He and the medical staff were confident he'd be fine to get through Lord's, although he might be a bit sore. KP was a slightly different situation because I think he was beginning to lose confidence in his ability to manage his Achilles, and he was really down. The way he batted in both innings in Cardiff, you could see he was being distracted by the injury. You could understand why. He was concerned about what was wrong with it and how long it would take to get better.'

Pietersen also knew that if he was going to play at Lord's at all, he owed it to the team and to the captain to do everything in his power not to let his strife affect team spirit.

'Normally I'm quite a jovial guy in the dressing-room. People are abusing me. I'm abusing them. Just having a real good banter. But in Cardiff I moped around and I was not a good influence'

Kevin Pietersen

'It was touch and go. I was desperate to play. I wanted to try and get on the honours board as an individual and to be part of an England team who could make history on this ground by being the first to beat Australia since 1934. But I didn't want to disrupt the team environment by playing and not being right. I said to Andy Flower, "I promise you that, if I play, I will make sure that nobody sees I'm injured and no one sees me down in the dumps."'

'Inside my attitude was, "I'm going to go and enjoy this Test match because if the Achilles flares up again, this will probably be my last chance to make an impact on the series."'

To give Pietersen every reassurance possible, the England medical team invited an assessment from leading Achilles surgeon Håkan Alfredson, who was holidaying on his boat off the coast of Malmo, Sweden when he got the call.

Peirce recalls: 'Clinically the Achilles had shown signs of improving, but Kevin was suffering from a very sharp pain that was disproportionate to the injury. He managed to get through Cardiff, but we went to see a back specialist when we arrived in London to exclude the possibility that the back was causing the problems. Then we contacted Håkan Alfredson. We discussed the findings from various scans, and he gave his advice that confirmed the situation was fairly unusual. Later, he agreed to break off from his holiday after the Lord's Test and fly to London to see Kevin in person but, as the week progressed, Kevin seemed to be responding to painkillers, did some aggressive batting in the nets and pronounced himself ready to play.'

Strauss's other issues were to do with selection. Two spinners had been the order of the 'dai' in Wales due to the dry and dusty surface. Here at Lord's, however, as Strauss knew only too well, if the pitch was going to help anyone it would help swing and seam bowlers.

Durham's Graham Onions had impressed in the Test series

against the West Indies with his swing at a lively pace, but had been left out in Cardiff to accommodate the extra spin bowler. At Lord's, however, it looked as though the final place in the team would come down to a straight choice between him and Monty Panesar, with Swann having confirmed his status as the team's number-one spinner.

Not surprisingly, most of the column inches and airtime on the eve of the action were filled by the news of Flintoff's impending retirement, with opinions expressed focused as much on the timing of the announcement as the fact of it happening.

Shane Warne wrote in *The Times*: 'Maybe Fred spoke to Andrew Strauss before deciding to reveal his intentions now rather than at the end of the series. Freddie is a team player through and through, so he must feel it will help the side to gel. At the same time, if you want to be devil's advocate, there are similar instances where teams have suffered.

'When I think back to Steve Waugh announcing his retirement before a home series against India in 2003–04, every Test match then became a farewell to him. It had a knock-on effect on the other guys, and on the focus of the team as a whole.'

Warne also had some selection advice for Andrew Strauss. Steve Harmison had been drafted into the squad, officially only as cover for Flintoff, but the scourge of so many England Test batsmen for the best part of two decades advised the England selectors to play the bowler formerly known as 'GBH' – Grievous Bodily Harmison – ahead of his Durham team-mate Onions. Warne, in his typically understated fashion, said: 'I cannot believe that England are serious about picking Graham Onions ahead of Steve Harmison today. Australia will just smash Onions around the park. He needs conditions to be in his favour, which is why he does well for Durham. Otherwise he is a very flat bowler. England could be about to make a decision they regret.'

With his head still spinning from having to deal with all of the aforementioned issues, Strauss took some time out on the eve of battle to try and gather his thoughts.

'I hadn't really managed to get any quiet time for myself between Cardiff and Lord's,' he said. 'I was tired, because Cardiff had been emotionally exhausting, and I remember spending the night before the game on my own. I just really didn't want to speak to anyone. I wanted to give my brain a break and try to clear my mind. There was a lot going on in my head.'

Flintoff was duly passed fit to play on the Thursday morning and so was Pietersen. Somehow Strauss also managed to resist Warne's suggestion, and England settled for the predicted switch of Onions for Panesar. Now all he and his England team-mates had to deal with was Australia in an Ashes Test at a venue where they had not known victory over these opponents for 75 years.

Strauss did his best to keep a cool, calm, rational grip on things, but he wasn't finding it easy. 'It was such a special thing for me,' he said. 'It was my first Ashes test match at Lord's, my home ground, if you like, as official captain. The Lord's Ashes Test match is probably the number-one Test match in world cricket and I'm thinking to myself, I'm leading England in an Ashes campaign and this Test match may be pivotal in the potential outcome of the series and it's my home ground and, yes, there were a lot of motivating factors for me.'

Once again, England's plan was simple, if different this time to Cardiff. Win the toss, bat first, see if Jimmy Anderson could

'Australia will just smash Onions around the park. He needs conditions to be in his favour . . . England could be about to make a decision they regret'

Shane Warne gets it wrong

regain his command of swing, Onions could rise to the Lord's occasion, Broad could get back some of his bite and Flintoff could underpin all their efforts with some seriously fast, throat-high deliveries.

Before any of that, however, Swann, sensing nervousness amongst his colleagues, felt the need to remind them to enjoy the occasion. If not now, when?

Pietersen recalls: 'We were sitting on the grass discussing various aspects of our performance at Cardiff, knowing we hadn't done ourselves justice and, because we were so keyed up and nervous, Swann said, "Look, lads, we're at Lord's, one of the greatest places to play cricket in the world. We're playing Australia and we're play-ing for the Ashes. Just bloody enjoy it."'

Looking back on that moment, Swann says: 'We had a little team meeting and there was all sorts in the Aussie press, saying it's easy to win at Lord's because the England players aren't that bothered, but for the Aussies there's 75 years of a winning record to maintain. And I remember just saying, something along the lines of "**** it, for the next five days let's absolutely soak everything up. Actually look around – don't just get stuck with tunnel vision on the game – look around and enjoy these five days because this is incredible." This is as good as it gets. England–Australia at Lord's, the architec-ture and all the paintings in the Long Room, the whole history of the game is here. All the ghosts of past players seem to go back to Lord's, not to haunt the place, but to give it an atmosphere, a mystique. I told the guys to feed off that.

'For me the whole week at Lord's was magical. Two days before the start I bumped into Stephen Fry at Andrew Strauss's benefit dinner. He's one of my absolute favourite comedians – Fry, not Strauss, that is – and I loved that message of support he recorded for us. "I don't want to put any pressure on you," he said, "but my entire happiness and well-being depends on you winning the Ashes."'

'I introduced myself to Stephen at the reception beforehand and I said, "Let's go and have a look at the Ashes." So there we were, in the Lord's museum at the MCC, standing in front of the glass case, staring at the Ashes urn, talking about *Blackadder*.'

At the toss, Ponting called heads again, and lost again. Strauss had no hesitation in taking first use.

> 'I don't want to put any pressure on you but my entire happiness and well-being depends on you winning the Ashes'
>
> *Stephen Fry to the team*

One spectator had more reason than most to soak up the atmosphere. Marcus Trescothick had been one of England's Ashes heroes in 2005, but was sadly absent from their thoughts since he announced his retirement from international cricket the previous winter. In 2005, he had been one of those players to have been hit by a wall of noise from the MCC members as they walked through the Long Room at Lord's on the first morning of the greatest series of their careers. This time he decided he wanted to be one of those leading the cheers, so he made his way to the heart of the old pavilion to await the entry of Strauss and his opening partner Alastair Cook.

Jostling for position with the MCC members, Trescothick stood a few rows back from the door through which his great friend Strauss and his successor, Cook, would pass into the Long Room, then heard the click-clacking of studs as England's longest-running opening pair made their way down the stairs from the home dressing-room, and finally lent his West Country burr to the uproar that followed.

Once he stepped through the pavilion gate and onto the billiard green grass, England's captain turned to England's vice-captain and said simply: 'What was that like?'

Strauss was ready, Cook was ready, and Lord's, bathed in sunlight, was bursting with readiness.

LORD'S, DAY ONE: ENGLAND 364 FOR 6

Cook says: 'I will remember that noise for a very long time. Ravi told me later that, up in the dressing-room, someone called for quiet as we walked out so that they could listen to the sound that came out of the Long Room. Jimmy Anderson called it "posh cheering". And when we emerged to go down the pavilion steps I thought to myself, Just please don't get nought after all that noise, because they won't make the same noise if I go back in with a duck.'

'I was expecting it,' says Strauss, 'but it still blew me away. It was ridiculous. It's very hard not to be emotional after going through that, but we had a job to do and, fortunately, the Australian bowlers made it a bit easier for us than they would have liked.'

In the event, Strauss and his partner responded emphatically to the challenge confronting them and Australian captain Ricky Ponting was powerless to halt the onslaught of runs that came before lunch, chiefly because of the glaring deficiency of his attack. Left-armer Mitchell Johnson, the new spearhead, was clearly battling both himself and his unorthodox low-slinging action. What made it worse for Johnson, Siddle and Hilfenhaus is the difficulty Lord's almost always poses for first-time callers, with the slope carrying the ball away from the batsman or into him, depending on which end you bowl from, and the fact that swing occasionally seems impossible to predict, let alone control. Furthermore, Johnson in particular seemed to be having all manner of problems controlling the Duke ball. In the match against the England Lions at Worcester, it was noticeable that Johnson had held the ball across the seam for long periods. Some believed this was to try and speed up the scuffing process and, therefore, encourage reverse swing for Brett Lee to exploit. However, few observers realised it was also because Johnson, who had only ever used the Kookaburra ball before in his short Test career, was finding it almost impossible to handle with any confidence a Duke ball that is noted for swinging far more.

Strauss recalls: 'Alastair Cook and I both realised pretty early that Johnson was struggling, as a lot of good bowlers tend to do the first time they play at Lord's. He was dropping the ball a bit short and wide, and we were cashing in on those deliveries. We wanted to set the tone. I don't think we were approaching it in a hot-headed manner as we had done in Cardiff, just saying we're going to try and smash everything. We just felt that the conditions were in our favour, Johnson obviously wasn't bowling very well and, though both Siddle and Hilfenhaus bowled spells where you could just leave balls alone, there were other times when we could hit more aggressively.'

Try as he might, Johnson simply couldn't settle. Of the 22 boundaries Strauss and Cook shared through the morning session, exactly half of them came from Johnson's bowling. Operating from the Pavilion End, the Queenslander's first seven overs cost 47 runs. When Ponting switched him to the Nursery End at the start of the second hour, there was no discernible improvement, as Cook twice latched on to wide deliveries to thrash two successive boundaries through the offside in the first over of his second spell.

Frustration spilled over for Johnson, who unleashed a primal scream into his baggy green cap as he trudged away into the deep. But while his batting colleagues might not have shared his sentiments, Anderson remembers empathising with his opposite number.

'I've huge sympathy for any bowler who goes through that. Whereas the majority of our top six, when that was happening, were going, "Wey-hey, he's lost it here," I think all the bowlers were going, Yeah . . . but.

'Three months ago he was the spearhead of their attack, and then the first couple of games he was a bit off. So it does happen to people, and you just hope it's not you. I recall having a nightmare in Johannesburg on the last tour there when I didn't know where the bloody thing was going.

'I was bowling so badly that even when I took a wicket I was almost embarrassed to have done so, so I did feel a real connection with the pain he was going through.

'The Lord's slope is very tricky. You have to get used to feeling a little off balance when you land on the crease. From the Pavilion End, you just end up getting pushed into the stumps. It's not that obvious to the naked eye, but when you get to the crease, all of a sudden you're closer than you want to be to the stumps. And the opposite applies from the Nursery End.'

Nor was Johnson the only Australian bowler to suffer a crisis of confidence. Siddle, too, was thrown by the Lord's slope, and lost his direction in spectacular fashion. Wicketkeeper Haddin saved a couple of runs by getting a paw on a delivery that kept going beyond first slip, but was helpless when an overcompensation from Siddle sent the ball scuttling down the legside for four byes. Only Hilfenhaus, who began with three maidens, held things together. Nasser Hussain, summarising for Sky Sports, summed it up: 'That's as poorly as I've seen Australia bowl for a long, long time,' said the former England captain.

Cook, Strauss and their team-mates could not have cared less about that. England's opening pair reached 50

> 'The Lord's slope is very tricky. You have to get used to feeling a little off balance when you land on the crease'
>
> *James Anderson*

after just 49 minutes. The hundred was posted at 12.43pm, and the stand had blossomed to 126 by lunch.

The sunshine that had bathed the morning's play disappeared after the break and the changing conditions appeared favourable to the Australian bowlers, but they were still on the ropes. What made it worse for Ponting was that a couple of fielding mishaps were greeted with a scornful lack of respect by English supporters all around the ground. When Haddin allowed four byes to go between his legs off Marcus North's gentle off-spin, the more vociferous members of the crowd wasted no time in reminding the Aussie keeper to try using his gloves and, later in the same over, when Ponting himself misfielded in the covers to allow a single, each replay on the giant screen was met with a greater volume of ironic cheers.

Ponting's state of mind was hardly eased by an incident in the 36th over that summed up his and Australia's day so far. With England 136 without loss, Hilfenhaus found the edge of Strauss's bat with the England captain two runs short of his half-century, but the bowler had overstepped the mark and, to compound his frustration, Haddin then floored the one-handed attempt.

Just when Ponting must have believed things could not get any worse for him, they did, three overs later, when Strauss, now on 52, survived a chance that did lasting damage to the Australian cause. A ferocious straight drive thrashed through the fingers of bowler Nathan Hauritz like a hurricane through a haystack, and left them pointing in diametrically opposed directions. The middle finger of his spinning hand, eerily at odds with the rest, was in obvious need of attention, and the more queasy among his colleagues shied away as he tramped off to get the dislocation reset.

The days when Australia could rely on Shane Warne and Glenn McGrath to steady the ship were over and, without the injured Brett Lee, the Australian attack suddenly looked, well, ordinary.

Finally Johnson unleashed his mystery delivery – the straight one – and the surprise element proved too much for Cook, who played around it to become Johnson's 100th Test victim and leave England on 196 for 1 from the penultimate ball of the 48th over. Cook received warm applause from the Lord's crowd, but could not hide his disappointment at falling just five runs short of what would have been his second Ashes ton. The Essex left-hander had been appointed vice-captain before the start of the series and had not enjoyed the greatest of starts to this Ashes series, but Strauss was impressed by how he'd stuck to the task even though he was still searching for his form.

'What's great about Cookie is that he doesn't get fazed by the situation. If he plays and misses a couple of times, he doesn't let it affect him. Mind you, how he didn't let that roar affect him when we came out to bat, I'll never know.'

Now Strauss settled himself again to follow the example of the Australian bastmen at Cardiff and cash in on a promising start and, although England lost Bopara at 222 for 2, leg before to Hilfenhaus after another bright flurry, Pietersen helped his captain to complete a well-deserved and potentially crucial century. Strauss couldn't help but notice, however, the strain on his partner's face.

'Kevin was struggling,' said Strauss. 'I was delighted he was playing, but it had been touch and go. He did his best to put his Achilles injury to the back of his mind, and to play as if it wasn't a concern, but he didn't look good. In fact, I realised very quickly that if this was as mobile as he was going to be, he would have to miss some cricket to get himself right.'

Strauss reached his hundred, which included 15 boundaries, when he cut the penultimate delivery before tea, sent down by Hilfenhaus, for three. It was his fourth Test ton at Lord's, his third against Australia and, in terms of its significance, the hope started to grow among his team-mates that it might be up there with the magnificent ton he made at The Oval in 2005 to keep England's noses in front.

'It was a great moment. I suppose I had a bit of a point to prove after Cardiff, and it was against Australia as well. It was a great occasion and to score a hundred on it . . . that's got to go down as one of the best days of my career.'

Pietersen has grown to appreciate just how good a batsman his skipper has become since returning to the side after missing the tour to New Zealand at the start of 2008.

'He's really come back to himself since being left out. He's obviously got a very good head on his shoulders. He approaches the game very simply and he sticks to his gameplan. When he's playing well he plays brilliantly well, because he's got that pull shot that he hits on length. Anything that is slightly short he pulls through or over midwicket, and to have that in your locker as a batsman is huge, because the bowler knows he can't miss his length.

'The boys in the dressing-room loved this innings because they love him as a skipper and he leads them well. The great thing about Strauss is that you can take the mickey out of him. Matthew Hoggard was merciless in 2005, calling him a "posh twit" and other words to that effect because he went to public school at Radley. Mind you, you wouldn't think his parents paid for his education when you see his area in the dressing-room, because he's the messiest player I've ever come across. I don't like it. My place is absolutely spotlessly clean, but I look down and suddenly there's Straussy's jockstrap in my bag and other stuff all over the place and I say to him, "Strauss, sort your life out!"'

Sadly for him, Pietersen's day was cut short when he was caught at the wicket as Siddle got one to move away from him from the Pavilion End and England were 267 for 3.

Whether the need to block all day at Cardiff had got under Collingwood's skin, he paid the penalty for a loose shot with

England on 302 when he holed out to Michael Clarke. And when Matt Prior fell shortly afterwards to leave the score on 317 for 5, Andrew Flintoff entered the arena for the first time in his final Lord's Test to a chorus of cheers and left, after edging Hilfenhaus to Ponting to reduce England to 333 for 6 to a chorus of groans.

'Maybe my shot was a reaction to the way I batted in Cardiff,' says Collingwood. 'I was in two minds – should I play it, should I not? And if you don't commit yourself a hundred per cent to it, you've had it. But thank goodness for Strauss. We'd spoken in depth about making big runs, and to finish the day on 161 not out was exactly what we were talking about. I think all the way through the innings we felt as though the ball was doing things, either swinging around or the odd one was moving down the hill, but he just played in such a balanced way. You knew it was one of those knocks that might win you the match.

'It was a great effort from him after everything that had happened at Cardiff and since then, but he seems to get into his own bubble when he's batting. I think the captaincy actually spurs him on a lot more and seems to make him concentrate a lot more. To have the mental toughness to go out and do what he did, even though he was knackered and his head must have been spinning, was exceptional. It was a make-or-break partnership with Cook, as simple as that. It was exactly what we needed as a team, and it certainly gave us confidence for the rest of the match.'

'I felt great overnight,' said Strauss. 'But the close-of-play score of 364 for 6, though handy, was fewer than we might have made. I enjoyed getting to the hundred and the 150 even more. The big-screen operator put me under a bit of pressure at one stage when it suddenly showed that I only had four to get to get reach 5,000 Test runs. I'm not sure quite what was going on there. Fortunately I got a big full toss from Hilfenhaus that ran down to third man.

'But I definitely didn't think the job was done. I was utterly and absolutely determined to come back the next day and push on through 200 and beyond. I wanted us to get a massive score to put pressure on Australia, and I was ready to make a big contribution to that.'

LORD'S, DAY TWO: ENGLAND 425, AUSTRALIA 156 FOR 8

Sadly for Strauss, things didn't quite work out as planned.

'I should have known,' said Strauss. 'Maybe I got too focused on what I was supposed to be doing. Maybe I should have taken a leaf out of someone else's book and gone out and got hammered the night before.'

The first ball of the day, bowled by Hilfenhaus from the Nursery End was, according to the England skipper, 'just a regular ball that swung in. I can't quite work out why I decided to leave it.' And neither he nor Hilfenhaus, nor anyone else, could quite believe that it crashed into his off stump to reduce England to 364 for 7.

Strauss had been warned. One of the newspapers pointed out that Strauss had always struggled after ending a day on an unbeaten century, and Stuart Broad had brought this scary truth to his attention. Overnight hundreds in both innings in South Africa in 2004–05 were followed by a further six and three runs respectively the following morning. In New Zealand in 2007–08 he added just four runs to an overnight 173, and in the West Indies earlier in the year he added just three to a first-day 139.

'I've been a hundred not out in my career seven times overnight, and the most runs I've scored the next day is six,' says Strauss. 'Yes, Stuart Broad came up with that stat and I wish he hadn't. I've no idea why it happens. Maybe I should bat slower in future and make sure I'm about 98 not out overnight.'

'Maybe I got too focused on what I was supposed to be doing. Maybe I should have taken a leaf out of someone else's book and gone out and got hammered the night before'

Strauss once again fails to build on an overnight century

Nevertheless, any fears Strauss may have felt that the innings was about to crumble soon disappeared as his tail-enders once again attacked to good effect. Broad, then Jimmy Anderson and Graham Onions, helped push England past 400 and beyond to 425. Bearing in mind how much the pitch had offered the seamers, and how the overhead conditions had encouraged swing, England were quietly confident that this was a more than serviceable score.

Anderson's audacious backfoot drive was the first of his five boundaries off Johnson during a rapid 29, and his 47-run partnership with Onions for the tenth wicket helped England regain the momentum. Johnson appeared less than impressed, exchanging words with Anderson when it was all over.

Anderson recalls: 'I can't remember when it started. I'd hit him for four a few times through the offside and he wasn't best pleased, so I think he was just getting frustrated and angry. And I just gave him some back.

'I've always had a short fuse. I'm very competitive, and it tends to come out when I'm playing sport. When I'm bowling it comes out as me having a go at someone. I actually have to try and control it a little bit because a few years ago I got into strife for shoulder-barging Runako Morton in a one-day match against the West Indies at Edgbaston. But it happens in everything I do, even playing golf.

91

'Admittedly I've never shoulder-charged anyone playing golf, not yet, anyway. I normally end up lobbing my clubs into the trees. But I did actually nearly kill Graeme Swann with my driver once.

'I've just got to have an angry swing after hitting a bad shot, and this time the club slipped out of my hands and whacked him straight in the chest.'

In the event, having done the job with the bat, England were hoping that Anderson could find the swing he just couldn't lay his hands on at Cardiff. Andrew Strauss at slip and Matt Prior next to him realised he had relocated it almost straight away; they were soon followed by the rest of the England side and, more importantly, by the Australian batsmen.

'That was a massive moment,' said the captain. 'When Jimmy managed to swing the ball right from the off, that was a huge shot in the arm to us. At Cardiff, we'd only taken six wickets in the whole match. Now he got Phillip Hughes out early and then, more importantly, Ponting as well. But it wasn't just the fact that he got Ponting out that was so significant. Before he did so he probably bowled him 20-odd balls, and Ponting didn't look comfortable at any stage. I'm sure the rest of their batsmen were watching that going on and thinking, if Ponting's struggling, we're in trouble here.'

Hughes, on his 'home' ground at Lord's, was tucked up for space and was caught by the keeper for four. With Anderson swinging the ball both ways at will, and Flintoff supporting him with his pace, Ponting survived until the Burnley Express swung one into his pads late to which he had no answer.

The Australian captain aimed to push the ball through the onside, but the ball ducked under his bat, whacked into his pad, then spooned to the England captain at first slip. Anderson led the appeals and the England supporters who had watched the Aussie skipper amass a brilliant 150 less than a week before held their breath while the officials began their attempts to sort out what had happened. Prior was not exactly certain for what Ponting should be given out, only that he must be.

'Initially I was going up for an lbw shout, 'Says Prior.' Then there was a feeling that Ricky had hit the ball onto his pad. So then I thought, well, if he's hit it he's out caught and if he hasn't he's out lbw, so either way he's got to be out.'

First umpire Rudi Koertzen consulted with his partner Billy Doctrove at square leg to see if he could confirm that the ball had carried to Strauss and, by doing so, he indicated he believed the ball had indeed travelled into his pad via an inside edge. The pair then decided to refer the issue of whether the ball had been taken cleanly to the television umpire, Nigel Long.

The legitimacy of the catch confirmed, to an explosion of cheering, Koertzen used his slow finger of death to send Ponting on his way.

The Australian captain was clearly aggrieved to be given out caught, as he felt he hadn't got a nick on the ball. He was proved right by television technology on that count but, as Hawkeye also showed, the ball would have cleaned up all three stumps had the pads not got in the way. To the England supporters, at least, it felt that justice had been done, though Ponting may not have seen it that way at the time.

Leaving the controversy aside, Anderson and Strauss were delighted because a pre-prepared plan had worked to perfection. Anderson explains: 'It happened just as we wanted: to set him up by dragging him right across his stumps with the away-swinger and then bowling one into him.'

With Australia in trouble on 10 for 2, and with probably the best batsman in the world already out, England, cheered on by an army of celebrities including the ubiquitous Fry, Daniel Radcliffe and Mick Jagger, as well as the Barmy Army, sensed blood.

Flintoff had shown no signs of an adverse reaction to his injections while batting, but one or two players were already picking up warning signs that his knee might be feeling the strain.

'I can't remember which over it was,' said Collingwood, 'but I did catch a glimpse of him grimacing. I was watching from second slip and I said to Strauss, "Be careful, Fred's limping." And he said, "Is he?" Someone else passed me in between overs and said: "I think Fred's cooked."

'He never said anything himself, but when he ended his spell I went and stood next to him at slip and asked him if he was OK. He said: "It's strange. When I run in to bowl I can't feel it, but when I walk it feels like I'm being knifed." I said: "Well, keep bloody bowling then!" Then he said: "It's funny you should say that, because that's exactly what I was thinking."'

Strauss says: 'If I asked him how he was, he'd say: "Yes, fine. It's more sore when I'm fielding than bowling." And I said: "Well, you're just going to have to let us know. It's hard for me to tell what I need to do. You know your body better than I do, so if there's a real issue then let me know." He said: "No, I'll be fine." So that was pretty much the last conversation we had about it that day.'

Flintoff admits: 'To be honest. I may have been a little bit economical with the truth. Whatever I told Strauss and Colly, the knee was hurting all the time. But I didn't want to leave the field, miss any games or not play the full series.

'I was watching from second slip and I said to Strauss, "Be careful, Fred's limping." Someone else passed me in between overs and said: "I think Fred's cooked"'

Paul Collingwood

'The one thing I did truly believe was that, however much it hurt, I could still bowl on it, and could still make a difference. From the time it first flared up in Cardiff I modified my action and found a way to bowl that took as much strain off the knee as possible – basically by using my upper-body strength and my shoulder and not worrying about the finer points of my action. I was struggling, but I was determined to do whatever it took to keep going.'

With Australia on 27 for 2, England's progress was halted by lunch, and the break was extended while Her Majesty the Queen met the players on the field.

As is the custom, the players from both teams were presented to the Royal party, which included HRH Prince Philip. Ravi Bopara was clearly dazzled because when asked what he thought of the great lady he replied: 'I thought she was cute.'

> **'I may have been a little economical with the truth. Whatever I told Strauss and Colly, the knee was hurting all the time'**
>
> *Andrew Flintoff*

Prior recalls: 'Actually, I've met the Queen a few times. I met her at Loughborough when she opened the Academy there, and I met her at Lord's on my debut, against the West Indies. So we're in regular contact. She didn't say anything to me, though Prince Philip asked me if I was the wicketkeeper because I had my pads on at the time and we were in the field. He said, "Do those pads actually work?" and I said, "Well, you're meant to use your hands most of the time, but every now and again the ball does get you on the shin, so yes, they're OK." Then he saw I'd got a strapping on my injured finger and he said: "Well the pads may work, but the gloves obviously don't."'

Paul Collingwood was just desperate to avoid repeating the unfortunate experience of Rowan Atkinson in his notorious 'film premiere' scene from television's *Mr Bean*. And he was also surprised to find that the Royal visit meant the usual sumptuous lunches on offer at Lord's had been replaced by a rather more mundane buffet.

The effect of such relatively meagre pickings, and a spot of rain, which interrupted proceedings twice in the afternoon session, was to slow England's progress to a virtual crawl. By tea, Simon Katich and Mike Hussey had steered Australia to 87 for 2, and it looked as though the initial burst of enthusiasm might come to naught.

Then, at 4.56pm, Onions enjoyed a moment he will never forget.

He explains: 'I'd seen Steve Harmison bounce Katich out when we played together in the Lions match and I thought to myself, OK, I'm going to give him a go here. I positioned my fine leg slightly squarer, I bounced him, he got in position to hook and then hit it upwards. I just remember thinking, catch it, and then Stuart Broad came running round and he did catch it. It was brilliant. I just remember there was a massive smile on my face, running as fast as I could to try and congratulate him. You've got to get yourself going. I don't care whether or not it's the first game of the season for Durham, or your first Test wicket, it's good to get off the mark. It's a massive thing because the longer you go without getting it, the more pressure you're under, so it was like, Phew, I've done it now. After that, maybe I was guilty of being a little too enthusiastic and trying a little too hard, but when you're playing against Australia you want to do so well you can be suckered into that, so I had to take a step back and think to myself, just enjoy it. I suppose that's just taking care of the emotions really.'

Australia were 103 for 3 and the door was once again ajar. Flintoff and Anderson charged through it.

First, Flintoff sent down a monster of a delivery at 95.1mph, which Hussey either decided to leave, or was simply beaten for pace, as it nipped back and bashed into his stumps. Flintoff was proving his theory right. The faster he ran in, the less pain he felt. Now the pain was all Hussey's. Australia were 111 for 4.

Next it was Anderson's turn to strike, in the very next over, when Michael Clarke, on one, fell straight into the short-midwicket trap sprung by Strauss to be caught by Cook, and the curse of Nelson, to leave Australia on 111 for 5. Almost out of nowhere, England had reduced Australia to scrapping for all their worth to avoid the follow-on, with the target figure still 112 runs away.

Marcus North became Anderson's fourth victim for the day, bowled for nought attempting an ambitious pull to reduce Australia to 139 for 6, then, with the murky light in need of boosting by Lord's four new floodlights, Stuart Broad's policy of bowling short and fast at Mitchell Johnson paid off – Australia were now 148 for 7 – and, almost unbelievably, did so again against Brad Haddin soon after to leave the visitors reeling on 152 for 8.

For Anderson, the day's work was rather more satisfying than his experiences in Cardiff.

'When the ball starts swinging straight away, you feel a real wave of energy. The fielders can sense it too, so they're buzzing and everyone gets the feeling that things are going to happen. Instead of thinking, How the hell are we going to bowl these guys out?, there's a real sense that if you stay patient and ask enough questions, you've a chance of putting them under real pressure.

'And from a personal perspective, it's huge. You're given the ball to take wickets. That's your job and when you actually do it, it's fantastic. When the captain is asking you, "Are you OK? Can you bowl another one?" rather than taking you off, it does give you a lot of confidence.'

Lord's was bouncing, and Strauss knew that if his team held its nerve from here they could change the complexion of the entire series. They would have to wait to do so, however, as the umpires decided that the artificial light was projecting shadows and, there-fore, interfered with the batsmen's vision. As a result, play was abandoned for the day at 6.23pm.

Strauss recalls: 'That was a huge day for us. After what had happened in Cardiff, when we just never looked like taking wickets, we were able to exert real pressure on their batsmen. All the bowlers did brilliantly, and showed that we were going to be able to compete with Australia all summer. I slept a lot more soundly that night.'

LORD'S, DAY THREE: AUSTRALIA 215, ENGLAND 311 FOR 6

The celebrities just kept on coming through the Grace Gates and the other entrances to the home of cricket. England's performance over the first two days at Lord's had rekindled the hope that Strauss and his men may yet gain revenge for the hammering they had suffered in 2006–07 and that they could unite cricket supporters across the nation in celebrations reminiscent of 2005.

Now came Russell Crowe, otherwise known as the Gladiator Maximus, Captain Jack Aubrey and Robin Hood, and the cousin of New Zealand Test-playing brothers Martin and Jeff Crowe (the latter now an ICC match referee). The Hollywood star was there to entertain listeners to *Test Match Special,* and he certainly impressed Jonathan Agnew with his in-depth knowledge of the game and with the fact that he had his own cricket pitch back home in Lalaland. Now *that's* entertainment.

For the moment, however, the only thing on the England player's minds on that third morning was to bring down the curtain on the Australian innings.

On the way to the ground Strauss considered his options. He was keen to enforce the follow-on, but decided he would only do so if two things happened. One, if England picked up the remainder of Australia's wickets quickly and cheaply so that his bowlers were not overexerted. Two, that bowling conditions remained conducive to wicket-taking. The last thing he wanted to do was let Australia have a bat if the sun was shining and the pitch became more benign than it had been the previous day.

In the event, the first of the two conditions was not met. England employed Broad to keep bowling short and straight and Onions and Anderson to swing it, but the sun had cheered up the pitch to such an extent that Hauritz, Siddle and Hilfenhaus were able to put on another 59 for the remaining two wickets. Strauss, also mindful that he wanted to protect and preserve Flintoff for an all-out attack in the second innings, was reluctantly on the point of bringing the talisman on to end the tail-end resistance. Flintoff was willing, at one stage turning to him in the slips and asking: 'Do want me to have a go?'

Strauss recalls: 'I said to the guys before going out that my intention was to enforce the follow-on. I thought it was a great opportunity to go and bowl them out again, but I wanted to see how the wicket played before deciding absolutely. The Australian batsmen hung around, didn't look in a lot of trouble and, as the morning went on, the conditions started saying to me that this was a great day to bat.

'When they got to nearly 200 before the ninth wicket fell (when Onions had Hauritz caught by Collingwood with the second ball of his spell to reduce Australia to 196 for 9), I was still saying to the lads, "We'll probably enforce it." Then, when Hilfenhaus and Siddle hung on for the tenth wicket I just thought, No, no. Let's bat well, give the bowlers a rest and then give them lots of time to bowl Australia out. As for Fred, I was mindful that, with the possibility that the pitch would flatten out here, we would need everything we could get from him in the second innings, and I wanted to preserve him for that.

Anderson just failed to put himself on the honours board again, finishing with 4 for 55, but it was he who had done the damage. Graham Onions performed creditably in his Ashes debut, finishing with 3 for 41 off his 11 overs, including the final wicket of the innings when he had Siddle caught by Strauss in the slips, to cheers of relief and anticipation, to dismiss Australia for 215. It had been a frustrating hour for England but, with a lead of 210 and more than half the available playing time remaining, the task facing them now was to bat Australia out of the game.

Onions was happy just being there.

'I was disappointed not to play at Cardiff,' he says. 'I'd bowled well in the nets beforehand, then I took seven wickets for England against Warwickshire the week before. I felt good within myself, and ready. It's been a massive plus for me that I've played about ten or 12 games at Lord's for Durham, for the MCC or for England, because for someone who generally bowls reasonably straight, you're always in the game on that slope. I knew if I could get the ball to swing a little bit as well, then great.

'I've got some big memories of Lord's. At the MCC game at the beginning of the year, Daniel Radcliffe, the actor who plays Harry Potter, came rushing over and asked me for my autograph. I said to him, "I'm sorry, this is really weird for me. Can I have *your* autograph?" He just said, "No, look, I've been impressed with your bowling and you'll play for England one day." And I thought to myself, well, that's OK. Maybe he'll put a spell on my bowling.

'I can't deny I'm thrilled to have got my name on the dressing-room honours board so early in my career, having got five wickets against the West Indies. When we pitched up in the home dressing-room, the last name on the bowling list was mine, and when Strauss said I was playing, he also said, "You're under absolutely no pressure at all. Go out and enjoy yourself." They told me on the morning of the game because they were waiting on Fred's fitness.

And when the time came, I didn't actually feel nervous. I was just so excited.'

Collingwood was impressed by his Durham team-mate's Ashes bowling debut: 'As well as using the slope well, he surprises people with his pace.' Maybe that was what first attracted the attention of singing star Lily Allen, attention Onions was blissfully unaware of at the time.

Miss Allen's thoughts over Strauss's decision not to enforce the follow-on are unknown, but the England captain was criticised by some as being ultra-defensive. Former England captain Mike Atherton said he would have enforced it, but then added: 'I don't think it makes that much difference either way. England shouldn't be worried about chasing any total against this attack.'

Stuart Broad agrees: 'The follow-on was an option but, personally, I think it's the most overrated thing in cricket. I think it's always best to let your bowlers get fresh, get the opposition back in the field and then you're ready go at them as a fresh, collective unit again. Keep them running around in the field for as long as you can to tire them out and then really tear into them.'

Onions didn't mind either. 'I was delighted to finish off the innings like that, to have made a personal contribution to our effort.'

Strauss mouthed, 'We'll have a bat,' as he ran off, and he and Cook moved serenely to 57 without loss by lunch. Nine boundaries were scored in the first ten overs alone, and England looked ready to kick on. But they stumbled, losing both openers in quick succession and, at 74 for 2, less than 300 ahead of Australia and mindful of the fact that Australia had scored nearly 700 runs in the first Test and that, in recent times, Lord's pitches have had a habit of gradually falling into a deep sleep, there was still work to be done.

Now Bopara, who had been accused of being too 'shot happy' in the first Test, and Pietersen, who is rarely accused of anything else, knuckled down to build one of the key partnerships of the series. It may only have raised 73 runs but, in taking up sufficient time without allowing Australia another breakthrough, must have dampened Australia's ambitions of getting out of this match with anything other than a draw.

Bopara admits he was struggling to restrain his attacking instincts. 'My partnership with Kevin Pietersen was not exactly an example of us at our fluent best. It was tricky checking the impulse to play shots, but our aim was to establish a platform.'

Strauss immediately understood just how important this stand was. He says: 'That was a tricky spell. Hilfenhaus bowled brilliantly and both batsmen were really struggling to find the ball. You could sense from the crowd that they thought we should be pushing on and attacking, and there was an element of that among ourselves, but also we knew that with Johnson struggling, once Hilfenhaus was finished, they would have to bring on the spinner again and it would be a lot easier for us. And that was the way it proved. So Ravi and KP did an excellent job, and gave us the opportunity to really go out and have a bash.'

While Strauss and his team-mates were happy with that, they were equally devastated by the sight of Pietersen hobbling between the wickets, according to one newapaper, like 'Long John Silver without the parrot'. They knew the significance of this. Put simply, Pietersen might even be playing in his last match of the summer.

Pietersen said: 'It was a very important partnership. Ravi and I understood the situation. There were two and a half days left in the Test match. We set ourselves to bat until teatime, even if we only scored about 20. We had to take the game away from the Australians. Take away all their momentum and shift it back our way so that after tea we could then go out and attack.

'"We cannot let them back into the game." We kept saying that to each other.'

'But I was struggling. In fact, I'd known from the previous evening that I was almost certainly playing my last match of the series because, when I came off the field at the end of that second day, I was virtually in tears with the pain. I tried not to show it in the dressing-room. I kept laughing and kept going with the boys because I thought I owed it to the team.

'So, even with the strongest painkillers, batting on that third day was agony. I could barely run between the wickets at all, and when I reached for a couple of balls wide of off stump from Siddle, I knew that any runs I was going to score in that innings from that point on were going to have to be boundaries.

'Once Ravi was out, Colly hit a ball into the outfield that, under normal circumstances, was an easy three, possibly four, but I just couldn't manage it. I had to send him back and I just felt terrible about it.'

Collingwood remembers: 'He was in a lot of pain. When I hit that ball off Siddle towards the boundary, I knew it would be three and I was even thinking of running four, but KP just couldn't manage it. He didn't say much at the time, but after the end of the day's play he couldn't stop apologising. Having seen how bad he was, I feared the worst. The Achilles was just too far gone for him; he needed something doing there and then.'

In the event, Pietersen and Bopara did last until tea with England on 130 for 2, but after they departed in quick succession soon afterwards – Pietersen's Test average dipping below 50 in the calendar year for the first time as a result – Collingwood, Prior and Flintoff took full advantage.

Ponting, sporting one of those faces your mother warned you to lose sharpish in case the wind changed direction, chewed his gum feverishly as his team were forced to concentrate on damage limitation. Where was Warne? Where was McGrath?

Where Bopara and Pietersen had scratched, albeit to good effect, Prior and Flintoff smashed. Unfurling some gorgeous cover drives, the England wicketkeeper/batsman once again underlined his growing value to the side. Many had considered him the best batsman among the contenders for the wicketkeeper's gloves. Now, having improved his glovework beyond recognition, thanks to sessions with former England keeper Bruce French, he was quickly developing into the finished article in both departments. Fred, cheered to the rafters in his final Test innings at Lord's, played with the freedom the occasion merited and an aerial drive and smash to third man for four in one Johnson over, were Bothamesque. Make that Flintoffesque.

Those beauties took England's lead beyond 500, and Strauss had already sent messages onto the ground to alert his men of a desire to declare and have 20 minutes at the opposition openers. Rain at 6.23pm scuppered that idea, but England supporters left the ground believing that only a storm of biblical proportions could prevent England from ending 75 years of Ashes hurt at the game's headquarters.

LORD'S, DAY FOUR: ENGLAND 311 FOR 6, AUSTRALIA 313 FOR 5

Knowing what they knew about Flintoff's current condition and long-term prognosis, some within the England set-up feared he might only have one last great performance with the ball in the Test arena in him.

Those who had paid to come to the ground for the fourth day of the 2009 Lord's Ashes Test may not have been fully up to speed with the medical condition of the man the Barmy Army love to call 'Super Freddie Flintoff'. There was even speculation in some of the papers that this could be Freddie's last ever Test.

Either way, what everyone wanted to see was Flintoff getting among Ricky Ponting and his team-mates and bringing the country's Ashes hopes back on track.

Strauss, seeing the wet weather blowing across the ground as the players practised on the fourth morning, made up his mind to declare straight away. Fifteen minutes were knocked off the start of the day, with the threat of further showers cutting the 196 overs at his disposal to dismiss Australia, persuading the England captain to waste no further time.

He had been pilloried by some for taking too long to declare in the Caribbean on a couple of occasions. This time, with Australia requiring 522 runs to win, the target, if reached, would obliterate the previous world record Test chase of 418 for 7 made by the West Indies against the Australians in Antigua in 2002–03.

Strauss recalls: 'The weather wasn't promising and the forecast bad, so we thought we might possibly miss a whole session. I discussed the declaration with Andy Flower and I remember him saying, "Look, if they make that many runs, they'll deserve to win, so let's give ourselves as much time as we can."'

The stage was set for Flintoff and he filled every inch of it. Relishing his new-ball role, Flintoff's opening barrage of bouncers to Phillip Hughes was followed up with some equally aggressive words, and the England supporters recognised immediately what they might be about to witness – a cricketing force of nature at his magnificent best, conceivably for the very last time. Charging in from the Pavilion End, his every step a drum beat inspiring an echo from the crowd a notch louder than the last, England's talisman was fuelled by emotion, driven by desire, and seemingly unstoppable, despite the occasionally crippling pain in his right knee.

Katich was the first to find Flintoff impossible to resist. When he was well held at gully by Kevin Pietersen at 11.29am, England's plan to get the ball full and down the slope outside off stump to the left-hander had been executed to perfection. The English voices among the 28,000 crowd at Lord's roared with delight. Flintoff acknowledged the plan and its formulator, bowling coach Ottis Gibson, by pointing to him on the dressing-room balcony.

Australian fingers were pointing at umpire Rudi Koertzen, however, as television replays showed Flintoff had sent down a no-ball.

England's supporters saw a rather different picture, however – their minds raced back to all those memories in which Flintoff lit up the 2005 series, of those great efforts of will with which he demoralised Australia and invigorated England. With Jimmy Anderson supporting him at the other end, and Australians to bowl at, Flintoff was, simply, in his element, a fact Ponting understood when, in Flintoff's next over, he took one amidships. Strauss, at first slip, was just as enthused as anyone else present by what he was witnessing.

'When Freddie bowls like that no one needs to say anything or do anything. He just dominates proceedings. And as a batsman, even watching from that distance in the slips, you think to yourself, good grief, thank goodness I'm not facing that. Indeed, sometimes you think, Good grief, how on earth do you face that?'

Flintoff went about his craft with perfection, using the width of the crease, coming over the wicket, coming round the wicket, and each ball was banged into the turf as though he was demanding it to behave exactly as he wanted. Just before the hour mark one did, when Hughes nicked one low to first slip. Strauss dived forward to claim the catch, and his former Middlesex colleague Hughes was on his way after turning to check with the England captain that the ball had carried.

As England's fielders celebrated, however, Ponting, anticipating the umpires would refer the incident to the television umpire as they had done when he was given out off Anderson on the second morning, halted Hughes's progress back to the pavilion. So the Australian captain was understandably surprised when Koertzen confirmed the dismissal on the field. Once again, he felt a sting of injustice when replays cast doubt on whether the ball had, in fact, reached Strauss on the fall. Strauss has no doubts that it did.

'This was a tough incident for me,' he says. 'I know in my mind the ball carried. It hit my hand. It hit my fingers, landing on two of them, and as far as I was concerned that was that. I saw Hughes asking if it had carried and the umpire said, "Yes." The umpires didn't actually ask me, they just went and consulted each other. Looking at the television replays, obviously, it appears as though there's some doubt, but, of course, this foreshortening of the pitch makes things look a bit weird sometimes. We all know that people have tried and succeeded in demonstrating that the camera lies and, suddenly, people were calling me a cheat for claiming it was a catch . . . all I'd done was catch the ball. It was up to the umpires whether they referred it, not me. If they had referred it, because of uncertainty over these issues, it may well have been given not out. It doesn't mean it wasn't a fair catch. As far as I'm concerned, it was.'

> '**Looking back on the TV I thought, Crikey, that actually looks a bit dodgy**'
>
> *Prior on Hughes's wicket*

Matt Prior, standing next to his skipper, was similarly convinced. 'I had the best view in the house because, obviously, I'm looking straight down at it on my left-hand side. I just thought it went straight in, that there was absolutely no doubt. Looking back on the television I then thought, Crikey, that actually looks a bit dodgy, but I still have absolutely no hesitation in saying that the ball went straight into his hands. Straussy is not that type of character anyway. If he had any doubt he would have held his hands up and let the umpires refer it, but there just wasn't any doubt in his mind or in my mind, and there still isn't.'

Not that that appeased Ponting one iota. Strauss was also concerned, but not by the dismissal. For, once again, there were signs that, although Flintoff's initial spell of seven overs, two maidens, 2 for 9, had provided the perfect start to England's bid to end 75 years without beating Australia at Lord's, his body might be creaking.

Prior observes: 'Every now and then, if a ball was struck back towards him and he had to move, he grimaced a bit. You could tell sideways movement wasn't good for him, but he was equally determined not to let on. This was serious stuff for him.'

With physio Kirk Russell ready to come on from the pavilion, it was clear, though, that Flintoff needed some immediate attention at the very least. At 12.30pm he went off to huge applause. It was acknowledgement of a job well done so far, but was it also tinged with concern that he may not be able to complete it?

'We all knew the possibilities,' recalls Strauss, 'but even if he took no further wickets, getting out Hughes and Katich so early, leaving them 34 for 2 and so far behind, it was worth having him on the field just for that.'

But Flintoff was not finished yet. 'To be honest with you, with the injuries I've had over my career going back to probably age 13 or 14 and having a back problem, it's something that you deal with as a bowler. If you ask any bowler, I don't think you're actually a hundred per cent fit any of the time. There's always something niggling away, whether it be some part of your body or your big toe, whatever, so it's just something you have to get on with because the incentives are so high. Playing for England, playing in an Ashes series, I think people will probably do more or less anything to get through that.'

With Ponting and Hussey not only digging in but also continuing to play positively, Australia reached 76 for 2 at lunch and England were forced to wait for the next breakthrough. Fittingly, when it came, in the second over after the break, it was provided by the man nominated by many to emerge eventually as Flintoff's natural successor, when Broad induced Ponting to play on.

'I'd not been overly happy with the way I bowled either at Cardiff, where I got nothing out of the wicket and didn't feel threatening at all, or in the first innings at Lord's,' admits Broad, 'even though I managed to bounce out Brad Haddin and Mitchell Johnson. But for me this was the biggest wicket so far . . .

'We'd set a plan of keeping the ball wider for Ponting outside off stump because he doesn't like leaving if he can help it. He'd far rather hit it. So, with plenty of time on our side, we planned to keep the ball outside of his eye line and to see how long he could leave it before having a go and, in the end, he couldn't leave it any more.

'He went for a ball that probably wasn't there for the shot and chopped it onto his stumps.'

Once again Ponting, still sporting remnants of the scar Steve Harmison had inflicted upon his cheek four years earlier, had failed to make a 50 in a Lord's Test. And though he could have no complaints about being out-thought, the Aussie captain's growing sense of being hard done by increased further when Swann got in on the act ten overs later as Hussey was adjudged to have nicked a ragging off-spinner to Collingwood at slip to reduce Australia to 120 for 4 when, in reality, the ball had spat viciously out of a foot-hole.

Swann's castling of Marcus North with a well-concealed arm-ball gave the England spinner even greater satisfaction, even though he was stunned when a leading analyst asked him afterwards if the ball had been a fluke.

Swann says: 'We'd recognised in Cardiff that North had a very high backlift. I said as soon as there is a wicket with a little bit of pace in, I'm going to get him lbw with a quick one because he won't get his bat down in time. It actually hit his leg, it would have been lbw, but it bowled him as well. It took middle stump out, so that was brilliant for me; bowl a few slow, slow deliveries, and then just fire one in about 7–10mph quicker.

'One of the TV experts said afterwards, "You didn't really mean to do that, did you?" At that point it was still seen as very much of a fluke, despite the fact that I'd done it against the West Indies on the same Test ground and I even said, "It's the same ball with which I got Sulieman Benn out in the Test match here, go and look at that, then look at this."'

'He said, "Yes, but there's no discernible difference in your action." I said, "Well, that's sort of the point." It took them until the end of the series to pick up that I was actually doing it on purpose.'

Swann's two quick wickets left Australia reeling on 128 for 5. Shouts of 'easy, easy' rang around the ground. Strauss wondered whether it had been too easy.

'It's hard to put the feeling into words,' he recalls, 'but it had so obviously been our day; everything had gone according to plan so perfectly that you always had the feeling in the back of your mind that we were almost doing too well and that something might be about to happen to come and spoil it all.'

By the close of play, a few of his colleagues knew exactly what he meant.

As England were only too aware, this new-look Australian team bat deep and their form player of the past 12 months, Michael Clarke, glided to a half-century off just 58 balls before tea. His fellow New South Welshman Brad Haddin proved a determined ally at the other end and, with the ball softening on the good batting surface, England found the going tougher as Australia headed into the final session on 178 for 5.

At that stage, 49 overs were still scheduled to be bowled and the possibility remained, not to mention the anticipation among the crowd, that Strauss's men would finish the job before the close. Within one hour, however, the Australian sixth-wicket pair had extended their stand into three figures, England's limbs were straining (Pietersen spent a lengthy period off the field) and the deep-set fields suggested Strauss was happy to tread water until the second new ball became available. Clarke went on to record his 11th Test hundred and when, shortly afterwards, Haddin passed fifty, devotees of sod's law might have been wondering whether Australia were in the process of surpassing their record for the highest successful chase of 404 for 3 against England at Headingley in 1948.

With his team displaying signs of weariness, Strauss caused a stir by calling an impromptu huddle as the officials received the new ball at 287 for 5. Was it a sign of panic? Or was it an inspirational rallying cry? Some compared it to Hull City manager Phil Brown's half-time hairdryer on the pitch at Manchester City the previous Christmas. 'And Hull only won once more all season,' quipped Nasser Hussain from the commentary box.

'It was time to refocus minds,' says Strauss. 'I just felt I saw a little trepidation creeping into our play.'

Indeed, when the umpires offered Clarke and Haddin the refuge of the dressing-room for bad light, their unbroken partnership was worth 185. On balance, England clearly held the upper hand, but Australia, being Australia, and sleeping on a score of 313 for 5, which was already the highest-ever fourth-innings total at Lord's . . . ooo-errrr.

LORD'S, DAY FIVE: AUSTRALIA 406. ENGLAND WIN BY 115 RUNS

Andrew Strauss admits his sleep was not as deep as it had been the previous night. When he returned home on the eve of this day of destiny he was frustrated for two reasons: one, that he'd suffered what he considered unfair stick following the Phil Hughes catch; and two, that Australia ended the day still, in theory at least, with a chance of pulling off an amazing victory.

Bearing in mind Flintoff's fragile physical state and the obvious signs of the Lord's pitch being on the verge of nodding off, did he harbour any doubt at all that England may not, in the end, be able to force a victory?

'I was very confident that we had set them an enormous target, and that if we took one more wicket they would be exposed,' Strauss remembers, 'so I felt the odds were massively in our favour. But somewhere in the back of my mind I also had the nasty feeling that this could be an absolute nightmare. There were nerves, no doubt, and they showed when we got to the ground when we started our slips catching practice. It was shocking. Catches were being shelled all over the shop – Colly missed a couple of "straight-inners" and Swann missed one that whacked him on the forehead.'

Swann confirms: 'Myself, Straussy and Colly, we were literally dropping them left, right and centre for no reason. I got hit flush on the head by one. I went to catch it and missed and it hit me, on the forehead, and I just wandered off in a bit of a daze and went to the back of the changing-room thinking, Uh-oh.'

Not that the players needed any pre-match memo about the significance of what they were about to attempt, but just how much it meant was underlined by the response to their journey through the Long Room at the start of play. Every time the team had entered the playing arena the noise had been huge. This time, however, it almost blew the roof off.

And Flintoff seized the moment. Bopara was walking ahead of the all-rounder as they made their way through the wall of noise. He recalls: 'As we went through them, the MCC members were urging us on, shouting: "Raaaahhhhhhrrrr!" Fred tapped me on the shoulder and said: "Watch this, Rav." I turned to see him as he stopped in his tracks, swung round to face them, pumped the air and shouted, "Raaaahhhhhhrrrr!" right back at them. Then they came back with an even bigger: "RAAAAHHHHHHRRRRR!"'

'It was a completely brilliant moment. They loved it and he loved it, and I realised nobody or nothing could possibly prevent him from doing what he wanted to do that day – win us the match.'

The sequence of roars made some of the players who were already out in the fresh air jump. Cook recalls: 'I was thinking, What the hell was that all about, and then I saw Fred emerge and I knew straight away.'

The fact that the man most likely to be the key to their fortunes was so obviously and utterly up for the challenge gave Strauss huge reassurance, not to mention the rest of his team. Jimmy Anderson recalls: 'There were a few butterflies, but Fred just told us, "Don't panic, lads. It's in the bag."'

'I wanted to show the Australians what I could do,' admits Flintoff. 'To make a statement. I wanted to bowl them all out. From my point of view the game was won on the Sunday, not the Monday. From the position we were in overnight, my attitude was that we could not lose that match.

'There was a bit of tension knocking about, but they were five down-there was no way they were winning that game.'

Strauss recalls: 'Fred had said to me: "Don't even bother trying to take me off." He just told me, with no ifs or buts or maybes, that he was going to keep bowling until the last Australian was out.

> **'Fred had said to me: "Don't even bother trying to take me off"'**
>
> *Andrew Strauss*

'He was incredibly confident we would win. Before the off, when we came together for the last chat, he more or less told everyone so. I don't think he even allowed the possibility of defeat to enter his head. You could see the effect of his certainty on the younger players and I think the crowd, who might have turned up a tad twitchy, soaked it up as well.'

According to Flintoff: 'The reasons I told Strauss I wanted to bowl until they were out were twofold: first, I wanted to make a big contribution, and second, I didn't think there was any chance I could come back for a second spell.'

In the event, charging in from the Pavilion End like a man possessed, his creaking frame energised by the challenge, Flintoff produced an immense performance to rank alongside any bowling spell by an Englishman in the past decade.

The mood was set from the first over of the day, bowled by his new-ball partner Anderson, in which Michael Clarke's pads were struck twice, on the second occasion encouraging a huge shout, due to the fact the batsman had declined to play a shot.

With Anderson swinging, England were already buzzing, but, as Bopara had already gathered, nothing and nobody were going to stand in Flintoff's way now.

There had been no addition to the overnight score when Brad Haddin pushed at Flintoff's fourth delivery of the day and the ball began its journey towards Collingwood at second slip. It seemed to the Durham man that it might never actually arrive.

'Just at first I thought, That's not going to carry,' says Collingwood. 'We knew exactly what it meant. If I had dropped it, everybody would have been devastated and, judging by my practice that morning, when I shelled about five, there was every chance. But it just went in beautifully, right into the middle of my hands, and I sort of had the sensation that my heart had actually stopped beating for a second, until I saw Fred standing there with a knowing nod of the head, milking the moment before being mobbed by us all. That was the moment I believed victory was a formality.'

Flintoff recalls: 'Getting Haddin out straight away was a godsend. The one thing I thought when I saw the ball going to Colly from the outside edge of Haddin's bat was, Don't, please, call a no-ball. And I looked out of the corner of my eye, just to check there was no sign of an outstretched arm.'

Australia may have been 313 for 6, and Flintoff just two wickets away from putting his name on the honours board for taking five wickets in a Test innings at Lord's for the first time, but Mitchell Johnson was determined to prove they were not finished.

He and Michael Clarke were both forced to take blows and when the vice-captain was struck on the pad by a full toss, he was only saved from certain lbw death by Flintoff overstepping the popping crease.

In the circumstances, Johnson appeared disinclined to wait around for another ball with his name on, however, and dominated a 43-run stand for the seventh wicket with Clarke, despite his partner already having a hundred in the bank.

Flintoff was true to his word to Strauss, and Strauss knew to leave well alone, but an instinctive bowling change paid immediate dividends shortly before drinks. With Flintoff roaring in from the Pavilion End, Swann offered a change of pace and, while his introduction at that stage might have been considered something of a gamble given Clarke's nimbleness of foot and Johnson's clean hitting ability, the positive move reaped a positive result. Clarke advanced down the pitch to Swann's second delivery and fatally played inside the ball on the full, to be bowled. Clarke doubled over like a teenager with his first hangover as the realisation sank in. From an England perspective, any inhibitions associated with a Lord's audience were drowned in an ocean of joyful mayhem.

'It just went in beautifully, right into the middle of my hands, and I sort of had the sensation that my heart had actually stopped beating for a second, until I saw Fred standing there with a knowing nod of the head. That was the moment I believed victory was a formality'

Collingwood on Flintoff's first wicket of the day

'What I call cricket heaven,' says Swann.

Anyone able to spare a nanosecond to glance at their watch would have noticed it was bang on high noon. Australia were 356 for 7, needing 161 more runs to achieve an historic win. England needed three wickets, and their first win over Australia since 1934 was within touching distance.

And nothing and nobody was going to stop Flintoff taking them there. In the very next over he produced a bolt of pure red lightning, far too fast and far too good for Hauritz, who was bowled shouldering arms when it jagged down the hill. Australia were 363 for 8, and the look of utter bewilderment on the Australian off-spinner's face told the story England's fielders already knew.

According to Pietersen: 'When Fred bowls like this, when he is in this mood and when his body can stand it, there is simply no question about it – he is the best bowler in the world.'

Collingwood says: 'When I'd seen Fred struggling in the first innings I remember thinking, How much will we miss him in the second innings? Can we win without him? And here he was, pounding in bowling at 90mph-plus every ball. As a fielder it was awesome to watch, but it must have been absolutely horrible to play against.'

Broad agrees: 'It was just phenomenal. I was at fine leg for the whole time that morning, so I was a bit disappointed to be so far away from the action, but he bowled the length that brings the stumps into play and that made every ball a threat.'

Strauss says simply: 'Just too good.'

'C'mon,' Flintoff bellowed as team-mates laid their hands on him. In taking 4 for 69, he had just achieved his best figures in a Lord's Test. Now, surely, the five-for that would put the perfect full stop to this chapter of his career must come.

Try as he might, however, and as much as all England supporters were united with him in his desire to finish the job, a couple of overs during which his pace occasionally dropped below ridiculously fast encouraged Strauss to consider what might have turned out to be the most unpopular decision of his career.

Indeed, had Flintoff, and fate, not intervened, Strauss may well have become the first man to win a Test against Australia and been lynched by his supporters on the same day.

Strauss explains: 'Fred had done exceptionally well and with those eight wickets down I felt the job was done. I knew he wanted to carry on until it was actually over, but he was obviously starting to struggle a little bit. I had been considering taking him off, before he got Hauritz out as a matter of fact, but I just couldn't bring myself to do it.

'But now, I was ready to do it. Fred had bowled all morning and I decided this over (the 104th of Australia's innings) had to be his last. I even gestured to Jimmy Anderson to get himself ready to bowl.'

When running up to bowl the final ball of the over, Flintoff seemed unaware of what his captain was thinking, and that this was going to be his last and positively final chance to take a five-for at Lord's and provide the story his performance both demanded and deserved. When it came, however, the delivery failed to trouble Peter Siddle. Thankfully, the cricketing gods have always been fond of drama, and umpire Koertzen's shout of 'no-ball' gave him one final, final opportunity.

Turning halfway back to his mark and ambling in off a shortened run, Flintoff dragged a ball from the very depths of his spirit that rushed through Siddle's defences and sent the crowd delirious.

In the middle, eyes closed in a moment of sheer delight, Flintoff sank down on one knee and stretched his arms wide. All he needed, some said, was a globe between his hands and he would have looked like Atlas holding up the world. Others saw the angel of the north-west. All present and watching on television or listening on radio will have had their own indelible image implanted in their memory. Nothing and nobody . . .

'The reason I came in off my short run-up was that I just couldn't be **sed to walk all the way back to my mark.

'As for what happened next, I've no idea why I went down on the one knee. Last time at Lord's . . . milked it a little bit, didn't I? Enjoyed it, though.

'Strauss said he was thinking of giving me a rest,' Flintoff recalls, 'but I told him I wasn't coming off. It wasn't about five-fors or getting your name on the honours board. It never has been. I'm on the honours board for a century against South Africa in 2003 when we lost the match by an innings and plenty. You shouldn't be judged by those things, but by your contribution to the side. The most important thing was winning the game.'

And England's historic victory was duly sealed at 12.42pm when Johnson, who had survived a sharp caught-and-bowled chance off Swann on his way to a belligerent half-century, missed with a heave to leg and was bowled. All that remained for Flintoff was to lead the team from the field, sun hat, souvenir stump and match ball, retrieved by Anderson from umpire Billy Doctrove, clasped in the bucket of his right hand.

The scene in the dressing-room was one of tiredness, emotion and euphoria.

'I don't think anybody wanted to go home that day,' recalls Swann, 'it was all just so perfect. Standing out there on the dressing-room balcony, or having a quiet moment back inside, everyone just tried to take as much from the moment as they could, in their own way.'

Bopara noticed: 'Looking around I sensed the players believed they might just be on the verge of something special.'

Collingwood recalls 'the camaraderie' and, finally, Andy Flower called the team together and reminded each in turn of the contribution they had made to the team's success.

As Flintoff sat in the dressing-room to reflect on his efforts, he looked up to discover that his appreciative team-mates had already taped his name and figures of 5 for 92 on the home honours board. He had joined a unique club of only six men – Gubby Allen, Ian Botham, Ray Illingworth, Vinoo Mankad and Keith Miller the others – to be on the famous boards for hundreds and five wickets in Lord's Tests.

Graham Onions has an overriding image of Fred appearing a tad dazed by it all. He wasn't the only one.

'Walking off the field at the end with a stump in one hand and a sun hat in the other after beating Australia in my final Test match at Lord's, winning a Test match against Australia, was pretty special,' remembers Flintoff. 'I don't recall feeling particularly emotional at the end, I suppose because it takes times for these things to sink in.

'I'm glad that Jimmy grabbed the ball off Billy Doctrove at the end because we had a dinner for my charity foundation the next night and it raised £35,000 in the auction.'

For England, however, in the moments after victory, it would have been impossible to put a price on the value of what Flintoff had done with it.

Second Test, Lord's, London
16, 17, 18, 19, 20 July 2009

Result: England won by 115 runs
Toss: England, who chose to bat
Series: England lead 5-match series 1–0
Umpires: BR Doctrove (West Indies) and RE Koertzen (South Africa)
Match referee: JJ Crowe (New Zealand)
Player of the match: A Flintoff (England)

England 1st innings		R	M	B	4s	6s
AJ Strauss*	b Hilfenhaus	161	370	268	22	0
AN Cook	lbw b Johnson	95	190	147	18	0
RS Bopara	lbw b Hilfenhaus	18	20	19	4	0
KP Pietersen	c †Haddin b Siddle	32	38	42	4	0
PD Collingwood	c Siddle b Clarke	16	43	36	1	0
MJ Prior†	b Johnson	8	13	10	2	0
A Flintoff	c Ponting b Hilfenhaus	4	16	10	1	0
SCJ Broad	b Hilfenhaus	16	50	26	2	0
GP Swann	c Ponting b Siddle	4	6	6	1	0
JM Anderson	c Hussey b Johnson	29	47	25	5	0
G Onions	not out	17	40	29	2	0
Extras	(b 15, lb 2, nb 8)	25				
Total	(all out; 101.4 overs; 425 mins)	425	(4.18 runs per over)			

Fall of wickets 1–196 (Cook, 47.5 ov), 2–222 (Bopara, 53.6 ov), 3–267 (Pietersen, 65.1 ov), 4–302 (Collingwood, 76.3 ov), 5–317 (Prior, 79.3 ov), 6–333 (Flintoff, 82.3 ov), 7–364 (Strauss, 90.2 ov), 8–370 (Swann, 91.5 ov), 9–378 (Broad, 92.6 ov), 10–425 (Anderson, 101.4 ov)

Bowling	O	M	R	W	Econ	
BW Hilfenhaus	31	12	103	4	3.32	(4nb)
MG Johnson	21.4	2	132	3	6.09	
PM Siddle	20	1	76	2	3.80	(4nb)
NM Hauritz	8.3	1	26	0	3.05	
MJ North	16.3	2	59	0	3.57	
MJ Clarke	4	1	12	1	3.00	

Australia 1st innings		R	M	B	4s	6s
PJ Hughes	c †Prior b Anderson	4	10	9	1	0
SM Katich	c Broad b Onions	48	141	93	6	0
RT Ponting*	c Strauss b Anderson	2	19	15	0	0
MEK Hussey	b Flintoff	51	127	91	8	0
MJ Clarke	c Cook b Anderson	1	21	12	0	0
MJ North	b Anderson	0	33	14	0	0
BJ Haddin†	c Cook b Broad	28	28	38	3	0
MG Johnson	c Cook b Broad	4	13	11	1	0
NM Hauritz	c Collingwood b Onions	24	53	36	4	0
PM Siddle	c Strauss b Onions	35	65	47	5	0
BW Hilfenhaus	not out	6	20	14	1	0
Extras	(b 4, lb 6, nb 2)	12				
Total	(all out; 63 overs; 267 mins)	215	(3.41 runs per over)			

Fall of wickets 1–4 (Hughes, 2.3 ov), 2–10 (Ponting, 6.6 ov), 3–103 (Katich, 32.4 ov), 4–111 (Hussey, 35.6 ov), 5–111 (Clarke, 36.3 ov), 6–139 (North, 42.3 ov), 7–148 (Johnson, 45.5 ov), 8–152 (Haddin, 47.5 ov), 9–196 (Hauritz, 58.3 ov), 10–215 (Siddle, 62.6 ov)

Bowling	O	M	R	W	Econ	
JM Anderson	21	5	55	4	2.61	
A Flintoff	12	4	27	1	2.25	(2nb)
SCJ Broad	18	1	78	2	4.33	
G Onions	11	1	41	3	3.72	
GP Swann	1	0	4	0	4.00	

England 2nd innings		R	M	B	4s	6s
AJ Strauss*	c Clarke b Hauritz	32	64	48	4	0
AN Cook	lbw b Hauritz	32	54	42	6	0
RS Bopara	c Katich b Hauritz	27	136	93	4	0
KP Pietersen	c †Haddin b Siddle	44	156	101	5	0
PD Collingwood	c †Haddin b Siddle	54	121	80	4	0
MJ Prior†	run out (North)	61	50	42	9	0
A Flintoff	not out	30	34	27	4	0
SCJ Broad	not out	0	1	0	0	0
Extras	(b 16, lb 9, w 1, nb 5)	31				
Total	(6 wickets dec; 71.2 overs; 317 mins)	311	(4.35 runs per over)			

Did not bat GP Swann, JM Anderson, G Onions
Fall of wickets 1–61 (Cook, 14.1 ov), 2–74 (Strauss, 16.2 ov), 3–147 (Bopara, 44.4 ov), 4–174 (Pietersen, 51.1 ov), 5–260 (Prior, 63.2 ov), 6–311 (Collingwood, 71.2 ov)

Bowling	O	M	R	W	Econ	
BW Hilfenhaus	19	5	59	0	3.10	(3nb)
MG Johnson	17	2	68	0	4.00	(1nb, 1w)
PM Siddle	15.2	4	64	2	4.17	
NM Hauritz	16	1	80	3	5.00	(1nb)
MJ Clarke	4	0	15	0	3.75	

Australia 2nd innings (target: 522 runs)		R	M	B	4s	6s
PJ Hughes	c Strauss b Flintoff	17	46	34	2	0
SM Katich	c Pietersen b Flintoff	6	15	5	1	0
RT Ponting*	b Broad	38	88	69	6	0
MEK Hussey	c Collingwood b Swann	27	100	63	3	0
MJ Clarke	b Swann	136	313	227	14	0
MJ North	b Swann	6	26	25	1	0
BJ Haddin†	c Collingwood b Flintoff	80	187	130	10	0
MG Johnson	b Swann	63	94	75	9	0
NM Hauritz	b Flintoff	1	5	5	0	0
PM Siddle	b Flintoff	7	18	13	1	0
BW Hilfenhaus	not out	4	11	4	0	0
Extras	(b 5, lb 8, nb 8)	21				
Total	(all out; 107 overs; 459 mins)	406	(3.79 runs per over)			

Fall of wickets 1–17 (Katich, 3.1 ov), 2–34 (Hughes, 9.2 ov), 3–78 (Ponting, 23.4 ov), 4–120 (Hussey, 32.4 ov), 5–128 (North, 38.4 ov), 6–313 (Haddin, 87.4 ov), 7–356 (Clarke, 98.2 ov), 8–363 (Hauritz, 99.4 ov), 9–388 (Siddle, 103.6 ov), 10–406 (Johnson, 106.6 ov)

Bowling	O	M	R	W	Econ	
JM Anderson	21	4	86	0	4.09	
A Flintoff	27	4	92	5	3.40	(8nb)
G Onions	9	0	50	0	5.55	
SCJ Broad	16	3	49	1	3.06	
GP Swann	28	3	87	4	3.10	
PD Collingwood	6	1	29	0	4.83	

Close of play
16 Jul day 1 – England 1st innings 364/6 (AJ Strauss 161*, SCJ Broad 7*, 90 ov)
17 Jul day 2 – Australia 1st innings 156/8 (NM Hauritz 3*, PM Siddle 3*, 49 ov)
18 Jul day 3 – England 2nd innings 311/6 (A Flintoff 30*, SCJ Broad 0*, 71.2 ov)
19 Jul day 4 – Australia 2nd innings 313/5 (MJ Clarke 125*, BJ Haddin 80*, 86 ov)
20 Jul day 5 – Australia 2nd innings 406 (107 ov) – end of match

The fact that this series would be Freddie's last made him more determined to play in all five Tests. Before Edgbaston he said: 'I have three Test matches left and I'll do anything to get through.'

James Anderson acknowledges the applause for his five-wicket haul during day two of the third Test at Edgbaston.

Graham Onions ensured that it wasn't just Anderson who took all the limelight, removing Shane Watson and Michael Hussey with the first two balls of the second day at Edgbaston, before taking the wickets of Ricky Ponting and Ben Hilfenhaus soon after.

Rain in Birmingham on day three led to a wash-out.

The batting of Bell, Flintoff, Prior and Broad helped England to a first-innings total of 376 at Edgbaston.

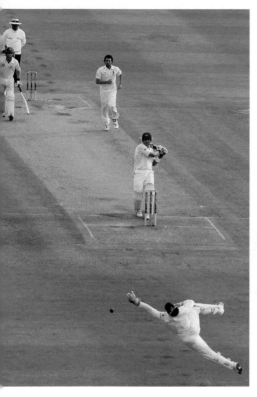

At the start of his career Matt Prior was regarded as more of a batsman than a wicketkeeper. But work with Bruce French has brought huge improvement to the quality of his work behind the stumps.

BELOW: Australia captain Ricky Ponting looks back to see that he is bowled by Graeme Swann.

LEFT: The scoreboard never lies. England dismissed for 102 on day one of the fourth Test, their lowest Test score for 100 years in Leeds.

ABOVE RIGHT: With uncertainity over Matt Prior's fitness, Paul Collingwood was preparing to keep wicket if the chance came about, even if others were unsure of the idea. 'As I'm standing there taking catches in practice, all the commentators were stood in a row behind me, just laughing.'

ABOVE: Strauss, Collingwood and Bell look on as England's innings falls apart.

RIGHT: Mitchell Johnson is congratulated by his captain as he takes the wicket of Alastair Cook.

ABOVE: Half an hour into the first morning, England were already 16 for two as Bopara saw the ball from Hilfenhaus lob to gully.

RIGHT: Graeme Swann ducks a bouncer from Hilfenhaus.

Stuart Broad celebrates the wicket of Ricky Ponting as his bowling steadily improved, but it was his 42-ball half century that rattled Australia at Headingley, even though they were already out of sight.

Third Test, Edgbaston: 30 July – 3 August

Everywhere you looked in the England dressing-room in the hours after the dramatic 115-run victory in the second Test at Lord's, there was joy and satisfaction. Everywhere you looked, except in one corner. Kevin Pietersen had succeeded in nursing his damaged Achilles through five days at the game's headquarters and a night of celebration with Stuart Broad, Paul Collingwood, Graham Onions and others, which reportedly cost the group a hefty bar bill at Tini Bar in Chelsea, while Andrew Flintoff chose to spend the evening in a Mayfair pub with his wife Rachael. Pietersen, England's star batsman, the man upon whom England had placed the bulk of their expectations, spent most of the evening considering the outcome of his appointment with the Swedish Achilles specialist, Håkan Alfredson, in two days' time, and whether his Ashes campaign was already over.

'I couldn't run for 30 seconds'

Kevin Pietersen faces up to the surgery that ends his Ashes

Alfredson cut short his holiday to fly to London to see Pietersen at 8am on Wednesday 22 July. His first glance at the ultrasound scan showed nothing too alarming, but when he asked Pietersen to get on the treadmill to try to speed some blood through the affected area, all that changed.

Setting the equipment for Pietersen to run at 8km/h, he suggested a five-minute run would be enough for the purpose.

'I couldn't run for 30 seconds,' said Pietersen.

At that point, the surgeon said, 'I think the decision here is simple. I have to operate.'

'I knew what that meant,' recalls Pietersen. ' I knew I was out of the series and I was gutted. I rang my wife, Jess, and I rang my parents and told them what had happened. It was a low moment. I'd invested so much of myself in this Ashes series. I really wanted to make a difference, and sitting in that room being told I was out of the series was just awful. I was close to tears. I knew the situation was bad at Lord's, and it wasn't getting any better. The idea of managing it to get through on a day-to-day basis was now obviously out of the question. We had the operation straight away and it was only when Mr Andersen opened me up that we realised what the problem had been – there were a mass of nerves trapped behind the fat pad attached to the tendon and that was where the pain was coming from.

'I'd known it was something very serious from the time I left Lord's. I did try to join in the celebrations and I was very happy for everyone, mostly for Fred, of course, and happy for Andy Flower that we'd actually changed history around and the team had shown what it was capable of. Even when I drove home I felt good, but then, when I started walking from my car to my house I felt the pain, and I thought, this is bad. All the euphoria just evaporated.'

The ECB issued the following media release the same day:

> 'England batsman Kevin Pietersen has been ruled out of the npower Ashes series after today undergoing surgery for an ongoing Achilles tendon injury. Pietersen was earlier today assessed by a leading specialist where the decision was made to undergo surgery, which will rule him out of all cricket for up to six weeks.'

ECB chief medical officer Nick Peirce said: 'Following a consultation involving scans and testing with the world's leading Achilles specialist, Kevin Pietersen today underwent surgery on his right Achilles tendon. The operation involved a small incision and trimming of the blood vessels and nerves around the inflamed tendon and appears, at this early stage, to have been routine. Kevin will look to undergo a comprehensive rehabilitation programme to ensure there is no risk of recurrence. This is expected to be approximately six weeks, but will be taken at an appropriate pace following constant review.

'Despite conventional conservative treatments to the tendon, with trial periods of rest and rehabilitation, Kevin continued to be in significant discomfort and is currently unable to run or even walk comfortably. He had a strong desire to get through the Ashes series but, despite this, he has recently been unable to achieve a maximum level of performance.'

Kevin Pietersen said: 'As an England cricketer the Ashes are the pinnacle of the game, so I'm absolutely devastated to be missing the rest of the series. I was pleased with the previous course of treatment, as it allowed me to take part in this Ashes series, but unfortunately the injury has recently deteriorated. I'll be supporting the team closely and wish them the best of luck as they look to build on the brilliant win at Lord's and reclaim the Ashes.'

Although Strauss had been expecting bad news, losing Pietersen for the remainder of the series came as a huge blow. 'We got the feeling at Lord's that we may lose Kevin temporarily, but it was not until now that the full significance of his injury became apparent.

'I was, of course, delighted by our performance in the match but, with Kevin out and Fred's knee continuing to be an issue, I was also pleased that we had a ten-day break before the next Test started at Edgbaston.'

The immediate priority for Strauss and for England was to decide on Pietersen's replacement. It didn't take the England captain long to make up his mind over who he wanted.

'For me, it was a straightforward decision to bring back Ian Bell. In a series like the Ashes you don't want to be stepping into the unknown with players, you want to be using players you've got a pretty good idea of. Though he had been dropped from the side after the first Test in the West Indies, I had been impressed by his response.

'He was left out then because he hadn't performed consistently enough. He'd done OK, but there was definitely a feeling that OK is not good enough and that we wanted to challenge the players to be better. He reacted exceptionally well. We told him he needed to get a lot fitter and that he needed to earn the right to play for England again and he did everything possible. He trained hard, then came back to Warwickshire at the start of the season and scored runs. I felt the experience would stand him in good stead when he came back in the side, as he surely would, because he would have felt like he'd sacrificed a lot to get back in and would be desperate to make that pay.

'I know from when I was dropped before the tour to New Zealand in 2008 that a spell out of the side can do you some good. In Bell's case, there was a suggestion that he had a psychological block over getting to fifty and not converting those scores to a hundred. Sometimes, the more you think about that kind of thing, the more it happens. So some time out to refresh himself and get rid of that baggage would have been useful.'

Bell himself had been stung by comments attributed to national selector Geoff Miller, which suggested the Warwickshire batsman may not possess the 'hunger' required to succeed at the top level.

'I was upset to be left out in the Caribbean,' he says. 'And then Geoff Miller's remarks did hurt. He's entitled to his opinion but, though I'm not the most vocal about these things, there's no one more passionate, no one who wants to play for England more or who is more determined to do well than me. Those comments, when I was told about them, did come as a bit of a shock, because they were questioning my commitment. I had a discussion about that with Geoff later, and he told me they hadn't come out as he'd wanted them to. Maybe they did some good, because they really reinforced my determination to get back into the England side.

'This was a big chance for me. I was sorry that Kevin wasn't going to be playing. No one likes to profit from anyone else's misfortune. But I'd liked what I'd seen from the England team in my absence.

'I think it was good for me and good for England that I'd been in and around the side for the previous four years. I was immediately comfortable coming back into the dressing-room and, though the next few weeks were going to be hugely important, I was pretty relaxed about what was in front of us.'

The press reaction to England's victory had been universally celebratory, on the home front, at least. One newspaper printed a photograph of the joyous scenes at Lord's in 1934, the last time an England side beat Australia at headquarters. There was no sign of an open-topped bus, ticker tape or sprays of champagne, but there was no disguising how much it meant to beat Australia even then. Bob Wyatt had led his side to victory by an innings and 38 runs on that occasion, 19 Lord's Ashes Tests previously, when hundreds from Les Ames and Maurice Leyland laid the foundations, and then Hedley Verity took 15 wickets for 104 runs to rout an Australian team featuring Don Bradman and Bill O'Reilly. For the record, the England team read: Cyril Walters and Herbert Sutcliffe, followed by Wally Hammond, Patsy Hendren (45 years old at the time), Wyatt, Leyland, Ames (the very model of the modern wicketkeeper-batsman), George Geary, Verity (who was to perish in World War Two), Ken Farnes and Bill Bowes (a veteran of the 'Bodyline' attack from the previous winter tour in 1932–33).

What most commentators neglected to point out about that victory in 1934, however, was that it came in a losing Ashes series, the first of six in a row between 1934 and 1953, 19 years later. In the circumstances, such an omission was understandable.

Meanwhile, Jeff Thomson, the Australian fast-bowling legend, aimed both barrels at his side's pacemen, placing the blame for their defeat firmly at the door of Mitchell Johnson & co. Not one to mince words, Thomo called Australia's bowling at Lord's 'rubbish', and claimed it had been a major blunder to leave Stuart Clark on the sidelines.

'Australia were cocky and complacent after they outplayed England in Cardiff,' said Thomson. 'It was a major blunder to omit Clark at Lord's. Fantastically as Freddie Flintoff bowled, the garbage Ponting's bowlers served up in the first two sessions was the difference between the sides. It's a long time since I've seen an Australian attack spray it around all over the place for so long and look so ragged.

'Dennis Lillee and I got a bit carried away against the West Indies in Perth in 1974–75 and copped some flak, but at least we won the series convincingly: these blokes will be lucky to win a wooden spoon unless they pull their fingers out.'

Ricky Ponting took even more flak, but made no attempts to find excuses. 'You can't change history,' said the Australian captain. 'There's no point in trying to blame it on the details.'

Meanwhile, Ponting's opposite number in 2005, Michael Vaughan, felt that, although England were going to miss Pietersen, they should still be able to cope. Indeed, he went as far as to predict that England would go on to win the series 3–0.

> 'Australia were cocky and complacent after they outplayed England in Cardiff'
>
> *Jeff Thomson*

'I think Flintoff is already inflicting a few mental scars on the Australian batting order,' he wrote. 'There were times in the second Test when they didn't seem to fancy it too much and, to be honest, I don't think anyone would have done. He was coming in at 90mph and making the ball lift and seam into the body. The ball that put paid to Brad Haddin – and with him any chance of a miraculous run-chase – was especially good because it held its line when all the others had tailed in.

'The way Flintoff bowled last week was up there with his spells at Edgbaston in 2005. He will be remembering the euphoria round the grounds during that series because the atmosphere at Lord's felt similar. He has the bit between his teeth, and he will be spying the opportunity of ending his Test career on a high. If he continues in the same vein, there can be only one result this summer.'

Strauss, who was in regular contact with his former captain throughout the series, may have reread the line 'if he continues in the same vein' because he knew, as did Flintoff, that there may be problems ahead.

Flintoff himself was determined that the pain in his right knee would not prevent him from making a major contribution to the rest of the series.

'There are no guarantees for anybody,' he said. 'I have three Test matches left and I'll do anything to get through, maybe put myself through things I wouldn't do if I was looking more long term. I will do whatever it takes to get out on the field. If I don't, it has to be something extremely serious.'

Unbeknown to Vaughan, or anyone outside the inner circle, Flintoff underwent two further jabs to ease discomfort in his ragged right knee on the eve of the contest and, though he pronounced himself fit for action, with back-to-back Test matches again coming up at Edgbaston and then at Leeds four days later, it was understood Flintoff may have to be nursed through, and there was a strong possibility he might have to miss at least one of the remaining three matches in the series. No wonder the skipper decided to clear his mind by taking the family to Legoland the weekend before the team met up at Edgbaston.

However much, or little, that helped to relax him, Strauss knew he was right back in the Ashes mix when, on the morning of the match, pre-Cardiff comments he had made regarding the loss of aura Australia had suffered after the retirement of Shane Warne, Glenn McGrath, Matthew Hayden and Adam Gilchrist were spread all over the morning papers, as in:

'An aura is when the opposition teams, even though they are on top, are not confident they are going to beat you. We certainly felt that in 2006–07. Even when we had good days we were thinking, What is going to happen now? Is Gilchrist going to blast a hundred, or Warne take five wickets from nowhere? It only comes with a consistent level of performance for a long period of time. Australia had that. Personally I don't feel that's where they are right at the moment.'

Encouraged to respond, Ponting did so emphatically. 'It's OK for him to say that now,' said the Australian captain. 'I'm not sure if he was saying that after Cardiff. I don't see how you can create an aura without winning everything and being on top. It's just impossible to do so. England's current Test rating at number 5 in the world rankings would probably indicate they don't have one.'

Edgbaston, Day One: Australia 126 for 1

Even before the players made their way onto the soggy outfield at Edgbaston, the third Test was already taking its first twist. The team bus had not even parked up when Australia's hand on selection was revealed, albeit unwittingly and unofficially, after Phillip Hughes chose to 'tweet' his bad news on his Twitter page. 'Disappointed not to be on the field with the lads today,' Hughes posted, several hours before the Australians intended to announce their team. 'Will be supporting the guys, it's a BIG test match 4 us. Thanks 4 all the support!'

News soon filtered through to the England camp; the knowledge gave them a significant upper hand in the psychological warfare before the start of what captain Andrew Strauss dubbed 'the pivotal Test' of the series. It was confirmation to Hughes that their plans had worked and that England had forced the Australians to end his personal torment and thrust Shane Watson into a makeshift opening role.

The Aussie management was inundated with calls about the Internet revelation, and the leak was not well received by Cricket Australia officials either, in the dressing-room or in the corridors of power back in Melbourne. As the day developed, the blame for the breach was pinned not on Hughes but his manager Neil d'Costa. Nevertheless, former Test batsman Dean Jones said Hughes deserved a 'good foot up the backside for that. He's broken a team rule and he's let the opposition know what's happened before the game's started.'

Although the two teams began their usual warm-up routines, the game was never going to start on time as light rain fell. Its presence and another later shower resulted in the cancellation of two scheduled inspections by umpires Rudi Koertzen and Aleem Dar. Furthermore, such had been the deluge in the days before that a couple of hours of sun and wind were nowhere near sufficient for the purpose of allowing play to get under way, no matter how hard the Blotter machines tried to soak up the excess water.

When the officials did finally make their long-awaited check at 3.30pm, it was a lengthy one, conducted in the presence of both captains. There was undoubtedly a desire to begin, but only in conditions fair to both teams. The biggest problem, aside from a boggy practice strip on the Rea Bank side of the ground, was the waterlogged bowlers' run-ups. Strauss and Ponting were both intent on checking the effects of pressure on the areas: Strauss rolled a ball across the turf to assess how much it soaked up while Ponting ran his hands through the grass to create a spray. In response, the crowd began a slow handclap, and the subsequent announcement that another check would take place at 4.15pm, with a view to begin at 5pm, was met with howls of derision. There would be 30 overs to be bowled.

Kevin Pietersen, at Edgbaston to support his team-mates, had already gone on record to back his replacement, Bell, by calling him 'world-class'.

'That was nice to hear,' says the Warwickshire man, 'but I didn't need any reminding that I had to improve my performance against Australia. Though I enjoyed every minute of 2005, it was a pretty fiery baptism and my last memories of playing against them, in 2006–07, are all pretty harsh. But I felt relaxed and confident. I was just eager to get out there and show them I was better than perhaps some of them thought.'

England's other big-game player, Andrew Flintoff, had his knee support applied by physio Kirk Russell in mid-afternoon, anticipating the start of battle. He also highlighted his potential extra menace at this ground, in particular when he held up the ball as though in delivery stride from the Pavilion End for Strauss, taking guard the wrong way round, to judge how difficult it was to pick up as a right-hander. It was a throwback to 12 months earlier, when South Africa's batsmen had found sighting Flintoff's deliveries from out of the commentary boxes at that end of the ground a nightmare – Jacques Kallis among those who had been spectacularly cleaned up by yorker-length deliveries.

As it transpired, Flintoff would get the chance to test the Australian batsmen's eyesight that evening after Ponting won his first toss of the series. Even if he had considered there might be the slightest case for inserting England, bearing in mind the decision that came back to haunt him in 2005, this time there was no chance that he would do anything other than bat. Shane Watson, it was confirmed, had been drafted in at the top of the order, despite averaging single figures in half a dozen first-class matches in the same position, thus becoming Australia's first right-handed opener for 93 Tests, a sequence stretching back to Michael Slater on the 2001 Ashes tour.

Wicketkeeper Brad Haddin's name also appeared on the Australian teamsheet when they were exchanged by the sides shortly after 4.30pm, only for the curse of Edgbaston to strike once more. Four years earlier, Haddin had been chatting to Glenn McGrath when his team-mate launched himself into a game of touch rugby and turned his ankle on a stray cricket ball, with significant consequences for both sides. Now, it was Haddin's turn to feel the pain. Haddin was keeping to the Australian pacemen when he was struck on the left ring finger by a loose delivery. Haddin knew immediately he was in trouble, but the incident happened so late in the warm-ups that the time permitted to allow Australia to bring in a replacement had already elapsed.

Australia team manager Steve Bernard immediately informed ICC match referee Jeff Crowe of the calamity. The laws of the game stated: 'Each captain shall nominate his players in writing to one of the umpires before the toss. No player may be changed after the nomination without the consent of the opposing captain,' and Crowe gave permission for Australia to seek England's approval of a change on the grounds that the willingness of both teams to start as soon as possible had cut the official practice time down to 45 minutes and had thus forced players to rush through their routines.

'To refuse is well within his rights,' acknowledged Australia coach Tim Nielsen. 'We asked the question, that's all we could do, and if he had refused we would have an issue on our hands of how we were going to deal with it.'

Strauss's consent to the request upheld the best traditions of sportsmanship, though the England captain did not spend too long over the decision.

'I was never tempted to say "no" for a moment,' Strauss says. 'Their manager came into our dressing-room with about 15 minutes to go and told us what the situation was. Andy Flower and I asked whether we could have a couple of minutes, but we both thought, This is the right thing to do; you want to play against their best XI players and you wouldn't have gained much out of victory in those circumstances. It was pretty much a no-brainer really.'

Or, as Nielsen called it, 'a fine gesture'.

So Australia turned to Graham Manou, a 30-year-old debutant, to fill the position behind the stumps, with the haste of his inclusion in the side precluding the usual ceremonial presentation of his baggy green cap.

Praise for England's attitude was forthcoming on both sides of the Anglo-Aussie divide. Even *The Australian*'s Malcolm Conn, an arch-critic of the England captain a fortnight earlier following the fifth-day finale in Cardiff, said: 'Strauss could not have done more to uphold the spirit of cricket.'

Sadly for Strauss, however, English generosity extended to the bowling, as the new-look Australian openers rattled along at breakneck speed. In contrast to its effect in the first innings at Lord's, the Anderson–Flintoff combination lacked threat and the pair was picked off as they strived for a breakthrough. There were simply too many four-balls on offer – 22 in the short session, in fact – and, despite a tense start for Watson, who had never before batted above number 6 in a Test, Australia raced to 50 without loss inside 13 overs.

Finally, Swann's knack of taking wickets in his first over of a spell did the trick for England. Having already had one confident shout for lbw against Watson turned down earlier in the over, Katich fatally rocked back to pull his first ball, which was delivered from around the wicket and rushed onto him. Edgbaston came alive to the sound of Bill Cooper's trumpet and taunting renditions of 'God Save the Queen'.

Now the Barmy Army's jeers to the Australian 'Fanatics' gave way to an ugly reception for captain Ricky Ponting as he made his way to the middle. The boos were arguably an inverted mark of respect, a similar reception to that which greeted Warne in 2005. Australia's long-term policy has been to attempt to undermine the opposition's best player. Now the English crowd were producing a variation on the theme.

'I have to say I think Ricky conducted himself brilliantly throughout the series,' says Strauss. 'As a visiting Ashes skipper you are always under the cosh, but I think he handled it well. My memories of 2005 were that, maybe, they were under more pressure and he allowed himself to get riled more easily, like he did with the Gary Pratt run-out in the fourth Test at Trent Bridge. But his comments during the presentation at Lord's indicated he was more relaxed. He was talking to Mike Atherton on the podium and gave a gracious little speech congratulating us and the crowd applauded and he said something like, "Can you keep asking me questions because that's the first time this match I haven't been booed."'

On the field, this time Ponting survived England's tactic to keep the ball full and wide and, by the close of play, Watson had justified Ponting's faith in him with an unbeaten half-century, from 89 deliveries. Australia had laid a platform.

> '**It was just one of those sessions when, for whatever reason, you can't get the ball to do what you want**'
>
> *James Anderson on a frustrating opening spell for England*

England's bowlers were far from content with their performance and some observers wondered whether their success in taking 20 Australian wickets to win at Lord's might have been a flash in the pan.

Anderson recalls: 'Nothing seemed to be happening on that first evening. I tried my best to get the ball to swing but it just didn't and sometimes that happens. I think we fell into an easy trap against Watson, thinking in the back of our minds, he's not a proper opener, he's a number 7, so it did take us a little time to get our heads around plans for him.

'But, generally, speaking it was just one of those sessions when, for whatever reason, you can't get the ball to do what you want.'

Edgbaston, Day Two: Australia 263 all out; England 116 for 2

Andrew Strauss sprang a genuine surprise on the second morning when he threw the ball to Graham Onions for the first over from Edgbaston's City End. After all, the Durham fast bowler had sent down a spell of 3-0-21-0 the previous evening, hardly the kind of figures to merit being called upon ahead of the usual new-ball operator Anderson.

'The way I'd bowled the previous evening, three overs for 21, I was thinking, I'm under pressure here,' Onions admits. 'So I said to myself, "All right, when you get that opportunity, just back yourself, just give it your best shot."'

'I remember Strauss having a team meeting beforehand and saying, "Look, as a unit we need to be slightly better, more on the ball straight away," and then, out of the blue, he said, "We're going to open with Fred and Graham." And I was like, "All right, OK." There, straight away, he just gave me a massive boost and made me think he was backing me.'

According to Strauss, there were two reasons why he chose Onions: 'I think he'd bowled three overs for quite a few the night before, and I remember speaking to Ottis Gibson before we started play, saying I thought it was important we showed a bit of faith in him now.

'The other aspect was I actually had a feeling he was going to get Ponting out. The way he bowls close to the stumps, he's hard to leave, and Ponting loves leaving early in his innings, so I actually felt he was a good option to bowl at him early on. In the end I suppose it was one of those hunches that came off.'

Indeed, what followed was beyond any plan Strauss could have devised. It was just sheer, *Boy's Own* Ashes drama. Before the majority of the capacity crowd had run through the whys and wherefores of Strauss's decision, two Aussie wickets were in the Onion bag.

'I actually had a feeling he was going to get Ponting out. The way he bowls close to the stumps, he's hard to leave, and Ponting loves leaving early in his innings'

Strauss shows faith and more in Onions

His first delivery, and the first of the day, nipped back to flummox Shane Watson and earn the plumbest of leg-before decisions.

Onions remembers: 'I felt as though I had a great chance of getting Watson out the night before, because he was playing deep in his crease and not actually getting forward at all. One of my strengths is that, when I hit the deck hard and people play back, the ball skids on. First ball, it was on the money straight away. Nipped back. Out. And I was absolutely pumped, because it doesn't matter who you are, when you get your first wicket in the match, you think to yourself, Right, I'm going now.'

Following England's profligacy on the previous evening it was the perfect start, and things were to get better. Instantly.

Onions made it two wickets in as many deliveries with a ball to Michael Hussey straight from the page in the coaching manual that says: 'Hit the top of off stump.'

Onions sent one down that angled in just enough to find its intended target, and left-hander Hussey's decision to leave alone proved fatal.

'I was absolutely pumped, because it doesn't matter who you are, when you get your first wicket in the match, you think to yourself, Right, I'm going now'

Graham Onions

'That was sweet, especially against my Durham team-mate. The ball was just probably slightly too close to leave. It held its line and came back. And my Alan Shearer salute came out.'

Suddenly, Australia were rocking on 126 for 3. Michael Clarke, having settled into a comfortable chair at 11am anticipating an hour or so to prepare for his innings, found himself walking to the crease after three minutes of play.

The crowd were awake and alive, wondering what Onions would produce for the hat-trick ball, and so were his energised team-mates. Onions recalls: 'Jimmy and Broady were asking me, "What are you going to bowl?"'

'I knew what I had in my head, to bowl a bouncer, but I also knew that if I told them, they would try and talk me out of it and say No, just try to hit the stumps again. So I told them I would bowl another fullish, straight one.

'I stuck to my plan and, as it happened, it was just slightly down the legside. For a moment, I thought he might have got a nick to Matt Prior. The slips went up, but I realised it must have brushed his jumper and didn't bother appealing. Who knows? If I had done, maybe I might have got lucky.'

Shouts of 'easy, easy' and 'cheerio, cheerio' rang around the ground and, though England's supporters finally showed their respect when Ponting passed Allan Border's career Test tally of 11,174 runs to become Australia's most prolific batsman of all time, they were soon singing their goodbyes to him as well.

At 11.42am, the Aussie skipper became Onions's third victim inside the first hour. Having survived a risky single in the previous over – had Ian Bell's shy at the non-striker's end been accurate, he would have been run out – Ponting was rushed by a second bouncer in succession and was caught behind by Prior.

According to Onions: 'He played the first bouncer as though he had so much time and, of course, his reputation says he can play the short stuff with his eyes closed. Without doubt he is regarded as the best player of short bowling in the world. So I thought the last thing he'll be expecting is another, maybe I'll let him have one here. Just to see.

'Whereas the first one had been a tad too high, this one was totally perfect. When I saw him top-edge it to Matt I didn't even appeal. I just ran. He stood there. My God, what a feeling!'

Paul Collingwood marvelled at his Durham colleague's front. 'That ball was a hell of a risk. Ricky doesn't get bounced out too many times and, with the shortish boundary on that side, the slightest mistake and it could easily have gone for four or six.'

Strauss concurs: 'One of the things I really like about "Bunny" is that he's naturally aggressive, and at no stage has he seemed overawed. His style of his bowling means there's a lot of ways he can take wickets, because he brings the stumps into play a lot. He can get you bowled, lbw, he's got a slippery bouncer and he's quite hard to line up as a batsman, but his biggest attribute is his mindset, which means he doesn't worry too much about reputations.'

> 'Trouble was, I had absolutely no idea who Lily Allen was'
>
> *Says Collingwood, aged 93, who lists among his musical favourites 'Whistling' Ronnie Ronalde*

Lord knows what Lilly Allen was thinking in these moments, though whatever it was its significance would have flown straight over Collingwood's head.

'The boys kept talking about the fact that Lily Allen had mentioned Bunny on her Twitter page and said she fancied him. 'Trouble was, I had absolutely no idea who Lily Allen was,' says Collingwood, aged 93, who lists 'Whistling' Ronnie Ronalde and World War Two Forces sweetheart Dame Vera Lynn among his musical favourites.

No matter. At 163 for 4, Australia were there for the taking and England took them.

With overhead conditions perfect for conventional swing, Clarke had already been afforded two lives off Onions – a plumb lbw shout and a rare drop at second slip by Andrew Flintoff, after the ball flashed off the face of the bat from an attempted leave-alone – when Anderson forced the innings into nosedive.

A huge inswinger, which may arguably have been doing too much, persuaded Koertzen to unfurl his finger of doom and Clarke's departure left Australia on 193 for 5. There were just 25 minutes left until lunch and, suddenly, Anderson was making the ball talk. Marcus North's struggles continued as, no doubt frustrated by a combination of two single-figure scores at Lord's, and England's tactic of bowling to him wide outside off stump, he chased one and edged behind for Prior to claim the Kodak moment for the morning: an aerial, left-handed grab to his left, in front of Strauss at first slip to reduce Australia to 202 for 6. And, from his very next ball, Mitchell Johnson was given out to a ball that struck above the knee roll to take Australia's score to 202 for 7.

'The ball that Anderson got Manou out with was as good as you'll ever see'

Andrew Strauss

Once again the hat-trick was denied, but Anderson brought the morning session to a delirious close when, with the final ball before lunch bowled from wide of the crease, the 'Burnley Express' angled the ball in and then got it to move away a fraction past Graham Manou's bat and into off stump.

Australia, having started the day on 126 for 1, had slumped to 203 for 8 at lunch. Strauss thought Anderson had saved his best ball for last.

'It was another one of those crazy sessions where we built up some momentum, the crowd got behind us, the ball was swinging, every ball looked like a hand grenade and both Jimmy Anderson and Graham Onions bowled exceptionally. The ball that Anderson got Manou out with was as good as you'll ever see.'

Anderson isn't arguing: 'I enjoyed that,' he says. 'I remember the ball just hooping round corners all morning. Days like that, and balls like that, are the reason I practise.'

Prior's 'super-catch', meanwhile, had gone a long way to persuading the doubters that he was now close to the finished article, not merely as a batsman who could keep, but a proper bona fide successor to Alec Stewart – a player worth his place in the side for his ability with bat *and* gloves.

Prior himself puts his undoubted improvement down to a change of approach to the job encouraged by his coach, the former Nottinghamshire and England keeper Bruce French.

French's mop of brown hair may have made him look like the fifth Beatle, and taken about 30 years off his appearance, but any relaxation of tonsorial discipline – short back and sides when playing – was not mirrored in his work with Prior.

> ## 'Now I'm treating wicketkeeping as a craft, as an art, rather than just the other thing that I do'
>
> *Matt Prior on the influence of Bruce French*

'I started working with him before the South Africa one-day series last summer and he's been absolutely fantastic,' Prior explains. 'He's an infectious character.

'He loves the craftsmanship of being a wicketkeeper, and has really tried to make that rub off on me. He's helped me immensely in every area of keeping. The things he asks you to do, the stress he puts you under and the training he does are absolutely brilliant.

'One of his main things is, if the ball's going to come at 90mph then you have to process your reflexes as if it's coming at a hundred, so then 90 doesn't seem that quick.

'We've worked on a lot of technical things on my positioning and footwork, but he's also helped a lot with my mindset towards keeping.

'It's no secret, I've always loved my batting and, in the past, I've probably worked far more on that than I did on my keeping. I thought it was enough to get by on good eye and athleticism. Now I'm treating wicketkeeping as a craft, as an art, rather than just the other thing that I do. This catch was the reward for all that.

'I knew Jimmy was trying to line him up with the away-swinger, I was seeing it particularly well and I thought, back yourself, because he's going to get an edge here. And I saw it, I went for it and it stuck. It was a great feeling, because it wasn't an accident and it wasn't a fluke, you've done the work, you've prepared yourself in every way to do that. Having said that, I'm very glad it did stick, because I'd nicked it from Straussy's pocket and he wouldn't have been best pleased if I'd grassed it.

'As for our performance that morning, I remember walking off the pitch after the first day and all the guys were annoyed with themselves. But there was just this feeling that, OK, that was a bad 30 overs, but tomorrow we're going to come back and it will be different.'

Even some late-order resistance after lunch failed to detract from England's effort. Anderson completed a maiden five-wicket haul in Ashes cricket when he enticed a routine edge from Peter Siddle and, although number 11 Ben Hilfenhaus was reprieved by Ravi Bopara's unsuccessful attempt at an over-the-shoulder catch running back from point, Onions got his man at the second time of asking when a slice to gully ended the innings. Nine wickets had gone down for 137 runs: it altered the position of the match drastically.

With Australia dismissed for 263, Anderson finishing with five for 80 and Onions four for 58, England were once again powered by the momentum that had swung in their favour at Lord's. Whatever the dreary weather forecast, if they batted well in their first innings, they could set up the victory that would secure them at least a share of the series and, maybe, ownership of the urn itself.

Now the England fans turned up the heat with ironic taunts of 'We want Mitch, we want Mitch' and 'Super Mitchell Johnson' at the start of the England innings. Given his performances in the previous two matches, Ponting no longer trusted the left-armer to open the bowling. Peter Siddle took advantage of his own promotion, however, to send back Alastair Cook in his first over. It was the only success before tea, however, as the in-form Strauss, accompanied by Bopara, drove confidently to collect regular boundaries.

A less-certain stroke accounted for Bopara soon after the interval as the diagonal bat offered to a Hilfenhaus delivery sent the ball crashing into the stumps. An out-of-sorts Bopara may only have amassed 104 runs in his first four Ashes innings, but his mentor, former England captain Graham Gooch, felt this might turn out to be a breakthrough innings.

Bopara recalls: 'Graham said to me, "I thought you batted brilliantly today. I know 20s and 30s are not want you want, but you were unlucky to be out when you had done the hard work. Keep at it and the scores will come."'

His dismissal afforded Ian Bell the chance finally to make a mark on an Ashes contest. Bell's career return of just 502 runs in ten previous Tests against Australia had filled former foe Shane Warne with confidence. 'They'll take Bell any day,' Warne wrote in his column in *The Times* that morning. 'I think Peter Siddle could really work him over in the same way Glenn McGrath used to. Bell doesn't like the ball coming back into him – he is bowled and leg-before a lot – and Siddle will show up the flaws in his technique.' Warne added: 'Bell's return will hopefully be greeted with, "Welcome back, Shermanator," the nickname I gave him in 2006. I remember watching *American Pie* in the team hotel with Michael Clarke on the fourth evening of the Adelaide Test, and when the dorky ginger kid appeared we both started laughing because he reminded us of Bell. The next day I was bowling to Strauss, with Bell at the non-striker's end. As I walked to my mark, he seemed to be staring at me, so I just said: "What are you looking at, Shermanator?" It brought a good laugh from the fielders. "I've been called worse," Bell told me. "No, mate," I said. "You haven't."'

Bell was unmoved. 'I'd heard what Warney said. Typical of him, he probably had a pop at every player in that England team. To me, you've got to go out and play the eleven players you're playing against, and you can't afford to worry about things that go on outside of the cricket. But it meant nothing to me. He wasn't playing. He was writing. No one ever got out to a clever sentence.

'I felt pretty good from the off. It was nice to be at Edgbaston, and I wanted to go out there and just play the way I'd been playing for Warwickshire, and make a statement that I'm here for this series and I believe I'm good enough.'

Indeed, Bell demonstrated his confidence immediately, using his feet to loft Nathan Hauritz for a sublime straight six.

Luck was also with him when Johnson swung one back to hit his pad a couple of overs before bad light stopped play. The pursing of Bell's lips and his fidget away from the stumps as he waited for umpire Koertzen's verdict suggested he feared the worst.

> 'But it meant nothing to me. He wasn't playing. He was writing. No one ever got out to a clever sentence'
>
> *Ian Bell deals with Shane Warne*

'I was worried,' Bell concedes. 'In hindsight it was absolutely plumb, but there are days when you get poor decisions against you, so I'm more than happy to take those ones.

'Watching the Ashes for the first two Tests from the outside, you're obviously listening along to the commentators, and Johnson hadn't been swinging the ball back at all. That was probably the first Test match he started doing it. We did a lot of preparation for the two days prior to the Test, for the ball going across and, all of a sudden, he clicked.'

In the Sky commentary box, Michael Holding was incredulous at Koertzen's decision. 'How is that not out lbw?' he asked. ' What is going through the umpire's mind?'

But with Strauss once again beyond fifty, England were well set on 116 for 2 when play closed at 5.45pm.

Strauss recalls: 'Batting down the other end there, I felt this was a very important phase of the game. When Bell came in at 60 for 2, the innings could have gone either way, so I was impressed pretty much straight away by his attitude. He went down the wicket and whacked Hauritz over his head. He looked busy and he had a bit of luck, but it was encouraging to see him play positively.'

Edgbaston, Day Three: No Play. England 116 for 2

England's hopes of pushing on towards a 2–0 lead against Australia for the first time since 1986 were dealt a significant blow when the curtains were drawn on a filthy day in Birmingham. Once again, overnight rain had left Edgbaston's playing area saturated, which delayed the start. Further wet weather meant play was abandoned at 2.38pm after two post-lunch inspections were flushed away. This was the first Ashes washout since Boxing Day at the Melbourne Test in 1998.

Technically, given their advantage in the series, being off the field suited England better than their opponents. To some observers, the Australians were having no luck at all, and this was symbolised when the early afternoon downpour soaked a group of their players as they dashed back from the indoor school to the pavilion. The smiles on the faces of Andrew Strauss and Andy Flower, as they trod the same path under the shelter of a vast umbrella, said it all. But such was the confidence gained from recent days in the middle that England's leaders rued the missed opportunity to drive home the advantage.

The only competitive edge to the day took place before the rain abated, as Ravi Bopara saw off Strauss, Alastair Cook, James Anderson and Graeme Swann in a dressing-room poker school, trousering £80 for his efforts. Meanwhile, the smart money on the outcome of the Test was on the draw, particularly given the optimism, or lack of it, from groundsman Steve Rouse for the penultimate day's outlook. However, Flower refused to give up on toppling Australia at Edgbaston once more. 'Looking at that outfield, I'm not sure how much play we're going to get tomorrow,' he said. 'Steve Rouse has said we might get in 70 overs. That would be a godsend. But we've seen here how fast things can happen, so a result is definitely possible.'

Flower also revealed the intention to use Andrew Flintoff in full capacity, whatever the danger of aggravating his knee. The precautionary route of avoiding the excessive workload may have preserved the all-rounder's body for another week and another Test, at Leeds, but Flower said: 'We don't look any further forward than this game. We've got to try to win it and then make decisions thereafter. I'm thankful Flintoff is playing. I think it is great that he is playing, given his injury record. I think he can play two Tests in a row, but we don't know what will happen over the next two days. He is a strong bloke, so it's possible. We would like him to be playing every minute of this game. There will be quite a lot of wear and tear on him.'

While England's dressing-room was bullish, Australia's was best described as 'sheepish' following reports the axed Hughes had been spotted drowning his sorrows in a Broad Street bar in the early hours of Friday morning. The decision to jettison the opener for Shane Watson had been criticised by Anglo-Aussie writer Peter Roebuck. Whatever the rights and wrongs, it had certainly been an unusual move by Australia, given their reluctance to compromise on previous visits. In their past three tours of England, in fact, the Australians had made only two changes to their batting – Justin Langer for Michael Slater in 2001, and Ricky Ponting for Michael Bevan in 1997. Even in 2005, when their batting rarely functioned effectively, they kept faith with their top six. To change things now appeared, to some, an admission of uncertainty, even – whisper it – weakness.

Edgbaston, Day Four: England 376 all out; Australia 88 for 2

Just as on the first day, wet weather had taken its toll on the bowlers' run-ups, and with the umpires concerned at the sogginess of the surface, England's progress was delayed for a further hour. The fact it was Ponting twirling his studs into a quagmire at mid-off, at the City End, to emphasise the sodden state of the turf, told its own story. For once he did receive applause from those on the terraces, albeit in the form of a slow handclap.

When play did get going, at noon, the allocation for the day had been reduced to 91 overs, but if the warm-ups were anything to go by the first hour was going to be something of an examination for England's batsmen. The ball had swung massively for the Australian bowlers during their run-throughs, and continued to do so, for Ben Hilfenhaus in particular.

Elsewhere on the square, Stuart Broad, concerned that he had so far failed to make a telling contribution with the ball, and aware of suggestions that his place may be in jeopardy, was beginning the process of finding a way to do so. Under the watchful eye of bowling coach Ottis Gibson, the six-foot-six paceman – nicknamed 'Baywatch' by the touring South Africans the previous year 'because they thought I looked like Pamela Anderson' – was intent on re-grooving an approach and an action he believed may have been confused by an over-aggressive intent so far.

According to Broad: 'I hadn't bowled well in the series up to this point and here, even though we got them out cheaply in the first innings, my poor performance had been masked by the brilliance of Onions and Anderson.

'So, at the halfway stage of the game, I sat down with Ottis and had a discussion about which direction I wanted to go. We came to the conclusion that maybe I had been trying to do too many different things with the ball, searching too much for perfect deliveries, trying to buy wickets with bouncers and yorkers and slower balls. I had been trying to bowl in an aggressive role, but that led me to end up losing my natural length and I wasn't looking dangerous. We both felt it was time to get back to real basics.

'Throughout my first-class career, I'd aimed to hit the same spot – top of off stump – and let the ball do something, not try and swing it, not try to seam it everywhere, just to get the ball in the right area and see what it does. And Gibbo said, "It's not what the ball does, it's where it does it from that matters," which made sense to me.

'It doesn't matter if the ball's swinging three feet if it starts from outside off stump, because the batsman won't be able to reach it, let alone edge it. But if you make the batsman play and the ball does anything either way, you're in the game.

'So I decided I was just going to put a cone down in practice where my best length is, sixteen feet away from the stumps, just outside off stump. When I'm in rhythm and bowling at my best, my natural shape makes the ball swing away slightly from that angle so I can attack the stumps or the outside edge.

'I just concentrated on trying to hit that cone every ball. And I did the same from then on every day in warm-ups right through to the end of the series.'

Strauss, who edged the first ball of the third over of the morning just short of first slip with no addition to the overnight score, continued his recent trend of falling early in the day when set overnight. He had managed only a handful of runs, in fact, when he attempted to cut a Hilfenhaus delivery that was far too close to him and edged behind to leave England on 142 for 3.

Bell was still battling to deal with a rejuvenated Johnson, whose first ball from the Pavilion End pitched perfectly and was going on to hit middle. To the batsman's relief, an inside edge made the shouts irrelevant. When Paul Collingwood succumbed to the impressive Hilfenhaus, however, Australia's most reliable bowler during the series, England were struggling on 159 for 4 shortly before lunch. Then Johnson finally had Bell lbw for 53 and, at 168 for 5, still 95 runs short, the ball appeared back in Australia's court.

But beware the wounded beast. Never was the great Gordon Greenidge more dangerous than when he began to limp. Steve Waugh proved as good on one leg as two on the 2001 Ashes tour. Now Flintoff, though hobbling at the crease, did what sporting superstars are supposed to do. Inhaling lungfuls of the Edgbaston spirit, he seized the moment, and the game, by the scruff of the neck.

His early combat with Johnson was enthralling enough. With two fielders set for the trap, bouncers whistled past the batsman's grille and views were exchanged through it, as memories were evoked of similar battles between Flintoff and Brett Lee.

> 'Forget thinking like a batsman and just hit the ball'
>
> *Andrew Flintoff races to 74*

By his own admission the all-rounder needs lots of innings to get into a batting rhythm, something denied him over recent years due to repetitive injury breakdowns and rehabilitations. Whereas he feels his bowling can be switched on like a light, his batting needs grooving. Each return in recent years had reminded supporters of his stellar form of 2003–05, if only by its huge distance from it.

Now, as he had vowed to do since the eve of the series, he concentrated on the strengths that had served him so well in Cardiff, and played on instinct first and technique second. For him it was time to forget thinking like a batsman and just hit the ball.

'I think, with the retirement looming, I was just going out and playing for enjoyment,' Flintoff stresses. 'I felt like I was in for the day.'

After easing a first boundary off Hilfenhaus, he clambered into a brief buffet course from all-rounder Shane Watson. Booming drives regularly found the ropes and the effect on the crowd was as uplifting as his innings of 68 and 73 had been back in 2005. Matt Prior proved a willing accomplice in stealing back momentum. They charged from 200 to 250 in just 38 balls. Such was their force, in fact, that they appeared to be taking the contest away from Australia when Prior miscued consecutive pulls off Peter Siddle, the second proving terminal. England were just six runs behind.

Flintoff brought the scores level with one hefty blow that cleared the boundary at long-on off spinner Nathan Hauritz, and was celebrating a 53-ball fifty later in the over when he dragged a sweep through square leg for his seventh four. There was more fluency to this innings than any other since the 31-year-old's comeback; emphasised by a pull careering into the rope in front of square on the legside when Siddle opted for a bumper four overs shy of the new ball. Flintoff's freescoring was infectious, and Stuart Broad soon had the bug.

However, moments after acknowledging another half-century stand, the Flintoff show came to an abrupt, and rather odd, end shortly before tea. Hardly renowned for his desire to leave anything from a spinner when in full attack mode, Flintoff decided to take a breather to a ball from Hauritz that pitched, reared up, spat and bounced off his glove to Michael Clarke at slip.

Flintoff's 74 was his highest Test score on home soil since an Ashes hundred at Trent Bridge four years previously, but how he would have cherished another with the second hand on his career clock moving too fast.

Flintoff says, 'I just couldn't believe how I got out. Me, leaving an off-spinner? It just doesn't happen. Normally, if a spinner gets me out, it's caught on the boundary.'

Runs kept flowing, however, from Stuart Broad and Graeme Swann, as England showed they were more than ready to stand toe to toe with their Australian opponents. Much had been made of team-mates not backing up Paul Collingwood during verbal exchanges Down Under two and a half years earlier; an indication, it was said, of a fragile team spirit. This time, when Graeme Swann, who angered Johnson with a slice over the slips for four to the second new ball, received a bouncer and a barrage of words as retaliation, the response was dramatic. Swann returned opinion in kind as he followed his opponent up the pitch and Broad let rip from the non-striker's end to show Australia that, exactly like 2005, this team was not prepared to be bullied. Swann guided the next ball behind square on the offside for four to add to the theatre. 'I love it,' quipped Shane Warne from beneath the roar of the Hollies Stand. 'This is what it's all about.'

Swann may have been out next ball, Johnson's first from around the wicket, but England's intent was unmistakable. Their response to a mini-crisis had been for the last five wickets to produce 208 runs from 35 overs, reaching 376 and a potentially match-winning lead of 113. Broad was the last man out, for 55.

Broad recalls: 'I think that first innings at Edgbaston was a bit of a turning point in the series for me, with the bat. If the Aussies see a weakness they can exploit that, and to get those useful runs within a pretty tricky situation gave me a lot of confidence.'

Strauss says: 'Freddie played exceptionally well in that game. He hadn't got many at Lord's, but he said to me, "I'm just going to go out and hit the ball," and that's exactly what he did.'

'His batting, and the runs of Swann and Broad, not only earned us a useful lead, but the way they did it was important as well. It was really encouraging to see Ponting scratching his head and bowlers not knowing where to bowl. It certainly reminded me of how Freddie played in 2005. And those three guys really took the game away from the Aussies.'

Now, after having wrestled back control, Strauss sensed a real chance to make it count.

Such had been the weather's effect on the match, Australia's only ambition now was to bat long enough to secure a draw and they began their task comfortably, reaching 47 without loss. Then the Sunday crowd erupted again, as wickets in consecutive overs sparked them, and England, back to life.

Onions, whose double-wicket opening over on Friday had transformed the match for the first time, appeared to have done so again when he slanted one away from Simon Katich, whose over-ambitious attempt to on-drive resulted in a thin edge to Prior.

Ponting was greeted by the customary pantomime boos, and Swann made sure he didn't overstay his welcome with his best ball of the series so far.

After having an lbw appeal turned down by the under-fire Koertzen, Swann fizzed down a ball that drew a lunge forward from Ponting before turning out of the rough and ripping through the gate. As the bails lay fatally on the floor, ten Englishmen accosted their team-mate somewhere near extra cover.

'Not bad,' says Swann, 'probably hit a foothold.'

Ponting remained transfixed for a moment before marching off briskly, and his sense of astonishment was followed by another, admittedly with a more sinister tone, as he reached the pavilion gate, where a fan had prepared his own personal send-off.

'He was actually leaning over the grandstand and gave me a bit of a gobful,' said Ponting. 'And, as it turned out, he was later thrown out of the ground, so he was probably in the wrong, doing what he did.'

Sky Sports opted not to broadcast the heated spat, during which both parties swore, perhaps mindful of the controversial screening of Didier Drogba's tirade after Chelsea were knocked out of the Champions League by Barcelona at the semi-final stage earlier in the year.

Ponting added: 'Where we walked on and off was very close to spectators, so if there's one place in the world where a security guard should have been standing, it was right there. It's been well documented in the last few weeks that I've copped a bit from the crowds, so it wasn't a big deal at all. It was just a few words that I didn't think needed to happen.'

England smelt green-and-gold blood and, had Strauss been a tad bolder with his field placings, the tourists might even have been three down at the close. The inside edge that ballooned from Mike Hussey's pad might have been snaffled by a short leg, but he survived a king-pair chance when Onions failed to scoop up the ball in his follow-through. As it was, England were content to settle for an Australia score of 88 for 2, which meant they entered the fifth day requiring eight wickets, and with a slender, but significant, lead of 25.

Edgbaston, Day Five: Australia 375 for 5. Match Drawn

Perhaps hoping for lightning to strike twice, Strauss once again threw the ball to Graham Onions on the final morning. As inspirational as such a move had proved 72 hours earlier, however, it seemed a bold choice given that the conditions appeared tailor-made for Anderson. Cloud hung heavy overhead and the ball was 28 overs old, just about the point at which the Duke, with the right care, starts to arc through the air.

The feeling in the Australia camp was that England had missed a trick. 'I was a bit surprised, yeah,' admitted Australia captain Ponting. 'Andrew Flintoff is always their go-to man to try to set up the day for them. Looking at the game and the way it had been, the ball started swinging at the exact time that England started the morning, so I was surprised Anderson didn't get the new ball.'

Flintoff roughed up both Shane Watson and Michael Hussey, the overnight pair, in his first over from the Pavilion End, but despite his undisputed hostility, England struggled for a breakthrough and the Australians negotiated the first hour without mishap.

In contrast, Anderson took just six balls to break the third-wicket partnership of 85 when, immediately after drinks, Watson fell for the third time in as many innings soon after celebrating fifty – this time from a nick behind. The introduction of Stuart Broad as Onions's replacement also reaped rewards shortly before lunch when Hussey, whose 64 signalled a much-needed return to form, nibbled at one from around the wicket. Australia reached the interval on 172 for 4, 59 ahead.

Increased security was called for around the dressing-room area during the interval, following what later proved to be a hoax threat to local authorities. There was little drama on the field, though, as the lack of pace in the Edgbaston surface made prising the Australians out a thankless task. Strauss needed quick wickets to inject some life into his team's pursuit of victory, but it soon turned into the least enthralling day of the series. There was a sub-plot developing during England's toil, however: the fitness of Flintoff. A fortnight after producing the finest spell of his career at Lord's to unman Australia, he was now being used more sparingly, despite the need to make incisions into the middle order.

Indeed, after his initial seven-over burst, he was not called upon until the ninth over of the afternoon session and, after failing to force a breakthrough during a four-over spell in which his left ankle folded in his delivery stride to cause a moment of panic, he was put out to pasture by Strauss half an hour before the arrival of the second new ball.

With Michael Clarke and Marcus North entrenched, England's chance to win the match had gone and Flintoff was not called upon again.

'I was struggling now,' Flintoff recalls. 'The pain was pretty much constant and, though I was trying to put a brave face on it, I don't think I was kidding anyone.'

It was the first time Flintoff had drawn a blank with the ball snce England surrendered the Ashes in Perth in December 2006, and his previous wicketless Test blank was against the South Africans way back in the summer of 2003.

Though encouraged by signs of a return to form from Broad, who took 2 for 38 in 16 overs, Strauss was disappointed that his side were unable to create more pressure. He says: 'When Swann got Ponting out the previous evening, I definitely thought we had a sniff. But what was a bit irritating was that the conditions on that final day looked absolutely a hundred per cent suitable for swing bowling and the ball never swung. It may be that the night before the ball had been whacked . . . Swanny had been whacked for a boundary and it got wet, and maybe that just affected the ball, so in a way it was disappointing that we weren't able to force the issue a bit more when the ball wasn't swinging.

'Fair play to Clarke and North for getting stuck in, but the wicket, if anything, died a bit, it lost a bit of pace, and they played well.

'I think we were in a great position to win that Test match. When rain interferes as much as it did, it's always quite a good effort to force a result from there. I still think we took a lot from that game but, I must admit, at the back of my mind I was a little bit concerned about the game coming up. I remember speaking to

Andy Flower about it that evening going, This Headingley game's a massive one for us, and I'm a little bit concerned about where we are, we've expended a lot of energy.'

Flintoff's growing discomfort was seized upon by the Australian camp. 'You could see he went downhill pretty quickly during the course of this game,' said Ponting. 'So his injury is probably having more of an effect than we realised . . . It's been visible over the last couple of days; he's been struggling more than he did during the Lord's Test. No doubt they protected him late this afternoon, knowing how big a figure he is for the team.'

Strauss attempted to play down the state of his hobbling hero when he countered: 'There wasn't as much in this wicket for him as there has been on previous wickets. It was one of those wickets where the more you hit the deck, the slower it comes off, and at the back of my mind I'm conscious that when the conditions aren't really helping him, there's no point in tearing him to death.'

Inevitably, questions over his availability for Leeds followed. 'The Headingley Test is a massive Test,' said Strauss. 'It's an opportunity to win the Ashes, and we want to play our best team in every game we play. But we've got to be conscious that, if he's not fit enough to do his job, he won't play. A lot of it comes down to how he feels with his own body – he's got to be honest about that, and he has been so far. He's obviously desperate to play in the last two games, and we're optimistic he'll be fine, but I think he realises that, if he's not fit, he won't help us.'

Clarke, playing his 50th Test, and North progressed relatively untroubled towards three-figure scores in the final session after Australia took tea on 293 for 4. North opened his shoulders to power past his colleague via a glut of boundaries, including three in a row from Ravi Bopara's medium pace, and was just one more such stroke away from joining a rather elite club when he perished to a brilliant catch from James Anderson in the gully. As North's bat flashed at a ball from Stuart Broad, it appeared to be on its way to the vacant third-man area, but Anderson spectacularly flung himself high to his right to cling on. Had it evaded his grasp, North would have become only the fourth Australian to have registered three hundreds in his first five Tests, after Arthur Morris, Sir Donald Bradman and Michael Hussey. North's fortune contrasted sharply to that of Clarke, who survived twice in the 90s. Firstly, on 92, when a Broad delivery clipped his off stump but failed to dislodge a bail; then four runs later when, with the gloom gathering, he sliced to third slip off Bopara and was saved by a shout of no-ball. Two overs later he celebrated a second hundred of the series and 12th of his Test career, which signalled the handshakes and an early settlement. Australia had lost just three wickets on a fifth day England began with a swagger, to close on 375 for 5. Was momentum shifting back towards Ricky Ponting's Australians?

The England captain admits the thought may have filtered into his mind. 'The finish line was getting closer,' says the England captain. 'We could see the possibility of winning the Ashes but, maybe subliminally, we were also thinking, There's potential here for either a batting collapse or a less good bowling performance.

'Maybe we were being a bit negative, but I just had a bit of a bad feeling about what was to come.'

30, 31 July 2009, 1, 2, 3 August 2009

Result: Match drawn
Toss: Australia, who chose to bat
Series: England lead 5-match series 1–0
Umpires: Aleem Dar (Pakistan) and RE Koertzen (South Africa)
Match referee: JJ Crowe (New Zealand)
Test debut: BA Manon (Australia)
Player of the match: MJ Clarke (Australia)

Australia 1st innings		R	M	B	4s	6s
SR Watson	lbw b Onions	62	130	106	10	0
SM Katich	lbw b Swann	46	83	48	9	0
RT Ponting*	c †Prior b Onions	38	88	47	5	0
MEK Hussey	b Onions	0	1	1	0	0
MJ Clarke	lbw b Anderson	29	94	55	4	0
MJ North	c †Prior b Anderson	12	63	49	1	0
GA Manou†	b Anderson	8	20	11	2	0
MG Johnson	lbw b Anderson	0	1	1	0	0
NM Hauritz	not out	20	78	50	1	0
PM Siddle	c †Prior b Anderson	13	31	26	2	0
BW Hilfenhaus	c Swann b Onions	20	37	31	4	0
Extras	(b 5, lb 7, w 2, nb 1)	15				
Total	(all out; 70.4 overs; 319 mins)	263 (3.72 runs per over)				

Fall of wickets 1–85 (Katich, 18.6 ov), 2–126 (Watson, 30.1 ov), 3–126 (Hussey, 30.2 ov), 4–163 (Ponting, 38.3 ov), 5–193 (Clarke, 49.4 ov), 6–202 (North, 51.4 ov), 7–202 (Johnson, 51.5 ov), 8–203 (Manou, 53.5 ov), 9–229 (Siddle, 61.5 ov), 10–263 (Hilfenhaus, 70.4 ov)

Bowling	O	M	R	W	Econ	
JM Anderson	24	7	80	5	3.33	
A Flintoff	15	2	58	0	3.86	(1nb, 1w)
G Onions	16.4	2	58	4	3.48	(1w)
SCJ Broad	13	2	51	0	3.92	
GP Swann	2	0	4	1	2.00	

England 1st innings		R	M	B	4s	6s
AJ Strauss*	c †Manou b Hilfenhaus	69	178	134	11	0
AN Cook	c †Manou b Siddle	0	7	4	0	0
RS Bopara	b Hilfenhaus	23	70	54	4	0
IR Bell	lbw b Johnson	53	147	114	7	1
PD Collingwood	c Ponting b Hilfenhaus	13	27	22	3	0
MJ Prior†	c sub (PJ Hughes) b Siddle	41	100	59	6	0
A Flintoff	c Clarke b Hauritz	74	116	79	10	1
SCJ Broad	c & b Siddle	55	92	64	9	0
GP Swann	c North b Johnson	24	23	20	5	0
JM Anderson	c †Manou b Hilfenhaus	1	7	6	0	0
G Onions	not out	2	20	14	0	0
Extras	(b 2, lb 4, w 6, nb 9)	21				
Total	(all out; 93.3 overs; 399 mins) 376 (4.02 runs per over)					

Fall of wickets 1–2 (Cook, 1.4 ov), 2–60 (Bopara, 19.2 ov), 3–141 (Strauss, 44.1 ov), 4–159 (Collingwood, 50.5 ov), 5–168 (Bell, 55.6 ov), 6–257 (Prior, 71.3 ov), 7–309 (Flintoff, 80.4 ov), 8–348 (Swann, 87.3 ov), 9–355 (Anderson, 88.6 ov), 10–376 (Broad, 93.3 ov)

Bowling	O	M	R	W	Econ	
BW Hilfenhaus	30	7	109	4	3.63	(4nb)
PM Siddle	21.3	3	89	3	4.13	(1w)
NM Hauritz	18	2	57	1	3.16	
MG Johnson	21	1	92	2	4.38	(5nb, 1w)
SR Watson	3	0	23	0	7.66	

Australia 2nd innings		R	M	B	4s	6
SR Watson	c †Prior b Anderson	53	183	114	9	0
SM Katich	c †Prior b Onions	26	55	47	2	0
RT Ponting*	b Swann	5	6	7	0	0
MEK Hussey	c †Prior b Broad	64	154	130	13	0
MJ Clarke	not out	103	281	192	14	0
MJ North	c Anderson b Broad	96	208	159	15	0
GA Manou†	not out	13	39	28	1	0
Extras	(b 4, lb 6, w 2, nb 3)	15				
Total	(5 wickets; 112.2 overs; 466 mins)	375 (3.33 runs per over)				

Did not bat MG Johnson, BW Hilfenhaus, PM Siddle, NM Hauritz
Fall of wickets 1–47 (Katich, 13.2 ov), 2–52 (Ponting, 14.6 ov), 3–137 (Watson, 43.6 ov), 4–161 (Hussey, 52.6 ov), 5–346 (North, 103.1 ov)

Bowling	O	M	R	W	Econ	
JM Anderson	21	8	47	1	2.23	(1nb)
A Flintoff	15	0	35	0	2.33	
G Onions	19	3	74	1	3.89	(1w)
GP Swann	31	4	119	1	3.83	
SCJ Broad	16	2	38	2	2.37	(1w)
RS Bopara	8.2	1	44	0	5.28	(2nb)
PD Collingwood	2	0	8	0	4.00	

Close of play
30 Jul day 1 – Australia 1st innings 126/1 (SR Watson 62*, RT Ponting 17*, 30 ov)
31 Jul day 2 – England 1st innings 116/2 (AJ Strauss 64*, IR Bell 26*, 36 ov)
1 Aug day 3 – no play
2 Aug day 4 – Australia 2nd innings 88/2 (SR Watson 34*, MEK Hussey 18*, 28 ov)
3 Aug day 5 – Australia 2nd innings 375/5 (112.2 ov) – end of match

Fourth Test, Headingley: 7–9 August

Who needs a crystal ball when you've got Andrew Strauss?

Inspired analysis or self-fulfilling prophecy? Either way, from the moment the England skipper and his enlarged squad arrived at Headingley for the fourth Test, due to start on Friday 7 August, the bad news he had been fearing came in waves, and it would only keep on coming.

Mindful that a second sequence of back-to-back Tests in just five weeks would stretch Flintoff's resilience to its very limit, England had sought back-up, adding Jonathan Trott, the in-form, South African-born Warwickshire batsman, in case they felt the need to bolster the batting. Steve Harmison, meanwhile, was put on alert to play at Headingley as a like-for-like replacement with the ball.

In an increasingly painful session on the eve of the match, just three days after the end of the third Test at Edgbaston, it became clear that, no matter how much he wanted to play, Flintoff just wasn't physically capable of giving a hundred per cent of himself for five days.

Given the choice, Flintoff would have played. He had already made it clear that only something exceptional would keep him off the field.

He recalls: 'I wanted to play the whole series, and I thought I could have done. I was not great at Birmingham and then, even though I wasn't at a hundred per cent in the nets at Headingley, I still felt I could play but the selectors felt differently. They had a

161

difficult decision to make, and ultimately it had to be their choice in the end about what was best for the team.

'I discussed the situation with Andrew Strauss and Andy Flower and they told me that afternoon that I wasn't going to be playing. I left my bags in the dressing-room, because if I'd taken them away with me the press would have sussed the situation and everyone would have asked what was going on.

'It was a pretty tough time. I didn't feel great about missing out, especially as this match could decide the outcome of the Ashes.'

Strauss was determined not to let sentiment get in the way of what he and the management considered was not just the right choice, but the only one. He had batted against Flintoff that afternoon in the nets and, in his opinion: 'Fred was struggling. He was well down on pace. We spoke to him pretty much straight after the net to gauge his feelings. Fred said: "What I've done today in the nets is probably what I've got left for this Test match." In his mind, he felt, if I can bat and bowl ten overs or so per day then maybe that's enough to merit selection. Our feeling was that he was the all-rounder and he had to be able to do his job with bat and ball, and with the Oval Test match coming up there was a case for making sure he was OK for that.

'I suppose the other aspect was the question of whether it was right for someone like Fred to be hobbling around on one leg in a

'In his mind he felt, if I can bat and bowl ten overs or so per day then maybe that's enough to merit selection. Our feeling was that he was the all-rounder and he had to be able to do his job with bat and ball'

Andrew Strauss on the decision to omit Flintoff

Test match. No matter how good a player is or how important he is to the side, it just doesn't look right. At the back end of the Edgbaston Test he had started to limp heavily and, in the end, we didn't really think it was fair on him or the team to play him when he was clearly in a lot of discomfort.

'We told him, "Unfortunately we're not going to play you." To be fair to him, even though he was obviously disappointed, I thought he took it well.'

Collingwood was in no doubt the decision to omit Flintoff was unavoidable.

'I faced him in the nets,' said Collingwood, 'and seven out of every eight balls went down the legside, which meant he wasn't getting through his action at all. In the end it was an important Test match and, personally, I didn't think he was fit or that his body language was right.'

Flintoff's efforts in the nets were genuine enough. He was trying hard to hide the pain but, with every ball he bowled, the truth became more obvious. To some, his performance resembled the scene in the film *Monty Python and the Holy Grail* where King Arthur, attempting to recruit new members to join him at his Round Table in Camelot, comes across the insanely brave Black Knight, who tells him 'None shall pass' without a fight. As King Arthur

> '**I had a bit of a rant and got a few things out and I moved on**'
>
> *Andrew Flintoff*

dismembers his plucky opponent limb by limb, the Knight responds to each loss by shouting, ''Tis only a scratch', or 'Merely a flesh wound'. Only when, armless and legless, he realises he can no longer budge an inch, does he finally concede, 'Oh, all right then . . . call it a draw.'

Now not even Flintoff's consuming desire to play a part in all of this Ashes series could mask the fact that, momentarily at least, his injured body had let him down. It was already an open secret within the camp that Flintoff would require more surgery at the end of the series, and he spent the evening with his physio and friend Dave Roberts, the man who had helped him come back so many times before, softening his sorrows.

'I had a bit of a rant and got a few things out and I moved on,' said Flintoff.

Meanwhile, doubts were also increasing over the health of Stuart Broad, who had started to show symptoms of tonsillitis. In addition, the team's general sense of well-being was not improved when, at 4.30am, they were forced from their beds into a cold, damp and grey Leeds morning by the hotel fire alarm.

Ignoring the first blast, they had to respond to the second and soon found themselves, with their wives and families, congregating in the road as the Fire Brigade came to check the building. Half an hour later they were back in their rooms at The Radisson, in plenty of time for Swann to twitter the world about their predicament, but very few got another wink of sleep. Broad, dosed up with a sleeping pill to help him get through the worst of his illness, was still groggy when his own alarm went off around 8am.

A female guest, it turned out, had washed out her underwear in the sink during the early hours of the morning and had left it to dry dangerously close to a light as she hit the pillow. When her smalls began smouldering, however, they set off the hotel's smoke detectors. Rumours that the guilty lady had checked in earlier under the name Vicky Bonting have still to be substantiated.

England's players made their way back to their rooms at about the same time residents were having their morning newspapers slipped under their doors. The back pages were full of the news cricket fans up and down the country were dreading – Flintoff had been ruled out of the match.

Headingley, Day One: England 102; Australia 196 for 4

The England and Wales Cricket Board confirmed Flintoff's absence at 9.20am, but even 'Mystic Andy' could not have foreseen what further misfortune was about to befall his team.

England had just finished their usual football match when Matt Prior suffered a back spasm. As the clock struck 10am, the wicket-keeper/batsman was prostrate on the turf, being attended to by physio Kirk Russell.

'I'd had it before, so I knew exactly what it was,' Prior recalls. 'I stopped running straight away and attempted to prevent the full spasm from coming on, but it was too late. Almost immediately I found myself doubled over on the outfield thinking, Oh no, here we go.

'The last time I had this problem was in 2006 in a county game against Hampshire, and my experience was that it would take about 24 hours to recover. The next day I played and was in the field and I managed to keep, so I knew it was going to get better, it was just a matter of how quickly I could sort it out and release the back to be able to move at all.

'I had no inkling of a problem before it happened. The only thing I remember thinking is that my legs felt heavier than usual and I wondered why, because I didn't feel particularly tired. It literally just came out of nowhere. It was like having extreme cramp in all the muscles around the spot, so what basically happens is you're paralysed. You can't move your arms or legs or anything. And because all the muscles tighten around your ribs, it then impedes your diaphragm as well, so you struggle to breathe, and you actually feel like someone's knocked the wind out of you. Fortunately, I had known the feeling before so I knew it would pass, but it's still quite frightening and at that moment I thought, I'm out of the Test match.'

And so, when they saw Prior's arms being yanked back and forth and his body twisted this way and that, did the rest of the England team.

While Prior was taken to the dressing-room for a Voltarol injection in his backside and a massage to his lower back, certain players started speculating whether French himself might be called up. Other possibilities included an SOS to either Alec Stewart, commentating for the BBC, or even a late cap for coach Andy Flower.

Meanwhile, Paul Collingwood, who loves the idea of keeping wicket rather more than his team-mates like the idea of him doing it, spotted his chance.

'I must admit that, while I felt for Matt, I was getting a bit excited,' Collingwood says. 'I couldn't believe what had happened to him. He looked like he'd been shot. We looked at him and he was on the floor and he couldn't move, and he was trying to shout, "I can't move!", except that he could hardly breathe either, so it was coming out like a whisper. It was literally like, "What the hell's going to happen here?" That's when I started thinking, I'm going to have to keep for the first couple of hours at least, while maybe Steven Davies would come down from Durham or something like that.

'Straight away I went across to Matty's kitbag and put the inners and gloves on and I got myself ready to keep wicket.

'I wasn't everyone's choice, obviously. As I'm standing there taking catches in practice, all the commentators were stood in a row behind me just laughing their heads off, and I turned to them and said, "I'm not that bad," and all of a sudden it dawned on me that this was the Ashes, and that if I kept wicket we were going to be absolutely ridiculed. I had that in my thoughts when the next ball came through and I did my usual reverse cup and literally clanged the ball straight on the floor. I turned back again and all I could see were the commentators with their shoulders heaving up and down.'

'I couldn't believe what had happened to him. He looked like he'd been shot. We looked at him and he was on the floor and he couldn't move, and he was trying to shout, "I can't move!", except that he could hardly breathe either'

Collingwood on Prior

Not surprisingly, it was at this point that England asked permission for the toss to be delayed in order to give them time to see if Prior would be fit to play.

Given their generosity of spirit in the previous Test, when they had granted Australia a change after the toss had been made to allow Graham Manou to replace Brad Haddin, England knew they were in credit. In contrast to that match, the toss had still not taken place, so, at 10.20am, Flower tracked down opposite number Tim Nielsen, who was giving throw-downs to Simon Katich in one of the nets on the square. After a brief exchange, Nielsen soon skipped off down the tunnel to back a formal England request to delay the toss for 10 minutes.

It provided just enough time for Prior, with the anti-inflammatories and injection now kicking in, to test his injury and he was back out on the field at 10.25am to keep to the fast bowlers. 'Quite honestly, I wouldn't have made it had the toss not been delayed,' said Prior. 'I was very grateful for it, and it was very good of the Aussies to agree to that.

'It was touch and go. It was risky, because if it had seized up again during the game we'd have been stuffed, but the only way I was going to know was to go out and try keeping wicket. So I went out and I took the bowlers with me, and I think the work that I'd done, the physio I'd had, plus the adrenalin, all kicked in. I was able, just, to move, take a few balls, do a few dives. And because I knew it was only going to get better from that point, I said, "I'm OK."'

In the circumstances it was probably a good toss to lose, and it summed things up that England won it.

Strauss says: 'Well, it was chaos really. As I said, I had a niggling thought in the back of my mind that we might confront some problems after Edgbaston, but I never anticipated anything like this. There was so much rushing around even after, and not just with Matty. We were trying to figure out who might play, what our alternatives were and, at the same time, we had the toss to deal with and I had on-field interviews and all of that, so it was just absolute mayhem.'

The one thing England had decided on in advance was that Harmison would play. With Flintoff out, they wanted someone capable of bouncing the ball off a length to keep Australia pinned on the back foot. The last man to know any of this was Flintoff, who had decided not to come to the ground until the match was in progress so as not to be in the way.

'The last thing they wanted was me getting in their way,' he admits. 'In fact when Jimmy Anderson saw my bags were in the dressing-room, without knowing that I wasn't playing, he thought for a moment that I'd overslept and started texting me, saying things like: "Fred, the match starts in an hour, get down here quick!"

'I was there for the first bit, about 40 minutes, but when wickets started to tumble I thought it best to go.'

Without Flintoff, the drafting in of the extra bowler meant Stuart Broad would bat at number 7. England had clearly thought this was no time to play for a draw. The problem was, their batsmen then took that message rather too literally.

Strauss should have known. On the eve of the match, he and his batsmen had discussed what not to do on this Headingley pitch.

Strauss recalls: 'We talked about being positive, but also about being patient. I reminded everyone how too many of us had been out driving against South Africa the previous year. This again did not look like a pitch to drive on.'

Strauss could have gone in a blink when he was struck in front of middle stump by the first ball of the match, sent down by Ben Hilfenhaus, but New Zealand umpire Billy Bowden somehow came to the conclusion it was not out. However, the reprieve was short-lived and when Peter Siddle sent down a fullish delivery in the fourth over, Strauss couldn't help himself. Marcus North produced a wonderful reflex catch high to his right at third slip and, at 11.15am, England were 11 for 1.

'In hindsight it was a very good toss to lose,' says Strauss. 'The head said bat, the heart said bowl. Maybe I should have followed my heart. If we could have got through the first session we would have been fine, but we weren't even near to doing so. It didn't help matters when, after having warned everyone against driving, I was out to a big waft 15 minutes into the game. Good to see the rest of the lads follow my example, though!'

'And that catch by North was one of those key moments when you can feel one team going up and the other going down.'

Just 29 minutes into the first morning, England were 16 for 2 as Ravi Bopara saw the ball lob to gully off the bowling of Hilfenhaus.

Sky Sports commentators Shane Warne and Ian Botham had

'. . . having warned everyone against driving, I was out to a big waft 15 minutes into the game. Good to see the rest of the lads follow my example, though!'

Strauss's Friday morning doesn't get any better

been vilifying Australia for discarding spinner Nathan Hauritz to make room for the returning Stuart Clark, but the pacemen were already justifying their selection and Mitchell Johnson was close to an immediate success when, in his opening over, Ian Bell sliced a ball between the slip cordon and gully for four. As it was, the tall left-armer did for him in his third, as a snorter left Bell with nowhere to go and the ball flew through to wicketkeeper Brad Haddin off his gloves. At 12.25pm, Collingwood's tentative prod extended his struggles against Clark, which had begun in the 2006–07 Ashes, and England were staring down the barrel at 42 for 4.

It meant that, instead of putting his feet up, Prior was into the action less than two hours after being passed fit. 'At the time I probably did punch the air when we won the toss but, obviously, I was having to walk out there fairly soon,' he reflected. By lunch, he had lost two more partners as Clark's nagging accuracy reaped reward. First, with a dozen minutes of the session left, opener Alastair Cook nibbled at a good-length delivery and then, on the eve of the interval, Stuart Broad fatally turned the ball straight to short square leg. England were 72 for 6 at lunch.

They only managed to last another 42 minutes in the afternoon as Siddle, the former woodcutting champion who was reportedly considered for the chop before the decision to go spinless was confirmed, roughed up the tail with four wickets for three runs. Graeme Swann was lulled into a false drive, Harmison edged behind trying to work the ball to the legside – having been clonked by a bouncer – and the short stuff did for James Anderson and Graham Onions in consecutive balls to end 162 minutes of batting hell.

At 2.22pm, England were dismissed for 102. It was their lowest score for 100 years in Tests at Headingley, the eighth-lowest score by an England team on home soil in an Ashes series and England's eighth-lowest Test score anywhere since the Second World War.

Prior was left unbeaten for a top score of 37. Without Flintoff, without early wickets, it was feared they would soon be without hope. The *Daily Mirror* branded them 'Yorkshire Puddings' and 'Fredless Chickens'.

Strauss says: 'During the series there were a number of sessions where one team really grabbed hold of the game and the other didn't react well to being put under pressure. This was our turn.'

Prior agrees: 'There were a number of things that you could say were distracting, but that's no excuse. We've all played enough cricket and we're all big enough and experienced enough to be able to adapt to things, put things behind us and get on with the job.'

The fact of the matter was England had made a pig's ear of batting at the home of the Hog. For these were the kind of conditions in which Matthew Hoggard, one of the Fab Four of 2005, learned the mastery of seam and swing movement.

And now, facing the task of reacting to being bowled out for 102, they simply tried too hard to bowl Australia out for 101.

Anderson, Hoggard's natural successor, had tweaked a hamstring while batting, which clearly hampered his opening spell, and his first two deliveries were crashed through the offside for four by Shane Watson and further runs flowed before tea.

England were then suckered into believing all-out violence was the required approach when, in Harmison's first over in Test cricket for six months, the second of the innings, extra bounce did for Simon Katich and the ball lobbed to Bopara at leg gully. After being out of the England side for so long, Harmison confesses he was desperate to make an impact.

He says: 'I think I'd been in the selectors' minds again following my performance against Australia for the Lions when I gave Phillip Hughes a going-over. If I hadn't bowled well there they might well have put a line through my name, but they kept telling me that I was in their plans and that I should keep myself ready in case the opportunity arose. Strauss told me the day before that I was probably going to play, even if Fred also played, and I was thrilled. I did feel there was unfinished business between me and Australia. I had great memories of what we did to them in 2005 – they will live with me for ever – but I also had memories of what happened in 2006–07. I didn't want my last experience of playing Ashes cricket to be a 5–0 defeat. Everyone recalls the way I bowled at Australia on the first morning of the Ashes series in 2005 at Lord's, and they were great memories. The only thing I was unhappy with was not going to check on Ponting after I'd drawn blood. Of course, we were trying to get in their face and all that, but there are two teams out there playing cricket, not having a war. But I also had other memories, like of that first ball of the 2006–07 Test in Brisbane. Memories I'd rather not dwell on.

'But I did feel I could make a contribution, and I was excited by that. I'd seen how the team had come together in my absence after I was dropped in the West Indies, and that made me think two things: (1) how much I was missing playing; and (2) that I would do everything in my power, playing for Durham, to make sure they couldn't rule me out. Even without Fred, my feelings that morning were all about getting out there and doing a job against Australia.'.

Were he and the rest of the England bowlers simply too keyed-up?

According to Anderson: 'I think we all may have been guilty of that. We were confident arriving at Headingley that day, but the optimism was a bit feverish. People had been saying, "If we win here, we win the Ashes," and I think we got ahead of ourselves. I recall seeing the big sign in front of the building works saying, "Roar for England", and it sort of struck me: what if we get rolled here? Who's going to be roaring then?'

Strauss considers: 'Harmy getting Katich out the way he did was the worst thing that could have happened, because it gave all the bowlers the incentive to try to bang the ball in. But after the initial movement, the pitch was so friendly that anything short just let their batsmen cash in, especially Ponting, one of the world's great pullers.

When Graham Onions was deposited by Ponting for six off the Durham man's first ball, Geoff Boycott greeted the ball with a 'roobish' on *Test Match Special*. 'The one thing you do on any Headingley strip is pitch it up and make the batsmen play,' he observed. Next ball, Ponting swivelled on another short one that flew to fine leg. It brought up the Australia 50 in just 6.2 overs. Words were now failing Boycott, and two former England captains were equally dumbstruck as they chatted on Sky Sports at tea. 'It leaves you speechless,' said David Gower. 'Absolutely abysmal,' quipped Michael Atherton. Australia had passed England's boundary count for the entire innings when they struck their 11th inside nine overs. To emphasise the relative comfort of the batsmen, England's best chance of dismissing Ponting came in the tenth over when, on 32, he inexplicably nudged to the offside and took off for a run – he had given up as Ian Bell's shy fizzed past the stumps.

Moments for Bill Cooper to blow about were few and far between. Had he been there, of course. Cooper, the Barmy Army trumpet player, was conspicuous by his absence after Yorkshire upheld a ban on musical instruments. No Fred. No fanfare.

Having reached 69 for 1 at tea, Australia were in credit only eight overs into the evening session, and Watson followed up by cracking three fours in Harmison's first over of a new spell. That trio of boundaries brought up a century share between Watson and Ponting, from just 133 deliveries. Strauss and England were in desperate need of a breakthrough and, once again, Onions showed the knack of striking at the start of a spell, snaring Watson two balls after Australia's 'makeshift' opener had acknowledged his third half-century in as many innings.

Two more lbw dismissals by Stuart Broad – Ponting falling over and Michael Hussey undone by one from around the wicket – made it three wickets in quick succession, but Ponting's majestic 78, for which he raised his bat to the notorious West Stand as he departed, not only put Broad's improving efforts in the shade, it also ensured the Australians closed the first day with a 94-run lead, with six wickets still intact.

England argued that it should have been just five, but umpire Asad Rauf deemed Michael Clarke not out when, on 27, a ferocious Harmison bouncer flew through to Prior after appearing to flick the batsman's wristband on his glove.

In fairness, England's bowlers knew they would have been flattered by that score.

Anderson says: 'There's no getting away from it. We bowled poorly. We weren't trying to bowl short. We just did. There was a feeling we had to get them out for a low total and, instead of sticking to our plans and trying to create pressure, we just went gung-ho at them and paid the price.'

Harmison agrees: 'They picked us off. It wasn't a 450 wicket, but it wasn't a 102 wicket either. We got sucked in. Very disappointing.'

Swann says: 'A lot of people blamed the way we played on our disrupted preparation. Every now and again you have an absolute nightmare and that game, collectively, nearly everything went wrong. I'm not pointing a finger or anything. I think they [the Australian bowlers] put it in more or less decent areas. They bowled it full and wide of off stump and we all had big drives and got caught. I don't think we adjusted to the wicket as we should have done. That's got nothing to do with what happened that morning. It wasn't ideal preparation, of course not . . . But being professionals, we should have been able to bounce back better than that.'

England's supporters, meanwhile, suspected they were about to witness a car crash unfold in super-slow motion.

Headingley, Day Two: Australia 445 all out; England 82 for 5

England began day two in a more positive frame of mind. After all, under Strauss and Flower this England team tend to counter their tendency to go off the rails at any given moment with an admirable ability to bounce back. With six wickets to aim for and the bowlers refreshed by rest, they were still clinging to the notion that limiting Australia to a lead of about 150 would bring them back into contention. Any remaining optimism, however, was short-lived.

Fears over Anderson's fitness were highlighted by the sight of him having his hamstring stretched on the outfield before play. He was able to open the bowling, but his first over featured two landmarks for the innings: Marcus North brought up a 50-run stand with a crisply punched four off the back foot, then the lead reached three figures after Anderson sent down a huge wide.

In all, 110 runs came in the opening session of 29 overs, with the prolific Michael Clarke denied a third hundred of the series by just seven runs. His dismissal, lbw to Graham Onions, proved the only victory for ball over bat in the entire session. It meant that, by lunch, Australia were 306 for 5, the lead now 204, with North, unbeaten on 53, once again making steady progress.

Australia's batsmen revelled in Andrew Flintoff's absence from England's attack – as their bowlers had in the absence of Kevin Pietersen since Lord's – and Flintoff's no-show was acknowledged by one leading Yorkshire business, the Mumtaz restaurant chain, who chartered a light aircraft to fly over the ground in mid-afternoon to trail the banner: 'Get well soon Freddie.'

Meanwhile, England's state of health was put into context by the fact that the deficit soon exceeded 261, the largest previous first-innings deficit from which they had ever come back to win, but any hope of bettering the class of 1894, who recovered to beat

Australia by ten runs in Sydney, was fanciful.

Australia's long-handle tactics, particularly those from Stuart Clark, who wiped three sixes into or over the stands, further demoralised the home team and left Clark's own team-mates in stitches, but it was North's six, slog-swept off Graeme Swann to bring up his second century of the series, which they appreciated most.

His innings had put Australia into an almost impregnable position. In terms of numbers it also brought up a damning scoreline for England – they now trailed 7–1 in the century count. This was perhaps no longer a statistical anomaly, but more a true reflection of how the series was shaping up. The difference between the bowling units was also marked. Even though there had to be some sympathy, given they had just 102 runs to work with, England's application in such a dire situation was poor. Just as had been the case 12 months earlier against South Africa, it was England who looked the strangers to the conditions rather than their opponents.

Amid the rubble of England's performance, however, one beacon of hope flickered. Though Stuart Broad did benefit from the Aussie tail's licence to slog, there was more to his best Test figures of 6 for 91 than simply happening to have the fortune to be in the bar during happy hour.

It may have gone largely unnoticed at the time, but the work Broad had started to put in at Edgbaston was obviously having a beneficial effect, and the success he was enjoying soon bred more confidence in an ever-increasing virtuous circle. Now, having come under pressure for his place from various ex-players in the build-up due to a lack of productivity with the ball, he had become England's joint-leading wicket-taker, with 12 scalps, from nowhere. In the circumstances, however, he was grateful to the medical team for getting him onto the pitch in the first place.

'I was desperate to play, even though I was feeling awful the night before the match,' says Broad. 'I'd heard a few rumours that my place was being looked at and, although I wasn't concerned, that sort of talk does get to you.

'I'm not a big reader of the press as such, but I had obviously heard little bits and bobs about me being left out, but that always happens in any series, and people have to have their say. They've got to fill pages. Within the England camp no one's too fussed about it, because it's what the people in the camp think and say and believe that's important, and I was delighted that Strauss and Andy showed faith in me. There were never any whispers or discussions that I'd be left out from their direction. They had full confidence in me. And that helped.

'I got a little bit of confidence back in my bowling with the work I'd done with Ottis Gibson at Edgbaston, and I was keen to continue that here. The doctor just dosed me up to the maximum so I was able to get out of bed and onto the pitch.

'My best wickets came on the first evening. I had been battling away with Ponting for five or six overs, swinging it away from him. Then I managed to turn the ball round and it swung back into the stumps and had him leg before. Then to get Hussey lbw two overs later meant we were still in the game.

'After that they batted well and took the game away from us, but I was still encouraged that I was asking more questions of the batsmen than I had done previously.'

Anderson thought: 'That was a crucial time for Stuart. A lot of people were saying he should have been dropped after the first three Tests, and I think he was definitely aware of that. A lot of guys choose not to read the papers but, at the end of the day, stuff always gets back to you whether it's your family reading it or whatever. So he was aware of it. But he believes in himself. He's very confident and he's a serious talent.'

Strauss says: 'I was pleased for Stuart because he had struggled for the first half of the series and you could see he was reaching a bit. Certainly his performance in the second innings at Edgbaston gave me a lot more confidence in his bowling. Then, at Headingley, though there were a couple of gimmes, he deserved them for the way he bowled throughout.'

Strauss and Cook, initially, were watchful in defence, playing only at what they had to, and the fifty came up without loss in the 19th over.

From that point on, however, it was all bad for England as they careered towards defeat in a dramatic 40-minute period in the final session. Wicket to wicket, five batsmen perished in the space of 44 balls. There was now no escape.

It was the industrious Ben Hilfenhaus, not fancied for a place in the XI when Australia arrived, whose return for a second spell started the chaos. In his second over, he trapped Strauss lbw with a ball that shaped into the left-hander and had him stone dead. To the very next ball, Bopara, his place already in jeopardy, was adjudged lbw by umpire Asad Rauf. He stood in disbelief moment-arily and meekly waved the bat before accepting his unjust fate. Replays revealed the chunkiest of inside edges.

Mitchell Johnson started in typically erratic fashion, but the sight of Ian Bell sharpened his focus and England's number 4 soon nibbled at a ball slanted across him.

Bell's struggles against the left-armer were already apparent: this made it three out of three dismissals since his return to the side. Johnson followed up with wickets in each of his next two overs: Paul Collingwood was lbw, before Cook, having again outlived four partners in making his way to 30, edged a swinger to the keeper.

Off the last ball of the day, Matt Prior was put down in the slips by the otherwise impeccable North. Had it been clutched, Australia would have requested the extra half-hour to finish the job that night and it would have been difficult to refuse. Just nine overs earlier the chants from a group of hardy souls on the Western Terrace had been: 'Stand up, if you're 1–0 up.' It was an advantage that would not last much longer.

Headingley, Day Three: England 263 all out; Australia win by an innings and 80 runs

The revelations to which the England XI awoke on Sunday morning were poignantly timed. The hosts, intent on saving face in the final throes of the match, instead received a huge slap in the face when former Australia batsman Justin Langer's private dossier was revealed by the *Sunday Telegraph*. Sent via email on the eve of the Ashes, its content had been meant for the eyes of Australia coach Tim Nielsen and his management team. It was designed to pinpoint the strengths and, more importantly, the perceived weaknesses of England's class of 2009. Much had been made of the benefits of Phillip Hughes playing for Middlesex earlier in the summer, and now Somerset captain Langer was making the most of his county position to produce a vicious critique.

English cricketers were condemned as 'lazy', 'shallow' and 'flat', and as players who 'love being comfortable'. In short, players who put the doss into dossier.

Anderson was cast as 'a pussy' when things are not going his way and captain Strauss, a former Middlesex team-mate of Langer, was accused of being too 'conservative'. It advised the benefit of deconstructing the 'egos' of Matt Prior, Graeme Swann and Ravi Bopara.

Twelve months earlier, Langer had praised the competitive nature of the top tier of the County Championship. Now, he claimed, 'English players rarely believe in themselves. Many of them stare a lot and chat a lot, but this is very shallow. They will retreat very quickly. Aggressive batting, running and body language will soon have them staring at their bootlaces rather than into the eyes of their opponent – it is just how they are built. Because of the way they are programmed they will be up when things are going well, but they will taper off very quickly if you wear them down. Because they play so much cricket, as soon as it gets a bit hard you just have to watch their body language and see how flat and lazy they get. This is also a time when most of them make all sorts of excuses and start looking around to point the finger at everyone else – it is a classic English trait, from my experience.'

Langer also warned this Australian side not to repeat the mistakes of the 2005 team, of which he was a part, and be too close to the opposition. 'They like being friendly and "matey" because it makes them feel comfortable,' Langer continued. 'In essence, this is maybe the key to the whole English psyche – they love being comfortable. Take them out of their comfort zone and they don't like it for one second.'

Instead, Langer dished out advice on how to break down individual opponents. Of Strauss, Langer suggested: 'He is a very solid character and excellent bloke. His weakness is possibly his conservative approach. He will tend to take the safer options in most cases.' Anderson, he said, was: 'Hugely improved, but can be a bit of a pussy if he is worn down. His body language could be detrimental to them if we get on top of him early.'

To Prior, Langer would 'chip away at him about his wicketkeeping. I would be reminding him about how it could see him out of the team. I would definitely work his ego.' For Bopara, however, there should be contrasting treatment. 'He is sure to wind the boys up by his strutting around, but I would leave him alone,' Langer recommended.

Langer later said he was 'shattered' that his words had been leaked. Worryingly for an England team whose campaign appeared to be coming apart at the seams, however, England's 2005 Ashes-winning captain Michael Vaughan seemed to be in agreement with much of what was contained in the document.

There was no change to the course of events on the field, however, as England lost two wickets inside the opening seven overs to the impressive Hilfenhaus: Anderson and Prior both nibbling at deliveries outside off stump. England were 120 for 7 and, on the verge of imploding for a second time in the match, needed something spectacular to lift a downbeat Headingley crowd. Days restricted to fewer than 10 or 25 overs guarantee part or full refunds, but there is no recompense for poor play and the public were about to be seriously short-changed.

Whatever Langer thought, or Vaughan for that matter, England coach Andy Flower believed the time had come for England to show some bottle.

According to Broad: 'On the morning of that last day we were gone, dead and buried, but Andy came to the lads who still had a part to play – myself, Prior, Swann – and just said, "In your own way, I don't care how you do it or what you do, fight. Just show some fight. Try and claw back a little bit of momentum and frustrate them. Whether you block every ball you can and try and survive five hours, or whether you attack them and whack the ball about, just make sure you fight." So there was a bit of a momentum change when Swann and I bashed it around for that hundred partnership. We could feel the Aussies getting a little bit frustrated and really not enjoying it, because they obviously wanted to be celebrating, so that really helped the side to claw a little bit of something out of the match.'

Feeding off the renewal of his confidence with the ball, Broad now unfurled his full repertoire of strokes. He and his Notts colleague rode their luck early in their partnership, but from the moment the former survived a chance to mid-off off Mitchell Johnson, they cashed in on their carefree approach. For the first time in the contest, Australian bowlers were being struck down the ground. When they dropped short, cuts and pulls fizzed to the ropes. In a heady spell between the 47th and 49th over of the innings, England scored an incredible 49 runs, with Broad's 42-ball half-century registered in the thick of the assault. Despite being out of sight in the match, Australia were clearly rattled: wides and no-balls added to the berserkerie and Ponting felt the need for a time-out with bowlers Mitchell Johnson and Peter Siddle. Twice Broad diced with dismissal via chances to fielders on the boundary in the very next over, from Siddle, but was rewarded with two fours for his endeavours. The 100-run share, greeted with more rapture than anything else by Englishmen in the crowd over seven and a bit sessions, spanned just 73 balls, with not-so-silent partner Swann contributing 42 runs to the partnership, one fewer than Broad.

The fun lasted just one more over, as Broad pulled straight to deep square leg. It was not the first time England's tail had frustrated Australia in the series, but Broad's boundary-laden half-century, 61 from 49 balls to be precise, coupled with his earlier six-wicket haul, meant he became the first England cricketer to achieve such an Ashes double (six wickets in an innings and a half-century with the bat) since Darren Gough at Sydney in 1994–95.

The previous evening he had promised to provide late-innings resistance, and he was true to his word. The thrilling eighth-wicket stand of 108 was spread over just 12.3 overs. The tempo of the stand, at more than eight and a half runs per over, was the second fastest for any partnership over a hundred in Test cricket, behind Nathan Astle and Chris Cairns at Christchurch in 2001–02 – a similarly futile endeavour. Broad's fifth fifty at Test level was followed by Swann's second, registered spectacularly before lunch via a hooked six off Siddle. In an extraordinary morning's play, England stacked up 163 for the loss of three wickets.

Swann recalls: 'We were determined that, if we were going to go down, we would go down swinging. People say it's very easy to bat in situations where there's nothing to worry about, and we knew we were going to lose, but it was a case of saying, Let's make a statement, and we both enjoyed it.

'Broad had a very good all-round game. He didn't put a foot wrong there, and deservedly got those six wickets and then the 60, more than anything just to shut up a few of the ignorant voices that were calling for him to not be picked.

'People are always looking for scapegoats, and they'd been looking for reasons to get Broady out of the team since the start of the series, which is ridiculous. Had that got to him? I don't think it did. He's very phlegmatic for a young lad. He's very level headed and, outwardly, it didn't appear to get to him, but you never know, do you? You never know what happens when guys lock their door and go to bed at night. I know if it was me, I certainly wouldn't show any outward emotion towards it. I'd shut my door and make a little stab list and think right, that bloke's at the top of it, because it's never nice to read things like that.

'If it did **ss him off, he certainly didn't show it. But he bowled magnificently. He did all the talking the right way.'

> 'We were determined that, if we were going to go down, we would go down swinging'
>
> *Graeme Swann*

The inevitable duly arrived when Johnson had Swann caught behind, despite the batsman appearing far from convinced, and then bowled Graham Onions. It gave Johnson his first five-wicket haul of the campaign and signified a perfectly timed return to form.

Australia's victory by an innings and 80 runs, England's second largest defeat at Headingley after the innings-and-148-run loss to Australia in 1993, put Ponting's men in pole position to regain the Ashes. The margin of victory was also Australia's largest since Shane Warne and Glenn McGrath retired, although at one stage it appeared England were to notch another mark in the record books: their heaviest home Ashes defeat, which remains an innings and 180 runs at Trent Bridge in 1989.

Other numbers were also being contemplated following the landslide loss. Estimates of the cost to the local economy over the early finish were pitched at £2 million. Experts reckoned a full five-day Test match would have generated a minimum of £8 million for

West Yorkshire, but with supporters checking out of hotels early and 18,000 ticket refunds for Monday, profit projections were severely downgraded. Yorkshire were left contemplating how to dispose of 1,800 corporate lunches due for the following day.

Ponting revelled in England's misery and the chance to address the one blot on his own captaincy CV. Australia, it was felt, were now heading to The Oval to complete the formalities of retaining the little urn. 'It's a chance I've been waiting for this whole tour, and a chance the whole team has been waiting for,' said the Australia captain. 'After we lost at Lord's, we've been wanting to play well to win a game to get back to 1–1. I've said from the start about how much it would mean to me to win here, and it's exactly the same for every other guy that's in our touring squad at the moment. We've been waiting for this moment to come around and, now that we've got things back on track and are playing good cricket, we're all very excited about it. It's going to be a special week for all of us.'

Neither was Ponting going to miss an opportunity to get further blows in after the final bell. 'Looking in the papers this morning, they were talking about Ramprakash coming back in and those sort of things,' Ponting noted. 'That's obviously all started, which for us is terrific. It will be difficult for them to bounce back now. Some of our guys who had been struggling for a bit of touch are probably now in the best form of their careers, which is great. Everything is heading in the right direction for us at exactly the right time of the tour.'

Well, almost everything. That night, at the team's hotel, England's players and management came together for a meeting to discuss what had gone wrong and those discussions were to alter their mood, utterly.

7, 8, 9 August 2009

Result: Australia won by an innings and 80 runs
Toss: England, who chose to bat
Series: 5-match series level 1–1
Umpires: Asad Rauf (Pakistan), BF Bowden (New Zealand)
Match referee: RS Madugalle (Sri Lanka)
Player of the match: M J North (Australia)

England 1st innings		R	M	B	4s	6s
AJ Strauss*	c North b Siddle	3	16	17	0	0
AN Cook	c Clarke b Clark	30	104	65	3	0
RS Bopara	c Hussey b Hilfenhaus	1	10	6	0	0
IR Bell	c †Haddin b Johnson	8	40	26	2	0
PD Collingwood	c Ponting b Clark	0	13	5	0	0
MJ Prior†	not out	37	76	43	5	0
SCJ Broad	c Katich b Clark	3	13	12	0	0
GP Swann	c Clarke b Siddle	0	21	15	0	0
SJ Harmison	c †Haddin b Siddle	0	8	6	0	0
JM Anderson	c †Haddin b Siddle	3	7	10	0	0
G Onions	c Katich b Siddle	0	1	1	0	0
Extras	(b 5, lb 8, w 1, nb 3)	17				
Total	(all out; 33.5 overs; 163 mins)	102	(3.01 runs per over)			

Fall of wickets 1–11 (Strauss, 3.6 ov), 2–16 (Bopara, 6.4 ov), 3–39 (Bell, 15.3 ov), 4–42 (Collingwood, 18.3 ov), 5–63 (Cook, 22.2 ov), 6–72 (Broad, 24.5 ov), 7–92 (Swann, 29.4 ov), 8–98 (Harmison, 31.4 ov), 9–102 (Anderson, 33.4 ov), 10–102 (Onions, 33.5 ov)

Bowling	O	M	R	W	Econ	
BW Hilfenhaus	7	0	20	1	2.85	(2nb)
PM Siddle	9.5	0	21	5	2.13	(1nb)
MG Johnson	7	0	30	1	4.28	(1w)
SR Clark	10	4	18	3	1.80	

Australia 1st innings		R	M	B	4s	6s
SR Watson	lbw b Onions	51	121	67	9	0
SM Katich	c Bopara b Harmison	0	9	4	0	0
RT Ponting*	lbw b Broad	78	119	101	12	1
MEK Hussey	lbw b Broad	10	16	10	2	0
MJ Clarke	lbw b Onions	93	193	138	13	0
MJ North	c Anderson b Broad	110	321	206	13	1
BJ Haddin†	c Bell b Harmison	14	25	23	1	0
MG Johnson	c Bopara b Broad	27	70	53	5	0
PM Siddle	b Broad	0	1	1	0	0
SR Clark	b Broad	32	24	22	1	3
BW Hilfenhaus	not out	0	6	3	0	0
Extras	(b 9, lb 14, w 4, nb 3)	30				
Total	(all out; 104.1 overs; 463 mins) 445(4.27 runs per over)					

Fall of wickets 1–14 (Katich, 1.4 ov), 2–133 (Watson, 27.3 ov), 3–140 (Ponting, 28.6 ov), 4–151 (Hussey, 30.3 ov), 5–303 (Clarke, 72.6 ov), 6–323 (Haddin, 80.2 ov), 7–393 (Johnson, 96.3 ov), 8–394 (Siddle, 96.6 ov), 9–440 (Clark, 102.5 ov), 10–445 (North, 104.1 ov)

Bowling	O	M	R	W	Econ	
JM Anderson	18	3	89	0	4.94	(1w)
SJ Harmison	23	4	98	2	4.26	(1w)
G Onions	22	5	80	2	3.63	(2nb, 1w)
SCJ Broad	25.1	6	91	6	3.61	(1nb, 1w)
GP Swann	16	4	64	0	4.00	

England 2nd innings		R	M	B	4s	6s
AJ Strauss*	lbw b Hilfenhaus	32	97	78	4	0
AN Cook	c †Haddin b Johnson	30	136	84	4	0
RS Bopara	lbw b Hilfenhaus	0	1	1	0	0
IR Bell	c Ponting b Johnson	3	12	12	0	0
PD Collingwood	lbw b Johnson	4	10	10	0	0
JM Anderson	c Ponting b Hilfenhaus	4	20	10	1	0
MJ Prior†	c †Haddin b Hilfenhaus	22	40	29	3	0
SCJ Broad	c Watson b Siddle	61	95	49	10	0
GP Swann	c †Haddin b Johnson	62	100	72	7	1
SJ Harmison	not out	19	43	28	4	0
G Onions	b Johnson	0	8	7	0	0
Extras	(b 5, lb 5, w 5, nb 11)	26				
Total	(all out; 61.3 overs; 275 mins) 263 (4.27 runs per over)					

Fall of wickets 1–58 (Strauss, 22.4 ov), 2–58 (Bopara, 22.5 ov), 3–67 (Bell, 25.5 ov), 4–74 (Collingwood, 27.6 ov), 5–78 (Cook, 29.6 ov), 6–86 (Anderson, 32.3 ov), 7–120 (Prior, 38.6 ov), 8-228 (Broad, 51.3 ov), 9–259 (Swann, 59.2 ov), 10–263 (Onions, 61.3 ov)

Bowling	O	M	R	W	Econ	
BW Hilfenhaus	19	2	60	4	3.15	(9nb)
PM Siddle	12	2	50	1	4.16	(1nb, 1w)
SR Clark	11	1	74	0	6.72	(1nb)
MG Johnson	19.3	3	69	5	3.53	

Close of play
7 Aug day 1 – Australia 1st innings 196/4 (MJ Clarke 34*, MJ North 7*, 47 ov)
8 Aug day 2 – England 2nd innings 82/5 (JM Anderson 0*, MJ Prior 4*, 32 ov)
9 Aug day 3 – England 2nd innings 263 (61.3 ov) – end of match

Fifth Test, The Oval: 20–23 August

England's Ashes winners of 2005 all agreed that one of the key moments in that series came when they held a meeting following their defeat in the first Test at Lord's.

When the fab four of Steve Harmison, Matthew Hoggard, Andrew Flintoff and Simon Jones first battered and then bowled out Ricky Ponting's world-class batting line-up for only 190 on that feverish first day, the tide of optimism was all but overwhelming. And that made Australia's subsequent recovery, and eventual victory by 239 runs, deflating enough to persuade some that England's challenge was a mirage.

What the papers love to describe as 'a full and frank discussion' before the second Test at Edgbaston four summers previously enabled Michael Vaughan's team to regroup, refocus and draw strength from each other's commitment to be positive. The little matter of Glenn McGrath tripping on a loose cricket ball helped as well, of course.

Now, after having surrendered the lead in what Swann described as 'a pretty abysmal two and a half days at Leeds', and with those pessimism-prone England supporters again viewing the traffic going only one way, a similarly forthright chinwag was called for.

Swann said: 'Initially I just wanted to get away from Headingley. Losing a Test match in that way leaves you with a pretty sick feeling. We just hadn't competed.'

Wicketkeeper Matt Prior admits: 'I don't think I've ever felt as low playing for England as I did after the end of the Headingley

Test. It just seemed like the momentum was with Australia.'

Paul Collingwood recalls that, when the players came together at the team hotel in Leeds on the evening of the defeat, the mood was downbeat. Fortunately it didn't stay that way for too long. 'We had to get together straight away after a defeat like that to try and understand what had happened, what we'd done wrong and where we could improve,' he says. 'What we all agreed on is that we had just got ahead of ourselves.

'When you get close to something, something so huge as the Ashes, which means everything to all of us, you can actually forget what you need to do to get it. We had played the situation and not the match.

'It was a good piece of management by Andy Flower and Andy Strauss to ensure we didn't dwell on it. And it was amazing how well it worked. Instead of letting the bad things fester, we came out of the meeting feeling refreshed and ready to go again.'

According to Prior: 'When we walked away from the ground it felt like everyone was thinking, That was it, we've had it now. It was almost as though we were 3–0 down. I wanted to get home, really. So when you're told we've got to get back to the team hotel for a meeting, you think, Well, what have we got to talk about? I left Headingley feeling, Oh my God, what happened there? Then I left the meeting thinking, I cannot wait to get to The Oval.

'In that time we collected all the negative stuff, all the crap, and dug a great big hole and shoved it all in. We left that meeting knowing two things for certain. One, that we were going to cop a stack of criticism in the papers and all the media, and two, we were strong and tight and sticking together.

'Instead of going our separate ways, parting for a week and reading and hearing stuff about, "What direction should they go?" or "Who should they pick?", we all knew.

'And, actually, we reminded ourselves it was 1–1 and still all to play for. Maybe we just got our bad game out of the way – everything terrible in one go.

Stuart Broad said: 'We cleared our minds and said our piece. It was important that we didn't leave Headingley thinking, Oh, we were rubbish. Terrible. It's over. We left Headingley very clear on what we had to do. We *were* rubbish, but that had gone.'

Strauss says: 'But by getting all of our thoughts out in the open, the post-mortem was done before the match was cold. That meant we could just concentrate on preparing for The Oval.'

Having taken their defeat at Leeds off the agenda, Strauss soon found plenty to replace it with, however. First, there was the matter of the Langer dossier, which, with impeccable timing, had been published in the middle of England's worst performance under his captaincy.

Strauss and Langer had shared a dressing-room at Middlesex in county cricket, and had become close in the process. Some were tempted to ask, 'With friends like Langer . . . ?'

'I knew there was going to be plenty of flak,' Strauss says. 'And I was worried it might overwhelm one or two – "doom and gloom", "this could be the end of our careers" – that type of thing. What Langer said certainly hadn't helped.

'To be fair to him, he rang me up straight away and he was pretty distraught about it. He said he felt absolutely awful that it had got out into the media, and he hoped that I could understand why he'd passed the information on to the Australian team and I could, completely.

'It was important that we didn't leave Headingley thinking, Oh, we were rubbish. Terrible. It's over. We left Headingley very clear on what we had to do. We *were* rubbish, but that had gone'

Stuart Broad

'I didn't have a problem with Justin doing what he did. We have various sources from whom we try to get information on their players, and you expect them to be doing the same thing. The language used was the kind of stuff one mate might use to another because it was never intended to see the light of day. I just thought that the dossier being in the public domain was not ideal.'

Prior, one of those singled out by Langer as possessing 'a massive ego' said: 'I was asked about it, but I made a promise to myself that I wasn't going to read anything that week. My attitude was, Well, I could read it, but how is that going to help at The Oval?'

What caused Strauss a potentially even more painful headache were comments from Andrew Flintoff's agent, Andrew 'Chubby' Chandler, revealing that his client had told him that he was fit and ready to play at Headingley and that he was upset that his offer had been rejected.

That information had already appeared in the *Mail on Sunday* but, when Chandler's quotes appeared all over *The Times* the day after the defeat, Strauss felt compelled to react.

Chandler had said: 'I've seen a few disappointed sportsmen over the last couple of months, but I've never seen anybody as low as Flintoff was on Thursday night when he told me he would not be selected. He told them he was fit enough to get through, that he felt no different to how he felt at Edgbaston, and that he could get through and do his bit. They didn't want him. He was prepared to do whatever it took, was prepared to put whatever needed to be put into his knee. The whole point of announcing his retirement when he did was to clear his head and prepare to do whatever was needed to be done to play in the final Test matches of his career.'

Chandler insisted that adrenalin would have helped Flintoff to beat the pain barrier at Headingley, just as it had done done during his body-defying heroics at Lord's.

'What they didn't take into account during Thursday's practice was that there was no adrenalin. That was why he looked as though he was struggling so much. He was hurting at Lord's, but the adrenalin got him through. It would have got him through this week as well. His presence would certainly have lifted the crowd and the team, because without him they don't have much inspiration.'

Strauss explains: 'Reports like that in the media, at that stage, just after the Headingley defeat, were unhelpful for our prospects at The Oval because there was a danger they would create a distraction we could do without when all our focus needed to be on the future, not the past.

'So I spoke to Chubby about it. Someone wrote that it was a conversation littered with expletives, but it wasn't. It was just me saying I was disappointed and I felt that, factually, some of what he said wasn't on the mark either. We had more important things to worry about, but I felt it was important I said something to him rather than just let it lie.

'Fred, obviously, was disappointed to have been left out. I spoke to him about it as well, and the good thing to come out of our conversation was that when we arrived at The Oval we were both very comfortable with each other's position and we could move on.'

And Strauss did have other things to concern himself with, mainly just who should play in the biggest match of any of their careers.

Pressure had been building on Ravi Bopara and Strauss, and the management had come to a decision. It was time for the young Essex star – so clearly full of promise, but so clearly battling for form and confidence – to be taken out of the firing line.

What Strauss wouldn't have expected was the 'Whatever you do don't panic, but AAAAAARRGHHH!' response to the question of who should replace him.

England skipper Alec Stewart, on radio, and others in print, had suggested the time had come to call for the return of Mark Ramprakash, the veteran but evergreen Surrey batsman whose form in county cricket had been consistently brilliant but who, for a variety of reasons, had never quite fulfilled himself at the highest level. Having planted that seed, some others turned their attention to the possibility of a return for 2005 Ashes-winner Marcus Trescothick.

Before England finalised their squad for the World Twenty20, Strauss had contacted his former opening partner and friend, testing the water to see if there was any chance of Trescothick considering a return to England's colours for the shortest form of the game.

Trescothick thanked him for the call, but told Strauss that his retirement from international cricket was final and that there was no going back. Even though he felt he could still do a job with the bat, his experience with depressive illness had also proved to him how wide the chasm can be between what you want to do and what you can do.

This time, a phone call from Strauss enquiring whether Trescothick could play in his Benefit Golf Day was seen by many observers as another subtle attempt to see whether 'no' still meant 'no'.

What also blurred the lines were quotes from a Somerset official saying he believed Trescothick might be persuaded out of retirement for a one-off match.

Somerset chief executive Richard Gould said: 'I believe Marcus would be more than willing to end his self-imposed retirement if he was told he did not have to be available for any tours due to his much-publicised medical condition. He is absolutely at the top of his game, still one of the best batsmen in the world, with an unabated hunger for runs.'

Trescothick admits that he initially found the thought appealing, but that it very quickly became clear to him that it was a non-starter. In a column in his local paper, he wrote of the dream that told him there was simply no point giving it another thought.

The classic version of the batsman's nightmare goes like this. A wicket falls. You are the next man in. You cannot find your boots, gloves, pads, bat or helmet in time to get out there. In Trescothick's variation, he recounted he was being called to take part in the official England team photo at The Oval and couldn't find his whites.

'That was it,' said Trescothick. 'It was nice to be thought of again, but that experience, which woke me up in the middle of the night, told me all I needed to know. There was no chance.'

Nor, in the event, would there be for Ramprakash.

With the squad for the final Test due to be announced on the Sunday between Tests, Bopara felt he knew what was coming. He said: 'It was a tough week and a tough time. I've no regrets, but, looking back at the series, I was unable to make the big scores I wanted to for myself and the team, and I did start to feel the pressure. After Lord's I found myself under the pump and I was very frustrated because I really wanted to make a contribution. By the time I got to Leeds, I was a bit desperate. I was thinking to myself, I have to get a score. I just wanted to prove to everyone – my teammates, the fans and the Australians – that I could play on this stage, and it didn't happen. It was a bitter pill to swallow. Mentally it was tough, but I'm not one of those people who just sits down and takes it. I was determined to respond well and keep going until things came right again. I have some great memories, particularly of Fred at Lord's, and I'd won a few bob at poker as well.'

Bopara, as the England management team would have noted, scored a double hundred for Essex the following week.

Strauss met with Flower and selectors Geoff Miller, Ashley Giles and James Whittaker, on Friday 14 August. But though some drew a link between the coincidence that they came together at the Trent Bridge ground where Bell and Jonathan Trott had been busy making centuries for Warwickshire against Notts, Strauss insists he was already clear in his own mind that the latter, drafted in as batting cover for Flintoff at Leeds, was the logical choice to replace Bopara.

'It was difficult to leave Ravi out,' says Strauss. 'He'd played fantastically well against the West Indies, and is still going to be a big player for us going forward, but part of me remembered what it was like when I struggled against Australia Down Under in 2006–07, with all the expectation, the attention and the media coverage, as well as playing a good bowling attack. When they get on top of you it's very hard to come back, and the way Ravi got out at Headingley, maybe a little bit unfortunately, you just felt it would be a massive ask to expect him to come out at The Oval and score big runs in that final Test match. As for who would play ahead of him, we had a very long selection meeting on the Friday, but the majority of it was taken up discussing the one-day squads. In all honesty, the Test team was picked within half an hour.

> 'It was difficult to leave Ravi out . . . but it was obvious to all of us that Trott deserved his chance. He was in the form of his life'
>
> *Andrew Strauss*

'We spoke about the likes of Ramprakash and Rob Key, but it was obvious to all of us that Trott deserved his chance. He was in the form of his life. We'd all been impressed by the way he'd played in the nets at Headingley, and also by the fact that he went away from there and got runs.'

Indeed, so confidently had most of the Saturday-morning papers predicted that Trott would be included, some believed there must have been a leak. There was, in fact, but it was totally unintentional. Covering the match at Trent Bridge, one or two of the more intrepid members of Her Majesty's cricket press had gone in search of clues, and found them in the room where the selection meeting had taken place earlier. Giles takes up the story.

'That was a bit of an oversight. I'd scrunched up my versions of the squads when the meeting ended and chucked them in the bin.

There was a reason they were in the bin, as in, they weren't the finished article, but I don't think I'll be doing that again.'

And still Strauss had more to deal with.

Flintoff had been to see the specialist the day after England had lost at Headingley and, though there had been no substantial change in his condition, which would require surgery at the end of the series, it was felt that, with suitable management, he would be able to get through the final Test at The Oval.

That was the good news. The slightly worse news concerned Jimmy Anderson, who was working all hours with physio Dave 'Rooster' Roberts to try to repair the damage he had done to his left hamstring running between the wickets at Leeds.

Anderson said: 'I'd gone for a tight single and just overstretched. The scan showed no tear so I was happy with that, but "Rooster" had a root around and said, "Actually I'm not certain. I think there's a bit of work in this." When Rooster said that I thought, Surely not.

'From then on I was pretty much going in every day for treatment – manipulation and massage – and they got me running straight away to try and build it up and put it under a bit of pressure. Fortunately, we got it right.'

And though Broad had recovered from his bout of tonsillitis at Leeds, there was another illness causing England concern, namely what Graeme Swann later called 'Swann Flu'.

'The biggest match of my life and I had the worst preparation possible,' says the off-spinner. 'I'd phoned Andy Flower on the way home from Headingley. Initially he'd asked me whether I wanted to play for Notts against Warwickshire and at first I'd said no, but then I thought, This is going to be better than netting all week. I told Andy I wanted to play after all, so, with the game starting the next day, I went home and had a take-away curry.

'By 11 o'clock that night I was enjoying the worst bout of food poisoning I'd ever had in my life. I was convinced I had swine flu.

It was horrendous. After a couple of days I went in to see the Notts lads at Trent Bridge to watch half an hour of play, and my team-mate Paul Franks just said: "I've never seen a man look worse than you."

'I got slightly better over the weekend, though I couldn't get out of bed until Saturday afternoon and even then it was just to pad downstairs to try to eat a boiled egg.

'It was terrible preparation as far as my health was concerned but, on the other hand, it was probably the best I could have had, because I didn't think about the cricket at all. I lay in bed with the Discovery Channel on watching endless war documentaries, interrupted on a ridiculously frequent basis by visits to the loo, sitting there reading *Viz* magazine over and over again.

'I didn't feel great even up until the night before the match. I'm so glad we batted first in the Test, because if we'd bowled first I'd have had to bowl all day and I'd have been absolutely cooked by the end of it.'

In the circumstances, it came as something of a relief for the England players to get into their pre-match practice routines and focus on only the biggest match most of them had ever experienced.

For five days in south London the Ashes would be on the line. All the talk, all the speculation, all the conjecture and all the detail of what had gone before were now irrelevant. It was time for the better of two evenly matched teams to reveal itself. It was time for someone to win the Ashes.

'I lay in bed with the Discovery Channel on watching endless war documentaries, interrupted on a ridiculously frequent basis by visits to the loo, sitting there reading *Viz* magazine over and over again'

Swann flu strikes the camp

The Oval, Day One: England 307 for 8

Not since 1965–66 had an Ashes series moved into its final phase all square, a fact that only added to the anticipation of the nation. It rose to fever pitch when Flintoff was passed fit to play in his last-ever Test match.

Those looking for clues in recent form on this ground were encouraged that England had finished the previous summer here in style, defeating South Africa by six wickets, and that they came into this winner-takes-all contest unbeaten in seven previous Tests in SE11, stretching back to the 2001 Ashes.

Strauss was happy to absorb all the good signs as he shared a morning coffee with Michael Vaughan, with whom he had tasted nothing but champagne four years earlier.

Strauss recalls: 'We didn't talk about 2005 because we had tried to steer clear of that. What Michael did say to me was: "As the game progresses, you'll see little things that will tell you whether it's meant to be or not, and the biggest sign of all will come at 10.30am." He was talking about the toss, and it was obviously going to be a massive one to win.

'Some people, the majority of them with Australian accents, called it a wicket made to order,' continues Strauss. 'Definitely not.

'To a certain extent, the Surrey groundsman, Bill Gordon, realised it was in no one's interest for it to be a draw pitch, but I think both sides misread it. You could see the surface was dry, but we thought it would offer some pace and bounce for the quicks for the first two days and then take spin later. Had we thought it would go sideways, we had the option of playing Monty Panesar as the second spinner, but we didn't.

'It was a little surprising the Aussies left out Hauritz and didn't play a front-line spinner, but you could understand why, having bowled so well at Headingley, they wanted to keep the same side.

199

'When the toss went my way again, for the fourth time in five, on the way back to the dressing-room I kept thinking about what Michael had said.'

Strauss did not hesitate in electing to bat and, though England lost Cook cheaply at 12 for 1, even as they set about recovering to 108 for 1 at lunch, with Strauss reaching fifty in 90 balls, Graeme Swann found himself struggling to contain a growing feeling in the pit of his stomach. Fortunately for England, the sensation had nothing to do with the condition from which he had been suffering so spectacularly in the build-up to the match, and everything to do with what might be on the menu for him later.

Instead of a batting-friendly surface, a run-fest and a draw, frequent puffs of dust as the ball exploded through the top showed it to be drier than an 007 Martini. Swann was not the only one shaken and stirred.

According to his colleagues in the Sky commentary box when, shortly after the break, Marcus North made one jump, turn and shout, 'Boo!', Shane Warne could barely sit still. It was enough to make the great leg-spinner rue the day he retired.

Swann says: 'I remember bowling on the net wickets a couple of days before. The ball was turning square and I was thinking, well, this practice is a waste of time because the Test wicket's not going to do this. It didn't look like it was either. It looked a fairly normal Oval pitch. No one could have predicted it would dust up and play as it did.

'Then, sat there on the first day when we were batting and watching North bowl and get some spin, well . . . You know you always want to play and make an impact and win the game, and the fact that we'd batted first so we would be bowling last bar something crazy happening meant, I thought, This is starting to set itself up for me perfectly.

'Knowing that the cameras would be straight in the dressing-room to try and spot my reaction, I sat there trying to not smile.

Inside I was doing cartwheels. It was like being in Mumbai.'

However much help Swann may be offered by the pitch later in the match, England's immediate priority was a first-innings total that would give him something to bowl at. After Strauss perished to leave the score on 114 for 2 to a ball from Hilfenhaus delivered from some distance over the popping crease, it was down to Ian Bell and new number 4 Paul Collingwood to build a meaningful partnership.

Warne had begun the morning with another loud blast at his number-one target. 'So Paul Collingwood is going to bat at number 4 for England? About time,' he wrote. 'Up to now, Collingwood has been looking after himself rather than the interests of his team by staying at five, while Ravi Bopara and Ian Bell have been taking the flak above him. Now, at last, he's going to take some responsibility. He owes England a match-winning hundred; perhaps then he'll deserve the MBE he collected for scoring seven and ten four years ago.'

Even Lily Allen, cheeks decked with St George Crosses, was on Collingwood's case by mid-afternoon, for once assessing a player on Twitter for their on-field performance rather than for their looks or stamina. 'Collingwood is dull,' she tweeted. 'He'll probably still be batting when I'm back here at The Oval on Saturday, having scored no runs.' Bearing in mind how the pitch was now behaving, England might not have minded that one bit.

As the afternoon wore on, however, so England's frustration mounted as they seemed unable to maintain momentum. Australia adopted the tactic of bowling wide of the off stump with scouts patrolling the deep to dry up the runs or force the batsmen to take risks. After all, a draw for Australia would be enough for them to retain the urn. In the event the plan worked even better than Ponting would have hoped when, after a spell of 11 runs in 10 overs Collingwood flashed Siddle to Mike Hussey in the gully for 24 at 176 for 3.

With Collingwood's departure, debutant Trott joined his Warwickshire colleague Bell to a rousing reception. Watching from the dressing-room, Kevin Pietersen felt utterly confident that the man who followed his path from the South Africa Under-19s to realise a dream of playing for England would rise to the occasion, just as he himself had done four years earlier, when his brilliant 158 here persuaded the millions watching to excuse him for wearing a dead skunk on his head.

According to Pietersen: 'With my background being almost exactly the same as his, I know what he had to go through to get to this point, coming to England, playing in England and making England his priority and wanting to achieve amazing things. You have to leave your family, your friends, you start off in a new country where no one is your friend, you have to play well in order for people to accept you because people have got their own agendas. Basically, after having experienced all that myself, though it may sound stupid for me to say, I knew he was going to be all right.

'I mentioned all that to Strauss after the Headingley game because, knowing how hard it had been to get to this point and what he must have had to deal with, I backed him to come through.

'As for the panic that seemed to infect some people after Leeds, everybody's entitled to their own opinion and, of course, anybody would have wanted Marcus Trescothick back in because on numerous occasions in county cricket he's shown he is just too good for it. Ramprakash, unfortunately, I didn't have the same confidence in, because we've seen before how he reacts under pressure. I thought it was ridiculous that people were talking about him playing in the Ashes decider.

'But one thing England selectors have done really well over the last few years is that they've been consistent. Trott was next in line at Headingley. For me it was obvious he should play here, and he batted as though he'd been playing at this level for ages.'

Trott recalls: 'Somebody told me on the morning of the match that the South African coach Micky Arthur had claimed I wouldn't get into their side. Fair enough. I can't control what other people say. The best way of answering is succeeding.'

Bell, meanwhile, though inhibited by a bruised knee that restricted his running between the wickets, was now approaching three figures. At tea he had made 72 of England's 180 for 3, and everything appeared in place for a second England century to set alongside Strauss's match-winning contribution at Lord's when Bell succumbed to his first delivery after the interval, chopping onto his stumps to hand Siddle his third success of the innings.

Strauss believes Bell's innings was vital. 'He played exceptionally well. Maybe he wasn't at his most fluent but it was tough out there and he kept his head. Sure we lost wickets when he was out, but we would have been in big trouble without those runs.'

Indeed, England were suddenly wobbling at 181 for 4 and, when Matt Prior became the latest victim of Mitchell Johnson's slower ball, to reduce England to 229 for 5, all eyes turned to one of England's most treasured sporting sons.

With the St George flags fluttering proudly in front of the gasometer, Flintoff strode out to the richest of receptions at exactly 5pm. Within minutes, however, he was heading back again, after losing an intriguing, but ultimately brief, skirmish with Johnson by slicing a wide one behind for just seven to leave England in a spot of bother at 247 for 6.

The feeling that their batsmen had not shown enough application, or discipline, nor put a high enough price on their wickets, was hard to escape. Then Trott gave Australia a further unexpected bonus when, on 41 and appearing well in control, he was brilliantly run out by Katich from short leg, fielding his on-drive cleanly then reacting instantly to the realisation that the batsman had strayed from his crease for a moment. England were 268 for 7.

Hard as it may have been to take at the time, the lesson England's newest recruit learned from his dismissal turned out to be invaluable.

He explains: 'Getting out like that reminded me how precious your wicket is at Test level and how it can be snatched away just like that.

'I felt focused and all right. I wouldn't say I was casual, but sometimes, when you are feeling relaxed, you are not always on your toes. Then, suddenly, I was out and thinking, how the hell did that happen in the biggest game of my life? I hope I won't regret saying this, but I made up my mind to make sure it never happens again.'

And when Swann was dismissed three balls from the scheduled close to leave England on 307 for 8, opinions were divided as to what kind of day they had had.

The headline on the back page of the following morning's edition of *The Times* left little room for misinterpretation. 'England toss away chance to ram home advantage . . .' it read. Was their dream really over?

The Oval, Day Two: England 332 all out; Australia 160 all out; England 58 for 3

England were intent on getting as close to 350 as possible on the second morning, no doubt encouraged by Broad's recent form with the bat, Anderson's obvious improvement over the past year and number 11 Steve Harmison's incredible Test batting average of 119 at The Oval. For all that, however, the innings was extended by a mere 32 balls. Anderson's record for the longest Test career without a duck came to an end in the first full over of the morning, dismissed for nought for the first time in 55 innings. 'Bit of a relief, to be honest,' he says.

Hilfenhaus doubled his tally for the morning when he also removed Broad to leave England 332 all out and still unsure of just how good a score that was.

Swann says: 'Judging that as being a typical Oval pitch, a lot of people probably thought we were about a hundred below par. Outside the dressing-room they might have been saying: "What are we doing? Throwing it away. Same Old England. Ashes gone again." Inside the dressing-room, the guys who had actually batted on that pitch knew it wasn't easy. As it turned out, it was a tremendous first-innings score.'

'Bit of a relief, to be honest'

James Anderson loses his record of the longest Test career without a duck

Strauss recalls: 'I was disappointed with our total. I thought we'd missed an opportunity. We were looking for 400 and we were behind where we wanted to be.'

Collingwood agreed. Flintoff, on the other hand, remembers: 'I thought that was right in the game on that wicket. It wasn't a typical flat Oval track. It was hard to score on, and I thought we were in the box seat.'

Flintoff might have made it through his fitness check, and was being thrown the new ball, but his long-term future was put into serious doubt when that morning's *Daily Telegraph* confirmed earlier reports that he had been booked in for surgery with specialist Andy Williams the day after the scheduled end of his final Test match.

Flintoff, it was reported, was to have an operation similar to the one carried out on Michael Vaughan, which involved creating microfractures of the bone to stimulate tissue growth and replace worn cartilage. The estimated recovery time was put at anything between six and nine months, should the surgery and recuperation be successful. It took Vaughan almost a year to recover after his operation in 2006, and he was still plagued by knee problems when he announced his retirement from all cricket at the start of the 2009 summer.

For now, Flintoff continued to shrug off any discomfort as he combined with James Anderson to provide the Australia openers with a serious new-ball test. Three lbw shouts against Shane Watson in the opening half a dozen overs roused the crowd, the last, led by Flintoff, for good reason, as it appeared to be missing off and leg but hitting middle just over halfway up.

'I wasn't too thrilled with Asad's explanation of why he didn't give it, but you never are, are you?' says Flintoff. But the pressure was still on Australia as the only runs scored in the first five overs of controlled hostility were from Watson's edge for four to third man off Anderson.

Australia's openers survived, nevertheless, and took lunch at 61 without loss after rain ended play three minutes prematurely. The earlier than expected time of arrival also appeared to catch the groundstaff by surprise. Cue an extraordinary exchange between Australia coach Tim Nielsen and head groundsman Bill Gordon, after the former bounded onto the field to suggest the covers could be brought on with greater alacrity. Nielsen even threatened to report Gordon to match referee Ranjan Madugalle.

Then, when play resumed following a delay to the afternoon session of exactly 100 minutes, up stepped an England all-rounder to begin one of the great spells in Ashes history and haul the initiative back in his side's favour . . . not Flintoff on this occasion, but the man considered his natural successor. It was the time for Stuart Broad to present his credentials as a hero for a new generation, a cricketer capable of taking over the moment and shaping a match, and a series, to his will.

At 2.40pm, having been introduced at the Vauxhall End for the second full over after the extended break, the 23-year-old struck with his sixth ball when he pinned Watson on the crease to reduce Australia to 73 for 1. Following his six-for in Leeds, he was now England's outright top wicket-taker in the series with 13. In his next over, prize scalp Ricky Ponting survived a close call when getting a nick on a full ball that missed his stumps by inches.

But Broad, now charging in with more purpose, confidence and menace than at any time in the series, and responding to the call of destiny, would not be denied. At 3.01pm, with the final ball of his third over, Ponting was forced to yield when an under-edge sent the ball unerringly into the timbers. Australia were 85 for 2.

So strong now was the force within Broad that Hussey was simply blown away by it. At 3.08pm the left-hander crumpled leg before for nought after just three deliveries (89 for 3) and when Michael Clarke was brilliantly held low down by Trott, specifically placed at short extra cover for the drive, it was evident that there was no stopping either the rot or Broad.

At 3.17pm, from 73 for no wicket, Australia had slumped to 89 for 4. Broad, rising to the biggest challenge of his career, had taken 4 for 8 in 21 balls, and 3 for none in 9. Each time he made his way to fine leg, with hand on cap, a roar bellowed from the pit of the OCS Stand.

'Before I went in to bat I thought we were well short in our innings,' Broad admits. 'I was thinking that, on that wicket, someone should go on and get 130 or 140 and that for none of our batsmen to score a century was a bit criminal. Then, when I went in on the Friday morning, I realised batting was a bit more tricky than I'd originally thought. The ball was bouncing awkwardly, so that gave me confidence when it came to bowling.

'I'd prepared very thoroughly, aiming at that cone again and felt ready to go, but I could never have dreamt what was going to happen.

'What really helped me, I believe, is that though the ball did swing, it didn't swing every delivery and that meant, once I got into my rhythm, the batsmen could never settle. It enabled me to get Ponting and Hussey in quick succession.

'I got Ponting out with a ball that swung away beautifully then nipped back. It wasn't a full-on cutter, because I didn't want to take too much pace off it, but I just ran my fingers down the back of the ball and it came back into him after bouncing.'

Prior remembers the moment. 'I saw what he'd done and I thought to myself, great skills. But it's more than skill. To be able to control a cutter like that, bowling at that speed, and to do it against Ponting in an Ashes Test, that takes what used to be called a "strong constitution".'

Broad continues: 'Then, against Hussey, I tried to bowl the same shape delivery three balls running, swinging it into him as a left-hander – and only the last one actually did. Two deliveries in a row, I saw him looking at my wrist position and watching the seam coming out as though the ball was going to swing back into him then, when it didn't, he was able to play inside it comfortably and leave it alone.

'Then the third came out, with the same wrist position and the same seam position, he shaped to leave it and it swung right into his pad and hit him plumb in front.

'At that moment I recalled what Ottis Gibson had said to me at Edgbaston: "It's not what the ball does, it's where it does it from that counts." Spot on.

'I enjoyed Clarke's wicket as well. He'd been driving fantastically well, but we thought that, on this wicket, the ball might just stop, and having catchers in on the drive might put some doubt in his mind. It worked, he was a bit more hesitant, and then he tried to impose himself by letting go the drive, and Trott took a great catch at short extra cover.

'The crowd's response was phenomenal. I bowled a 12-over spell between lunch and tea, which is quite rare in Test cricket, and every time I ran down to fine leg the crowd were cheering and celebrating. You can have all the photographs you like, but those memories never fade and they'll be with me for ever.'

Flintoff says simply: 'He bowled beautifully. It was just one of those spells when everything you try comes off. I don't think I've ever had one myself. He beat the bat from more or less ball one. It put us right in the game.'

When Broad turned down the riches of the Indian Premier League in April to give himself the best possible chance of being fresh and at his best for his first Ashes series, his decision raised both eyebrows and his own standing with the English cricket public. Now it was paying a different dividend. Charged with adrenalin, he had the stamina to keep going and, when off-spinner Graeme Swann, his Nottinghamshire partner, was brought on to operate in tandem, they sent the Australia innings into freefall.

'You can have all the photographs you like, but those memories never fade and they'll be with me for ever'

Stuart Broad comes of age in Test cricket during Friday afternoon at The Oval

Consecutive wicket maidens, which began when Pakistan official Asad Rauf failed to see the chunkiest of inside edges from Marcus North and ended with a similar connection on the bat to account for Simon Katich at short leg for 50, left Australia on 109 for 6 on the stroke of 4pm.

And when Broad cleaned up Brad Haddin with a beauty that extracted his off stump, to take his figures to 8.4-1-26-5 and Australia to 111 for 7, the Sky cameras focused their attention on the young lady standing on the England dressing-room balcony punching the oxygen out of the south London air. It was Stuart's sister, Gemma, the team analyst.

'It was a rare moment of emotion,' says Stuart. 'But it wasn't only that. She has a very detailed approach to what she does, and she had been involved in devising some of the plans I had worked on. She was very happy, obviously, and also very proud as well, that some of her ideas had been taken into our thinking.'

At that stage Australia still needed 22 runs to avoid the follow-on. Though they succeeded, after Prior's fine take to dismiss Mitchell Johnson from a thick edge off Swann shortly before tea left them reeling at 133 for 8, Broad led England from the field to a thunderous ovation.

What was that sweet smell? Could it really be the Ashes?

Half an hour into the evening session when, after Swann had somehow persuaded umpire Rauf to give Stuart Clark out caught at short leg by Alastair Cook when the ball actually missed wood by six inches at least, then Flintoff rounded off the innings by bowling Hilfenaus all ends up, there it was again.

This time, as Broad took the players off the field with the match ball in his hand, he looked self-conscious as he waved it to all parts of the ground. At 5.18pm, and to as much amazement as ecstasy among the sun-baked crowd, Australia were all out for 160–172 runs behind on first innings.

All ten wickets had fallen for 87 runs in 180 balls spread over just two hours and 18 minutes. Broad finished with 5 for 37 and Swann 4 for 38.

No one was taking anything for granted, but a result considered at best unlikely, and at worst ludicrously over-optimistic by England supporters not 24 hours earlier, now seemed more probable than possible.

'It was quite hard to take it all in, really,' Broad says. 'It was one of those moments when everything worked. Not a purple patch, more a golden one.

'Strauss has been fantastic as a captain with me, backing me when there seemed no real reason to. I remember he threw the ball to me in Antigua when Chanderpaul and Sarwan were going. New ball. I hadn't taken a new ball all series and he said, "Come on Broady, get me two wickets," and I was lucky enough that day to repay him by getting Sarwan and Chanderpaul out. So I think that gives him a little bit of confidence, sometimes, when he gets a gut feeling just to say, "Go on, have a bowl, see what you can do."

'Someone asked me afterwards what I had been doing when England won the Ashes in 2005 and I could remember very clearly. I was 19, playing for Leicestershire and it was my first-ever season. But I was at home on the final Ashes day, and when Fred was caught and bowled by Warne, I remember thinking, Oh no! We're 126 for 5. That's the end of it. They'll bloody go on and win now. I remember very clearly his reaction, his whole body language just dropped when Warne caught that ball. And I remember feeling very down for an hour or so until KP started bashing it everywhere.

> 'It was quite hard to take it all in, really. It was one of those moments when everything worked'
>
> *Stuart Broad*

'When I was sat there watching that back in 2005, I would never have believed I'd be playing in the next Ashes series in England.

'When it was announced that the 2009 World Twenty20 would be here, I remember thinking, Damn, that's a couple of years too early. God, I wish it was a couple of years later because that would give me a chance to get into the side by then.

'As for this Ashes series, no way on earth.'

Strauss believes: 'He showed all his skills. In the West Indies he tried to bowl line and length and not much happened, and he was forced to try cutters and all sorts. But now he went back to simple basics and the Aussies just had no answer to him.'

According to Swann: 'It was stunning. Stuart ran up and basically ignored what everyone else was thinking, that on that pitch you had to bowl at a fifth stump. He bowled fast and straight and even the most pessimistic of souls must then have believed, now we have got a chance. Someone said Broad will never have another day like that. I bet he will. I've absolutely no doubt. He is going to be a great Test player for England, and I want to be around to see it happen.'

Collingwood believes this passage of play was symptomatic of the inexperience both sides showed from time to time. 'Every so often, when they were batting and when we were at Headingley for example, you got the feeling that things could happen very quickly – bang, bang, bang and you're out. To me, that reflected the fragility in both sides.'

Even though wickets continued to tumble, England's position at the end of day two, 230 runs ahead on 58 for 3, meant that whatever happened in the interim, Australia would have to bat exceptionally well under extreme pressure to deny England a second successive home Ashes triumph. The loss of Cook, Bell and Collingwood cheaply barely altered the feeling within the England camp that they held a sizeable advantage and, for once, even the pundits agreed.

The Oval, Day Three: England 373 for 9 declared; Australia 80 for 0

England's players awoke to celebratory headlines on the third morning of the deciding Test following a weird-looking day two scorecard of 243 for 15 across three innings. With their sizeable lead it was undoubtedly advantage England, but no matter how determined Strauss and Flower might have been that they should not get ahead of themselves again, the press saw no reason to hold back.

'They're coming home . . .' proclaimed the front page of *The Times* sports pullout, across the image of Stuart Broad celebrating his fifth wicket of the previous day, anticipating a repeat scoreline of 2005. 'This is a series that has had more twists and turns, plots and subplots, than a Len Deighton thriller, but when Australia lost ten wickets for 87 . . . it felt like the storyline had taken its final decisive turn,' wrote Michael Atherton, one of the many persuaded by events at Headingley that the tide sweeping Australia to victory was now irresistible. 'Broad to their knees,' exclaimed the *Sun*, referring to the 138 minutes of joy England experienced in the field. 'The King is dead. Long live the King,' said the *Daily Express*, heralding Broad's succession to Andrew Flintoff's throne as the country's premier all-rounder. 'Was this the day England won the Ashes?' asked the *Daily Mail*.

In direct contrast to the joyous reflection in the English press, indignation Down Under about the state of the surface in south London filled the Australian papers.

'Ricky Ponting could not have picked a better toss to lose at Headingley, and a worse toss to lose at The Oval,' wrote Malcolm Conn in *The Australian*. 'At Headingley, Australia's fast bowlers sliced England apart during the opening session of the match on a surprisingly lively wicket, and went on to a huge victory in just two and a half days to level the series at one-all. Now there is the danger of a slow death on a wicket manufactured to ensure the result England so desperately needs to regain the Ashes.' Oh dear.

> 'I knew I hadn't hit it, but I also knew the sound made by the ball when it flicked my trousers sounded very woody'
>
> *Jonathan Trott is nearly out first ball of the day*

Even though England were now clear favourites, Australia must have believed that if one or all of their bowlers could do to Strauss & co. what Broad had done to them the day before, the match, and the series, may yet turn again in their favour and, when the first ball of the day from Peter Siddle to Jonathan Trott clipped something on the way through to wicketkeeper Brad Haddin, their excitement was palpable. All eyes were on umpire Asad Rauf. Strauss, at the other end, could hardly bear to look.

Trott recalls: 'I'd felt comfortable the night before, but we knew we had a hell of a lot to do to actually win the game, and the task ahead of us was still a tricky one. Then, first ball of the morning, Siddle bowled me a ball that exploded through the surface. I knew I hadn't hit it, but I also knew the sound made by the ball when it flicked my trousers sounded very woody. As Siddle and the rest of them went up for the catch behind I was holding my breath and thinking that if the umpire is going on sound, he may well give this. And he made an absolutely brilliant decision. Imagine the pressure on the umpire in that situation. Siddle nearly burst a blood vessel he was appealing so hard, and I could understand why. Umpires take a lot of crap when they get decisions wrong, but this was a hell of a decision to get right and I'm very grateful he did or we would have been 58 for 4 and, suddenly, the complexion of the game changed completely.'

Television replays confirmed the ball had indeed brushed thigh rather than outside edge and Strauss breathed again.

'Again I thought back to what Vaughan had said about seeing the signs,' says Strauss. 'I was concerned on that third morning because I remembered back to the Old Trafford Test against New Zealand the previous year when, from a similar situation against us, they got bowled out for 120-odd and we knocked them off as the pitch died. And I had a strong feeling this pitch wasn't too well either.

'I didn't think it was going to be like us getting 150 all out and them getting 100 all out. I felt it was crucial that we batted well and set them at least 350. I must admit, for a moment my heart was in my mouth.'

The replays also engendered a fair amount of excitement in the England dressing-room as the slow-motion camera highlighted the small mushroom cloud of dust rising from the spot where the ball hit the pitch.

For now, attritional cricket was the order of the hour. The scoring rate did not hit three an over in the opening half of the session and the half-century England captain Andrew Strauss acknowledged just after drinks, his second of the match, was the slowest of his Test career to date, spanning three minutes short of three hours and spread over 154 balls.

It was not until the eighteenth over, in fact, that Strauss found the boundary for the first time in the day, via a pull off Stuart Clark. Perhaps gaining confidence from that, and indeed from his side's growing dominance, Strauss seized the opportunity to change tempo. Rather than allow Clark, bowling from the Pavilion End, to settle into a rhythm from around the wicket, aiming for the debris around off stump, Strauss twice used his feet to beat the two men specially positioned at short extra cover with flowing drives. The England captain's positivity was infectious, and when Trott stroked a three through point in the next over, from Ben Hilfenhaus, England's advantage was in excess of 300. The 100-run stand between Strauss and Trott came up from 194 deliveries and also included Trott's maiden international fifty. His fifth boundary, worked through the legside during a costly Michael Clarke over, got him there shortly before lunch. By now, every run appeared to be another prick in the balloon of Australia's hopes.

'I was so impressed by Trott's batting,' says Strauss. 'He didn't look nervous at all. We were just trying to score five runs at a time. He seemed absolutely certain about what he was trying to do to each bowler, and the Aussies had long since given up trying to get under his skin. In the first innings they gave him some but, when a batsman is looking as assured as he was, maybe the fielding side doesn't feel like there's much of an avenue to explore there.'

Trott recalls: 'We just didn't know what a good score was on this wicket. So, at first, we concentrated on staying in and collecting and then, as we passed 300, the time came to try to be more aggressive.'

In the circumstances, Strauss's dismissal at 12.56pm, as he edged a turning ball from North to be caught by Clarke at slip, came as something of a jolt and, at 157 for 4, the lead now stretched to 329, it was crucial that England reached lunch without any further alarm.

To that end, Trott and new partner Prior agreed they should endeavour to make sure this was the last over before the break and the keeper was as good as his word when his off-drive bounced up and struck Ponting, positioned intimidatingly close at silly mid-off, flush in the mouth. A stream of claret confirmed the power of the shot.

Trott recalls: 'I was quite pleased with that, not because Ricky got hurt, but because it meant I didn't have to face another over.'

After Prior was run out at 1.50pm by Katich's direct throw, Ponting's next significant action was greeted with cheers rather than the usual jeers, a welcome departure from the chorus of disapproval with which his every move had thus far been greeted in Cardiff, at Lord's, Birmingham and Leeds.

Flintoff, emerging from the dressing-room to play his final innings of Test cricket, was carried to the middle by a surge of hope, expectation and genuine affection. When he arrived, the Aussie captain captured the mood perfectly by offering his hand.

The gesture seemed momentarily to take England's talisman genuinely by surprise and those supporters with long teeth might, for a split-second, have made a connection with the scene at this ground prior to the final innings of the great Sir Don Bradman in the last Ashes Test of 1948.

The 'Don', universally acknowledged as the greatest batsman of all time, walked to the wicket that day in 1948 with 40,000 inside The Oval and 10,000 locked out, needing just four runs to end his career with a Test batting average of 100.

All present stood and cheered his passage to the wicket and, when he got there, England skipper Norman Yardley shook his hand and led his team in a Pathé news-style 'caps off and three cheers'. Two balls later, however, leg-spinner Eric Hollies clean bowled him with a googly, prompting BBC radio commentator John Arlott to muse: 'How tragic, how tragic, how tragic . . .' and wonder whether Bradman's view of the ball might have been impeded by the tear in his eye.

Strauss remembers: 'Fred spoke to the lads in one of the team talks and insisted that, even though it was his final game, it was a Test match with the Ashes at stake, so forget sentiment.'

Some observers wondered whether this was another dastardly Aussie plan to kill Flintoff's threat with kindness. Ponting's action was heartfelt enough. He knew only too well that numbers alone do no justification at all to the Fred Factor.

'If you look through his bare statistics, they probably don't read that flatteringly,' said the Aussie captain, 'but he has an impact on how that team plays and performs and for that he has to be right up there. He just seems to be one of those guys that everyone really enjoys playing with. He plays the game in great spirit, everything he does is done with a smile on his face, and when we got him at his best in 2005 he was a match-winning player for them throughout that series.'

Before his final Test series began, Flintoff insisted victory in 2009 would be a far greater achievement than in 2005, not just because of what he had been through since then on and off the field, nor

'Jonathan Trott was playing one of the best innings you'll ever see. He didn't get ruffled after that first ball. He just looked in command. He looked cool. I don't think I've seen anybody make a debut like it. He looked like he was playing his hundredth Test'

Andrew Flintoff

because of the pain in his crippled right knee, but also because this team was by no means the finished article. For now he had only one thing on his mind: to make a contribution.

According to Flintoff: 'Ricky shook my hand and said good luck and I appreciated the gesture, but I wasn't thinking about anything other than making quick runs and winning the game.

'Jonathan Trott was playing one of the best innings you'll ever see, not so much the runs he scored, more the manner. He didn't get ruffled after that first ball. He just looked in command. He looked cool. To play like that on debut, I don't think I've seen anybody make a debut like it. Sure, people do well and get runs first time out, but they tend to look a bit excitable when they are doing it. Trott looked like he was playing in his hundredth Test.

'Then, when he did go after the ball, it wasn't as though he tried to just smash it. He played proper shots. Very impressive.

'I'd decided how I was going to play in that last innings. I was going to swing from the hip. It was the position of the game. The wicket was deteriorating and I felt vulnerable about defending against the spinner, so I thought it would be best to get a quick 30 here rather than to try and grind it out for the next four hours.'

Indeed, for the next 26 minutes, to be precise, Flintoff demanded centre stage and dominated a brief sixth-wicket stand of 32 with a rasping 22. His final Test knock ended, fittingly, when an attempted six off North, which would have been only England's fourth of the campaign compared to 36 in the 2005 Ashes, failed to clear Siddle at long-on. England, so cautious in developing their lead earlier in the day, had rocketed from 150 to 200 in just 60 balls.

All the while, Trott displayed his understanding of his proper place in the drama, allowing Flintoff to take the lead while he progressed in his assured, unflappable manner. For five hours the Warwickshire debutant was the rock upon which England built their match-winning total.

Trott's innings may not have been as flamboyant as Pietersen's

ABOVE: Andrew Strauss avoids a short ball from Peter Siddle on his way to 55 in England's first innings at The Oval.

BELOW: The Australian reply is sent in to freefall by Stuart Broad and Graeme Swann and the second day is brought to a close with Broad finishing on five for 37 and Swann with four for 38.

The Brit Oval – the site of seven unbeaten Tests for England stretching back to the 2001 Ashes.

Strauss recalls, 'Fred spoke to the lads in one of the team talks and insisted that even though it was his final game it was a Test match with the Ashes at stake and forget sentiment.'

For five hours, debutant Trott was the rock on which England built their match-winning total.

ABOVE LEFT: Sheer jubilation for Freddie as he celebrates the run out of Ricky Ponting.
ABOVE RIGHT: Recalling the wicket of Brad Haddin Swann remembers, 'Strauss was positioned perfectly and it floated straight to him.'

The second of two spectacular run outs, this time Andrew Strauss takes Michael Clarke for none.

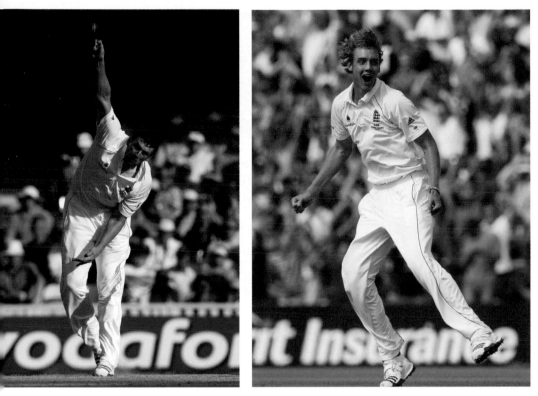

ABOVE LEFT: Steve Harmison beckons victory in a boisterous rush taking three wickets in 13 balls. ABOVE RIGHT: England's leading wicket taker across the series, Stuart Broad, disposing of Michael Hussey.

Graeme Swann delivers another fatal blow to Australia and later, at 5.48pm on 23rd August, the last day of the 2009 Ashes, celebrates his final, decisive wicket.

LEFT: Freddie gives his final wave as he leaves the field following England's triumph.

BELOW: England players thank the sun-baked crowd as they show their appreciation.

One hand or two? Strauss's dilemma over how to hold the urn.

Captain Andrew Strauss reflects, 'If I ever have a better feeling than this, I'll be a very lucky man.'

England regain the Ashes.

spectacular, series-clinching 158 here in 2005 but it carried all of KP's assurance. When the time came for his great personal milestone – reached with a flick off his pads to fine leg – the bemused look on his face as he waved his bat to his tearful mother Donna was genuinely touching.

'Surreal,' says Trott. 'It is one of those things you put in the memory bank. Hopefully, one day, I can look back and enjoy the moment a bit more.'

Trott had become the eighteenth England player to score a hundred on Test debut, and the first to do so in an Ashes contest since Graham Thorpe in 1993. More to the immediate point, his innings allowed his partners to concentrate on all-out attack. From 200 for 6 when Flintoff departed, a whopping 173 runs were scored in 30 overs, with Graeme Swann equalling his highest Test score of 63 with a mix of the audacious and the even more audacious.

Swann recalls: 'Because I'm so low down the order I almost have more of a licence to play my shots than people higher up in the order, and I joked with Strauss before I went out to bat that I was going to reverse-sweep North, even though it was turning and bouncing. He looked at me and said, "You're a buffoon." And, of course, I get out there and, third ball, when he let go of it, all I could think of was, Watch this, Straussy. So I got a couple of reverses out and, the ball before tea, I remember tearing down the wicket and smacking it for four over mid-off. It was quite deliberate because I

'Strauss said, "Go out and accelerate through the gears, but don't go mad." I nodded, of course, but inside I was thinking, I can't do that. If it's anywhere in my area I'm going to try and smash it'

Graeme Swann on the perfect second innings

219

always think it's the last thing they expect just before a break.

'And when I got into the dressing-room people were laughing, saying, "Oh, you blatantly didn't know it was teatime, did you?" I was going, Yeah, whatever.

'On the way back out Strauss said, "Look, we want a lead of 510, 520, so go out and accelerate through the gears, but don't go mad."

'I nodded, of course, but inside I was thinking, I can't do that. If it's anywhere in my area I'm going to try and smash it. It all came off and it was very enjoyable, and the best thing about it for me was, from looking to set them 510-odd, all of a sudden we were going to get a 550 lead, a world-record target if they'd made it and that gives you such a buffer, such comfort, knowing that even if they put on 300 for a wicket, they've still got another 250 to get. And the speed we scored those runs, and Trotty getting his hundred, it all just added up to a perfect second innings.'

With Stuart Broad (29) and James Anderson (15) also chipping in, England finally declared at Trott's dismissal for 119, caught by North off Stuart Clark, on 373 for 9, setting Australia a huge and, England hoped, nominal 546 to win in two and a bit days.

Australia's highest fourth-innings score in Tests was made in London, of course, and was still fresh in the memory – the 406 they managed in defeat at Lord's a month earlier. But though they reached 80 without loss at the close, surely now the match, and the urn, were England's for the taking.

'History is against us,' admitted North, 'but I think it is too early to look that far ahead. There is a lot of cricket to be played in this match, and what you will see is eleven guys come back to The Oval and show a lot of character and contest every over. If we do that, we can give ourselves a chance.'

'The selectors showed huge faith in me and I was pleased to be able to reward them,' Trott says. 'I felt I was in good form, and if the chance came I wanted to grab it with both hands. I was gutted to get out for 41 in the first innings. I remembered what Nasser

[Hussain] said when he presented me with my cap. He said if you get a chance, don't let them back in the game. That is what I tried to do. It is something I have worked towards my whole life since the age of three and being in the nets with my dad.'

The Oval, Day Four: Australia 348 all out. England won by 197 runs

If Strauss was still looking for signs, his vice-captain and opening partner Alastair Cook had a couple for him to think about.

Strauss had offered Cook a lift back to the hotel the previous evening and, as they left the dressing-room together, the Essex man drew his skipper's attention to events on the pitch.

Cook explains: 'It was way after play had ended and I saw people on the outfield setting up the winner's podium. They must have reckoned that the game could be over next day, so they were having a dress-rehearsal and I turned to Strauss and said: "Wouldn't it be nice if we were up there tomorrow?"

'Then, as we walked round the back of the stand towards the car park, I spotted something else that stopped me in my tracks. It was an advertising board for Vodafone featuring a photo of the England players celebrating their Ashes victory at The Oval in 2005, drenched in champagne and going berserk and, right in the middle, Michael Vaughan holding the urn with a hole where his head should be. The idea is that supporters can stick their head through the hole and have a picture taken of themselves as England's Ashes-winning captain.

'I'd seen it about a thousand times before during the series, but this time it had a real effect on me. I turned to Strauss and I could see he was thinking exactly the same thing – let's hope we don't cock it up now!'

The only player who admits to having any final-day nerves was

Paul Collingwood, who arrived at the ground suffering from 'the kind of fear you get when you go for your first driving test'. And he admits the feeling may have contributed to his out-of-character fielding display, including three dropped catches.

For the rest, early wickets from Swann and Broad were just the tonic these troops required.

Strauss had sprung surprises with his various choices to open the bowling on given days throughout the series. This time, however, his rationale appeared simple as he plumped for the two heroes of the first innings: Nottinghamshire duo Broad and Swann. They had shared nine wickets between them first time around and, given form, confidence and the evidence thus far presented in the match, seemed the boys most likely to conjure a breakthrough.

At 11:16am, Swann duly obliged, snaring Simon Katich with a delivery from round the wicket that angled in and kept on going until it hit his pads bang in front.

Ponting had barely composed himself following the shock of another warm ovation from The Oval crowd when, at 11.19am, in the very next over, Broad trapped Watson in front for the second time in the match.

Australia were 90 for 2 with Ponting and Michael Hussey, suddenly fighting for his place as well as for the Ashes, both on nought. Surely now the return of the Ashes was merely a matter of time.

For the best part of the next 40 overs, however, time appeared to stand still.

Ponting was struck in the midriff by a Swann delivery that ripped viciously in the next over but, during the next three and a half hours, the closest England came to breaking the third-wicket stand was when Hussey edged a sharp chance to Collingwood, who could not get a hand on it at slip.

Even the introduction of 'you-know-who' half an hour before lunch failed to deliver a third wicket. With the talisman now obviously hobbling and almost completely bust, and despite regular pleas from an expectant full house, including Lily Allen with a pint pot for a headdress to 'Come on England', Australia's two most experienced batsmen were still together at the break, at which point they had reduced the deficit to 374 runs, with eight wickets intact.

And by the time Ponting, on 51, having reached his forty-eighth Test half-century from 76 balls, survived another scare 13 minutes into the afternoon session, when his lobbed edge off the returning Swann struck Collingwood's boot at first slip, the Durham man was struggling to see the funny side.

Collingwood recalls: 'The pitch had gone to sleep by now, and they were making pretty comfortable progress. The closer you get to the prize the more nervous you get, and then you drop a catch and, though you try not to dwell on it too much, shooting through the back of your head is the thought, Oh f***. Have I just dropped the Ashes?'

His county colleague Steve Harmison was into the attack by the time Hussey reached his third fifty of the campaign, which represented 144 minutes of intense discipline. With both men cemented into a third-wicket stand that had now progressed comfortably into three figures, with the pitch visibly snoring great big zzzzs into the sweltering Oval sunshine and the crowd becoming increasingly restless, England were in desperate need of inspiration.

Strauss recalls: 'We allowed ourselves to get frustrated. They were still miles away, but you could sense the crowd was getting agitated that we weren't taking wickets and I think that fed through to the players.

'We had loads of runs in the bank, but we'd got to the stage where you thought, Someone's got to do something here because they're not looking under any pressure. The batsmen had got used to Swann's spin and the seamers were having to bowl a lot of cutters and they'd played everything well. So I was scratching my head for plan B.'

And then it happened.

At 2.34pm, Hussey drove a delivery from Harmison, operating from the Pavilion End, to the left of mid-on. Realising the fielder at mid-on was, in fact, Flintoff, and no doubt determined to work England's increasingly immobile all-rounder, he immediately called for a run. For a critical fraction of a second, though, instead of responding directly to his partner's call, the Australian skipper checked to see where the ball was travelling and who it was going to. Satisfied that Flintoff offered no threat in his present physical state, inasmuch as he could barely walk, let alone run, Ponting set off for the other end.

The next thing anyone knew, Flintoff's sidearm sling, faster than a speeding bullet and more powerful than a locomotive, arrowed straight into the off stump and smashed it from its mooring.

Athough Ponting lunged for safety, the England fielders knew what direct hits almost always mean and the television replays confirmed it.

Flintoff recalls the moment vividly. 'I don't think I've ever run anybody out like that in my career. In fact I know I haven't. I'd love to say it was reward for all the hours of fielding practice, but nothing could be further from the truth. I just picked the ball up and chucked it, and right from the moment I let it go it was knocking them all out.

'I remember watching Ricky and seeing him stretching his arm out for the line and I knew he was gone.'

So did Swann. 'From fielding at gully I was backing up behind the stumps, and I saw it come out of his hand. At first it looked wide to me, but then it tailed in, like a reverse in-ducker. As soon as the ball hit the stumps I looked up at where Ponting was and I thought, he's not made that . . . HE'S NOT MADE THAT.'

Strauss confirms: 'Straight away, I knew it was out. There was nothing textbook about it. It was a moment of pure talent. Talk about delivering when we needed it.'

'I don't think I've ever run anybody out like that in my career. In fact I know I haven't. I'd love to say it was reward for all the hours of fielding practice, but nothing could be further from the truth'

Andrew Flintoff runs out Ponting

'That was a great sight,' says Trott. 'From where I was standing, on the boundary, I could see the whole picture – the shot, the run, the throw, the stumps, the lunge for the line, the crowd's reaction, the big screen showing the decision and the word "OUT". Later, I tried to replay it all in my mind and I couldn't see a thing.'

To a man, the England players ran to Flintoff, who stood arms aloft. James Anderson, the first on the scene, embraced his Old Trafford colleague like a boy hugging a huge teddy bear. Sheer jubiliation cascaded through the team as they homed in on him. Ponting, the man with the biggest point to prove and the one most capable of doing so, had gone for 66. Australia were 217 for 3.

'We went through so many emotions – frustration, worry and despair – at times when it didn't look like we were going to take a wicket. But you can't keep Fred out of the game,' says Strauss, 'and that just set us in motion again.'

Ponting says: 'I felt in control, as much as you can on that surface. I was pretty determined to play well; with me being the leader, the captain wanting to stand up and perform when we were under the most pressure, I wanted to make a big score. We had started to wrestle some momentum back in our favour. I wasn't looking at the scoreboard, but Huss and I were going along nicely at that stage.'

Perhaps surprisingly, Flintoff's run out was England's first of the series. And just like the proverbial London bus, you wait 47 days for one to come and another one comes along in the very next over.

The victim this time, vice-captain Michael Clarke, used his feet to Swann and turned the ball to the legside, but, instead of finding the gap to get off the mark, it ricocheted off Alastair Cook's boot and Strauss collected it at leg slip.

The skipper had the presence of mind to palm the ball into the stumps, but those closest to the action – and they included Kiwi umpire Billy Bowden – felt, on first sight, that Clarke had almost certainly regained his ground.

According to Cook: 'Clarke skipped down the wicket like he normally does, and I knew nothing about the ball except that it hit me on the boot. It ended up in Strauss's hands, and he did well to throw down the stumps, but at first it was one of those where you just put the bails back on and carry on.

'Almost for a laugh a few of us were walking past Billy Bowden saying, "You might as well check that", and "You never know", and stuff like that. I honestly thought he wasn't going to bother, but then, possibly because of what had happened in the previous over, he sent it upstairs. Never at any stage did I think it was out, though.'

At this point Swann thought he heard a roar from one of the hospitality boxes and decided to check with Clarke. 'What do you reckon, mate?' I asked him and he said, "I think it's in, but you never know," at which point Gemma Broad and a few of the guys back in the pavilion started punching the air.'

Stuart Broad was one of them. 'At the time of Fred's run out, I was off the pitch,' he explains. 'I had a blister on my toe that needed taping before I could bowl again, so I'd actually nipped off very quickly.

'I heard the crowd go wild and thought, What's happened, what's happened? And I looked up at the tv in the dressing room and saw Hussey had flicked it to mid-on and then Fred hit the stumps.

'Then, when the Clarke run out was referred to the television umpire I was waiting at the bottom of the stairs to come back on, so I turned and looked up at the changing-room again to see the boys' reaction and saw Richard Halsall, the fielding coach, punch the air, so I ran out and shouted, "Boys, it's out, it's out, it's out!"'

Had Clarke's bat broken the popping crease before the bails had been dislodged? Fielders blocked one camera angle, complicating the decision-making process, and although cries from Down Under roared 'inconclusive', television umpire Peter Hartley believed he had seen enough.

With Australia 220 for 4, still 326 short of their improbable target and with only six wickets to account for, Collingwood's latest miss – failing to hang on to a chance offered by Hussey off Swann – would almost certainly turn out to be insignificant. But by this time he admits he was all over the shop. 'I'd gone. I was standing there thinking, How on earth have I just dropped that?'

In contrast, wicketkeeper Matt Prior's reactions were razor-sharp when Marcus North took a huge stride in attempting a sweep off Swann.

This time there was no doubt. The chalk belongs to the keeper, and North's foot was on the line at best, which meant Billy Bowden was confident enough to give this decision without referral, though Prior admits the excitement of the moment almost got to him.

According to the keeper: 'I'd been doing a lot of work with Bruce French about getting my hands back to the stumps quickly and I promise you, some of the time it's arduous. You're doing this work and you're thinking, Mate, why am I doing it, what is this all about?

'And then something like this happens and you realise why you go through all that. The ball spun and bounced, I took it high and to my left and now, because of my training, I automatically brought my hands straight back to the stumps.

'But I wasn't actually going to take the bails off until I looked at North's boot and realised his weight was on his toes and he was about an inch out of his ground.

'So now, having stopped the motion, I suddenly had to get my hands moving again and it was almost like one of those bad dreams where you're like, MOVE YOUR HANDS! and they don't budge. I've watched the replays and it almost looks like I've just nonchalantly knocked the bails off, but in my head I was like, MOVE YOUR F***ING HANDS – PLEASE! And then I finally managed to do it and I knew he was out because he still hadn't moved.'

It was 3.14pm. Australia had lost three wickets for 19 runs in 9 overs, and the excitement at the prospect of a four-day finish rippled through the stands. By tea, however, Hussey had guided Australia to 265 for 5, and when Strauss took the second new ball in the eighty-fifth over of the innings, he immediately encountered a couple of setbacks.

First, Broad was warned for a second time about landing on the business area of the pitch – which left him in danger of being forced out of the attack for the innings should he do it just once more. Then, at 4.38pm, substitute fielder Graham Onions shelled a high chance at short midwicket when Brad Haddin clipped a James Anderson delivery off his toes, a stroke that brought up the 50-run stand for the sixth wicket.

Swann, the man for whom Onions was deputising, recognised that, despite the state of the game, England's nerves were still jangling. 'When I came back out I said to Jimmy: "Hard luck, mate," and he said, "Why the f*** did you have to go off the field, you t**t!" Fortunately, Fred brought us together at drinks and said: "Listen boys, there's no point in getting shirty, they're still 250 behind. Just be patient."'

Moments after the missed chance off Anderson, Hussey was being congratulated by Haddin for Australia's eighth, and most stubborn, hundred of the series – 219 balls of pure concentration.

Having walked to the crease with a duck in the first innings, without a Test ton in his past 28 innings and a poor overall return in his second Ashes experience, Hussey was batting for his future. And his innings told you so. 'You could see in his eyes that morning that he was really up for the challenge,' said Ponting. 'To see him stand up and make that hundred in difficult conditions when the team needed him most and when he needed it most was great for us.'

But it could not stop England now. Despite signs that Haddin was intent on making England sweat overnight, at 5.11pm he succumbed as he greeted Swann's sixth spell of the day by dancing down the track and attempting to wipe him into the stands.

'I'd dropped Strauss back at midwicket, two-thirds of the way to the line,' recalls Swann, 'because on that pitch, if Haddin came after me and the ball spun, that was where he would mishit it.

'Strauss was positioned perfectly and it floated straight to him, but it was a lovely feeling when it was in the air, knowing that Strauss was underneath it and that, for me, was when I definitely knew, because the bowlers were coming in and it was turning that much. They'd got no chance.'

From 327 for 6 the end came in one big boisterous rush and it was Steve Harmison, one of the 2005 heroes, who beckoned it with a burst of three wickets in 13 balls.

Harmison summoned up enough hostility to send back Mitchell Johnson, Peter Siddle and Stuart Clark in quick succession, the latter two in consecutive deliveries. Suddenly, the extraordinary prospect of the Ashes being decided with a hat-trick came into view. 'One of the things that capped it off for me – I didn't take any wickets in the second innings – was the next best thing, to see Steve run in like that,' says Flintoff. 'I was urging him to get the hat-trick because, for me, it would have been the perfect way to finish.'

Harmison agrees: 'That afternoon I was chomping at the bit to get on and bowl at either end at any time. I was thinking, Just get them five or six down and I'll do the rest. Six down, you give me the ball and I'll bowl them out.

'I was glad to see Colly hold onto the catch to get Mitchell Johnson, because he'd had his feet on the end of his arms for most of the day. So was he, because he was running round shouting, 'I've caught one, I've caught one."

'And that just gave me that extra kick to say, "Right, these three aren't going to last that long, or if they do they're going to cop a few."

'Siddle did, and then he spooned one straight to Fred and it was just brilliant to see the big lad was awake because by this time, mentally, he'd already done his lap of honour and drifted off!

'Clark came in and, luckily for me, he got an inside edge that went straight up in the air to Cookie.

'Then came Hilfenhaus for the hat-trick ball. I bowled a yorker I was very happy with: I thought I was through him, but he jammed the bat down on it just in time. The he had the cheek to play a similar ball in the next over like the best batsman alive, straight through extra cover off the back foot for four.

'If I had taken the hat-trick to win the match I might well have called it quits there and then. But, to be honest, I was just thinking, after what happened four years previously when we found out we'd won the Ashes in the dressing-room we were off for bad light, however we did it, whoever took the wicket, this time I wanted to be on the field when it happened.'

And so he was when, at precisely 5.48pm on 23 August 2009, Hussey poked Swann to Cook at short leg and after seven weeks of drama, controversy, passion and perspiration, England had won the Ashes.

Swann momentarily lost the plot, sliding onto his knees, with clenched fists pumping skywards. He was finally caught and embraced somewhere near cover, first by his skipper, then, seemingly, by almost everyone in the ground and finally, through their tv screens, radios, laptops or mobile phones, by every other

England supporter on the planet. BBC *Test Match Special* producer Adam Mountford later revealed: 'We heard from people listening via satellite phone from the base camp at Mount Everest, from seal and penguin scientists tuning in online from the British Antarctic Survey on South Georgia [not to mention a few of the seals and penguins themselves] and from one listener who was following *TMS* sitting on a beach in Ghana, desperately trying to get in contact with anyone on the same beach who had a phone charger on them because his battery was flat.'

> 'It was just manic but it was as close to pure ecstasy as I've ever felt'
>
> *Swann takes the final wicket*

Swann says: 'I remember fielding at gully when they were nine down and Hilfenhaus drove a four and I was thinking quietly to myself, Don't get him out, because I'm desperate to get the last wicket and I'm desperate to get Hussey because he's my mate.

'Then I bowled him one that dipped a bit and didn't turn as much as the others, and as soon as it bobbed up in the air, I don't think I even watched it go into Cookie's hands, I just ran.

'I didn't know where I was going or what I was doing, and I ended up sliding on my knees and Strauss picked me up and it was literally pandemonium. I can't actually describe the feeling. I've seen it on video and it looks ridiculous. It looks like it's all pre-planned and everything, but I started running off and looking up to see where my mum and dad and fiancée Sarah were. It was just manic, but it was as close to pure ecstasy as I've ever felt. It was just a euphoric feeling of relief and satisfaction.

'The fact that was going through my head was, I've just taken the last wicket to win the Ashes and no one can ever take that away.'

Flintoff, meanwhile, took the time to ensure he shook hands with the Australian batsmen before joining in the celebrations. 'We played the ICC Champions Trophy final against the West Indies at The Oval a few years back and we lost,' Flintoff explained. 'The opposition ran around all over. We put our hands out, but there was no one to shake hands with. When you play in a series like this one, you have to respect the opposition. We'd got plenty of time to celebrate and enjoy each other's company.' Indeed, the hug he was about to receive from Harmison was described by Jonathan Agnew as 'the biggest I've ever seen.'

Ponting, who became only the second Australian captain to lose two Ashes series on English soil, and first since the nineteenth century, took his place alongside Billy Murdoch with great dignity. His Australia no longer number one in the world but as low as number four, his job now under huge scrutiny, Ponting said: 'We gave our all through the series but, unfortunately, we were not good enough. Full credit to England, and especially to Andrew Strauss. They have won the crucial moments.' His good grace was returned in kind by the capacity crowd, none of whom was prepared to leave for fear of missing out on the memories.

Strauss, man of the series for his calm under pressure as well as his outstanding contribution with the bat, was determined to take in everything he could, including, first of all, the physical sensation of holding the urn aloft.

'It was actually a little awkward,' he says. 'It's not often you get a trophy that small and you're not quite sure whether to lift it with one hand or two.

'It was a very special moment and the great thing about all those celebrations is that none of it has to be forced. You're not trying to show false excitement or anything like that, just genuine elation at having achieved something you were so desperate to achieve. It does make you very proud to be an England captain and I certainly remember back to Vaughan doing it in 2005. It's very easy when you start thinking about doing the captaincy to look at all the negative sides of it – having constant issues, not finding much time to get away from it – and it's easy to forget that actually the upside is massive.

'Unfortunately, I made a slip of the tongue when mentioning everyone who'd played except Ravi. That was not ideal and those things can happen in the heat of the moment. I imagine he was walking round with a voodoo doll of Andrew Strauss for a few days.

'My analysis of the series was that when we were bad we were very bad, but when we were good we were good enough to seize the moments that mattered.

'But my overwhelming feeling was that it was exactly how I expected it to be. It didn't happen in the way I expected it to happen. I thought games were going to be closer rather than a big seesawing affair, but the expectation, the attention, the way the country got involved in it, all that was exactly how I anticipated it would be and, in the end, exactly how I hoped it would be.

'It must have been bittersweet for Fred because it's a big thing when you know you're not to represent your country in Test cricket again. I'm just delighted for him that he was able to go out in perfect circumstances.'

For England's victorious 2009 Ashes winners, the celebrations lasted long into the night, first in the company of their opponents in the dressing-rooms, then with their families there and on the outfield – 'like a club side, we were,' recalls Collingwood – and later, back at the City Grange Hotel, where night turned into day far, far too soon for some.

Flintoff, though, was indeed experiencing mixed emotions. Though the bubbly tasted sweet as he prepared himself for a new chapter of his career, he admits the scale of the occasion got to him as he sought a moment of reflection in his usual corner of the dressing-room.

'I didn't think I would get emotional, but I did a little bit,' he says. 'I went up there and sat in the corner, the place I always sit at The Oval, on the left with my kit everywhere, and it was a teary moment while the lads were jumping around and celebrating. Then I saw the Sky Sports cameras coming into our dressing-room and I thought, No one's seeing me crying. I nipped into the toilets to give myself a minute and pull myself together.

'All those times that I have been with "Rooster" Roberts over the past few years training, this is why I have done it. Personally, through the series, I have not made that big an impact, but to be involved in a team that has won is everything. That's the reason I have gone through all the operations, done the work in the gym, the rehab, but I also knew I would never experience this kind of feeling again. All I could think about was, that's it for me. Over to you, Stuart.

'There was another moment in the dressing-room . . . Another moment when everyone was celebrating with all the families around. I was looking at the lads and how happy they were, which was one thing, but then I looked at my wife and kids and I thought, I've made the right decision here. I'm probably not going to get 25,000 people chanting my name again but you know, for me, spending time with my family and having the opportunity to do that is far more important, and something I'm really looking forward to.

'Now for the team. We've won the Ashes, fantastic, but if a lesson can be learnt from the past, it is now is the time to try to dominate. We've got the players to do it, we've got the captain to lead us and it's a realistic goal. Enjoy this celebration, get it out of the system and then move on. Almost be Australia-like in the way they've gone about it. They have won series in the past and continued to beat people. There are a lot of challenges in front of the team, but with what we've got we can live up to them.'

In contrast, Swann admits he wasn't too worried about the long-term future at this point.

'It was wonderful. We just sat there in the dressing-room with the Aussies and drank until the place was dry. Getting in the cars afterwards, literally with paparazzi chasing us, jumping out at traffic lights, throwing cameras in front of the car, amazing. I had this huge bottle of Veuve Clicquot, and Graham Onions was just pouring champagne in my mouth in the back seat.

'Every time I went to the loo that night, I just remember looking at myself in the mirror, and it was just making me laugh out loud how happy I was that I just screamed at myself, Yeahhhh! I still get goosebumps just thinking about it.

'I didn't last that long into the night because I was absolutely exhausted. I don't think I'd eaten all day, and I'd bowled a lot of overs. I was ready for the knackers' yard, to be honest.

'I know people say they try to savour the moment, but I go the other way. I live the moment. I'd rather be jumping up and down hugging everyone. Most people must have been sick and tired of me. Going off into the physio room by myself just to scream at the top of my voice and laugh, and have a bit of a cry about how happy I was. I'm very much into that, and I will never forget those moments, those feelings. If I'd just sat back and tried to take it all in, I always think you end up with a pretty peripheral view of things, like an outsider's view. And I thought, why should I have an outsider's view? I'm an insider.'

Broad switched on his mobile phone to receive the following message from his Ashes-winning dad, Chris: 'Bragging rights over to you.'

And amid all the mayhem, the waterfalls of champagne, all the tears of joy, Swann getting hit in the head by a cork when Corey Flintoff attempted to demonstrate what his dad had done to Ponting a few hours before, the laps of honour and the torrent of emotions, one man sat quietly trying to take in the fact that, though he had played in only one Test, his contribution to England's stunning victory had been every bit as significant as Flintoff's or Strauss's or anyone's.

Monty Panesar recalls: 'It was a very moving time, watching all the guys enjoy every minute of what we had achieved. And I sat there thinking, well, I had my little moment batting with Jimmy for 69 balls in Cardiff. Who'd have thought my *batting* would help win the Ashes?'

And when it was all done, somewhere on the balcony of the team-room on the top floor of the hotel, overlooking Tower Bridge and the lights sparkling on the surface of the Thames, Strauss turned to his Australian wife Ruth and 'suddenly realized what we'd achieved'.

'It had all been so frantic until that moment,' Strauss recalls. 'Then I thought to myself, if I ever have a better feeling than this, I'll be a very lucky man.'

Result: England won by 197 runs
Toss: England, who chose to bat
Series: England won the 5-match series 2-1
Umpires: Asad Rauf (Pakistan) and BF Bowden (New Zealand)
Match referee: RS Madugalle (Sri Lanka)
Test debut: IJL Trott (England)
Player of the match: SCJ Broad (England)
Players of the series: MJ Clarke (Australia) and AJ Strauss (England)

England 1st innings		R	M	B	4s	6s
AJ Strauss*	c †Haddin b Hilfenhaus	55	128	101	11	0
AN Cook	c Ponting b Siddle	10	19	12	2	0
IR Bell	b Siddle	72	222	137	10	0
PD Collingwood	c Hussey b Siddle	24	89	65	3	0
IJL Trott	run out (Katich)	41	125	81	5	0
MJ Prior†	c Watson b Johnson	18	57	33	2	0
A Flintoff	c †Haddin b Johnson	7	21	19	1	0
SCJ Broad	c Ponting b Hilfenhaus	37	89	69	5	0
GP Swann	c †Haddin b Siddle	18	43	28	2	0
JM Anderson	lbw b Hilfenhaus	0	5	6	0	0
SJ Harmison	not out	12	17	12	3	0
Extras	(b 12, lb 5, w 3, nb 18)	38				
Total	(all out; 90.5 overs; 414 mins)	332	(3.65 runs per over)			

Fall of wickets 1–12 (Cook, 5.3 ov), 2–114 (Strauss, 28.1 ov), 3–176 (Collingwood, 47.5 ov), 4–181 (Bell, 53.5 ov), 5–229 (Prior, 65.3 ov), 6–247 (Flintoff, 69.4 ov), 7–268 (Trott, 74.2 ov), 8–307 (Swann, 85.3 ov), 9–308 (Anderson, 86.6 ov), 10–332 (Broad, 90.5 ov)

Bowling	O	M	R	W	Econ	
BW Hilfenhaus	21.5	5	71	3	3.25	(5nb)
PM Siddle	21	6	75	4	3.57	(4nb)
SR Clark	14	5	41	0	2.92	
MG Johnson	15	0	69	2	4.60	(8nb, 3w)
MJ North	14	3	33	0	2.35	(1nb)
SR Watson	5	0	26	0	5.20	

Australia 1st innings		R	M	B	4s	6s
SR Watson	lbw b Broad	34	94	69	7	0
SM Katich	c Cook b Swann	50	169	107	7	0
RT Ponting*	b Broad	8	20	15	1	0
MEK Hussey	lbw b Broad	0	6	3	0	0
MJ Clarke	c Trott b Broad	3	9	7	0	0
MJ North	lbw b Swann	8	28	17	1	0
BJ Haddin†	b Broad	1	13	9	0	0
MG Johnson	c †Prior b Swann	11	27	24	2	0
PM Siddle	not out	26	54	38	5	0
SR Clark	c Cook b Swann	6	14	8	1	0
BW Hilfenhaus	b Flintoff	6	10	21	1	0
Extras	(b 1, lb 5, nb 1)	7				
Total	(all out; 52.5 overs; 226 mins)	160	(3.02 runs per over)			

Fall of wickets 1–73 (Watson, 22.6 ov), 2–85 (Ponting, 26.6 ov), 3–89 (Hussey, 28.3 ov), 4–93 (Clarke, 30.2 ov), 5–108 (North, 35.3 ov), 6–109 (Katich, 37.1 ov), 7–111 (Haddin, 38.4 ov), 8–131 (Johnson, 43.5 ov), 9–143 (Clark, 47.3 ov), 10–160 (Hilfenhaus, 52.5 ov)

Bowling	O	M	R	W	Econ	
JM Anderson	9	3	29	0	3.22	
A Flintoff	13.5	4	35	1	2.53	
GP Swann	14	3	38	4	2.71	
SJ Harmison	4	1	15	0	3.75	(1nb)
SCJ Broad	12	1	37	5	3.08	

England 2nd innings		R	M	B	4s	6s
AJ Strauss*	c Clarke b North	75	226	191	8	0
AN Cook	c Clarke b North	9	49	35	0	0
IR Bell	c Katich b Johnson	4	13	7	1	0
PD Collingwood	c Katich b Johnson	1	9	7	0	0
IJL Trott	c North b Clark	119	331	193	12	0
MJ Prior†	run out (Katich)	4	16	9	1	0
A Flintoff	c Siddle b North	22	24	18	4	0
SCJ Broad	c Ponting b North	29	43	35	5	0
GP Swann	c †Haddin b Hilfenhaus	63	57	55	9	0
JM Anderson	not out	15	34	29	2	0
Extras	(b 1, lb 15, w 7, nb 9)	32				
Total	(9 wickets dec; 95 overs; 408 mins)	373	(3.92 runs per over)			

Did not bat SJ Harmison

Fall of wickets 1–27 (Cook, 12.3 ov), 2–34 (Bell, 15.4 ov), 3–39 (Collingwood, 17.3 ov), 4–157 (Strauss, 54.3 ov), 5–168 (Prior, 57.6 ov), 6–200 (Flintoff, 64.1 ov), 7–243 (Broad, 74.2 ov), 8–333 (Swann, 87.4 ov), 9–373 (Trott, 94.6 ov)

Bowling	O	M	R	W	Econ	
BW Hilfenhaus	11	1	58	1	5.27	(4nb)
PM Siddle	17	3	69	0	4.05	(2w)
MJ North	30	4	98	4	3.26	(1w)
MG Johnson	17	1	60	2	3.52	(5nb, 2w)
SM Katich	5	2	9	0	1.80	
SR Clark	12	2	43	1	3.58	
MJ Clarke	3	0	20	0	6.66	

Australia 2nd innings (target: 546 runs)		R	M	B	4s	6s
SR Watson	lbw b Broad	40	101	81	6	0
SM Katich	lbw b Swann	43	98	68	7	0
RT Ponting*	run out (Flintoff)	66	157	103	10	0
MEK Hussey	c Cook b Swann	121	328	263	14	0
MJ Clarke	run out (Strauss)	0	5	4	0	0
MJ North	st †Prior b Swann	10	31	24	2	0
BJ Haddin†	c Strauss b Swann	34	95	49	6	0
MG Johnson	c Collingwood b Harmison	0	5	5	0	0
PM Siddle	c Flintoff b Harmison	10	14	14	1	0
SR Clark	c Cook b Harmison	0	1	1	0	0
BW Hilfenhaus	not out	4	10	8	1	0
Extras	(b 7, lb 7, nb 6)	20				
Total	(all out; 102.2 overs; 431 mins)	348	(3.40 runs per over)			

Fall of wickets 1–86 (Katich, 23.6 ov), 2–90 (Watson, 24.3 ov), 3–217 (Ponting, 63.6 ov), 4–220 (Clarke, 64.5 ov), 5–236 (North, 72.2 ov), 6–327 (Haddin, 94.4 ov), 7–327 (Johnson, 95.5 ov), 8–343 (Siddle, 99.4 ov), 9–343 (Clark, 99.5 ov), 10–348 (Hussey, 102.2 ov)

Bowling	O	M	R	W	Econ	
JM Anderson	12	2	46	0	3.83	(1nb)
A Flintoff	11	1	42	0	3.81	(1nb)
SJ Harmison	16	5	54	3	3.37	(4nb)
GP Swann	40.2	8	120	4	2.97	
SCJ Broad	22	4	71	1	3.22	
PD Collingwood	1	0	1	0	1.00	

Close of play
20 Aug day 1 – England 1st innings 307/8 (SCJ Broad 26*, 85.3 ov)
21 Aug day 2 – England 2nd innings 58/3 (AJ Strauss 32*, IJL Trott 8*, 28 ov)
22 Aug day 3 – Australia 2nd innings 80/0 (SR Watson 31*, SM Katich 42*, 20 ov)
23 Aug day 4 – Australia 2nd innings 348 (102.2 ov) – end of match

The Ashes Series 2009 Statistical Record

MATCH RESULTS

First Test, Cardiff, Wales, 8, 9, 10, 11, 12 July 2009
England 435 and 252/9
Australia 674/6 declared
Result: **Match Drawn**

Second Test, Lord's, London, 16, 17, 18, 19, 20 July 2009
England 425 and 311/6 declared
Australia 215 and 406
Result: **England won by 115 runs**

Third Test, Edgbaston, Birmingham, 30, 31 July, 1, 2, 3 August 2009
Australia 263 and 375/5
England 376
Result: **Match Drawn**

Fourth Test, Headingley, Leeds, 7, 8, 9 August 2009
England 102 and 263
Australia 445
Result: **Australia won by an innings and 80 runs**

Fifth Test, The Oval, London, 20, 21, 22, 23 August 2009
England 332 and 373/9 declared
Australia 160 and 348
Result: **England won by 197 runs**

Series result: **England won the series 2–1**

SERIES AVERAGES

England – Batting

Player	M	I	NO	Runs	HS	Ave	100	50
IJL Trott	1	2	0	160	119	80.00	1	0
AJ Strauss	5	9	0	474	161	52.66	1	3
KP Pietersen	2	4	0	153	69	38.25	0	1
GP Swann	5	8	1	249	63	35.57	0	2
A Flintoff	4	7	1	200	74	33.33	0	1
MJ Prior	5	9	1	261	61	32.62	0	2
SJ Harmison	2	3	2	31	19*	31.00	0	0
SCJ Broad	5	9	1	234	61	29.25	0	2
IR Bell	3	5	0	140	72	28.00	0	2
PD Collingwood	5	9	0	250	74	27.77	0	3
AN Cook	5	9	0	222	95	24.66	0	1
JM Anderson	5	8	2	99	29	16.50	0	0
RS Bopara	4	7	0	105	35	15.00	0	0
MS Panesar	1	2	1	11	7*	11.00	0	0
G Onions	3	4	2	19	17*	9.50	0	0

England – Bowling

Player	M	I	Overs	Mdns	Runs	Wkts	Ave	5
SCJ Broad	5	8	154.1	25	544	18	30.22	2
G Onions	3	5	77.4	11	303	10	30.30	0
SJ Harmison	2	3	43.0	10	167	5	33.40	0
GP Swann	5	8	170.2	30	567	14	40.50	0
JM Anderson	5	8	158.0	38	542	12	45.16	1
A Flintoff	4	7	128.5	18	417	8	52.12	1
PD Collingwood	5	4	18.0	1	76	1	76.00	0
MS Panesar	1	1	35.0	4	115	1	115.00	0
RS Bopara	4	1	8.2	1	44	0	-	0
IR Bell	3	-	-	-	-	-	-	-
AN Cook	5	-	-	-	-	-	-	-
KP Pietersen	2	-	-	-	-	-	-	-
MJ Prior	5	-	-	-	-	-	-	-
AJ Strauss	5	-	-	-	-	-	-	-
IJL Trott	1	-	-	-	-	-	-	-

Australia – Batting

Player	M	I	NO	Runs	HS	Ave	100	50
MJ Clarke	5	8	1	448	136	64.00	2	2
MJ North	5	8	1	367	125*	52.42	2	1
RT Ponting	5	8	0	385	150	48.12	1	2
SR Watson	3	5	0	240	62	48.00	0	3
BJ Haddin	4	6	0	278	121	46.33	1	1
SM Katich	5	8	0	341	122	42.62	1	1
MEK Hussey	5	8	0	276	121	34.50	1	2
NM Hauritz	3	3	1	45	24	22.50	0	0
GA Manou	1	2	1	21	13*	21.00	0	0
BW Hilfenhaus	5	6	4	40	20	20.00	0	0
PJ Hughes	2	3	0	57	36	19.00	0	0
PM Siddle	5	6	1	91	35	18.20	0	0
MG Johnson	5	6	0	105	63	17.50	0	1
SR Clark	2	3	0	38	32	12.66	0	0

Australia – Bowling

Player	M	I	Overs	Mdns	Runs	Wkts	Ave	5
BW Hilfenhaus	5	9	180.5	40	604	22	27.45	0
PM Siddle	5	9	161.4	24	616	20	30.80	1
NM Hauritz	3	5	103.2	17	321	10	32.10	0
MG Johnson	5	9	162.1	15	651	20	32.55	1
SR Clark	2	4	47.0	12	176	4	44.00	0
MJ North	5	4	67.3	13	204	4	51.00	0
MJ Clarke	5	5	19.0	1	75	1	75.00	0
SM Katich	5	3	10.0	2	27	0	–	–
SR Watson	3	2	8.0	0	49	0	–	–
BJ Haddin	4	–	–	–	–	–	–	–
PJ Hughes	2	–	–	–	–	–	–	–
MEK Hussey	5	–	–	–	–	–	–	–
GA Manou	1	–	–	–	–	–	–	–
RT Ponting	5	–	–	–	–	–	–	–

BATTING RECORDS

Leading Run Scorers (250 or more)

Player	Team	Runs	Ave
AJ Strauss	England	474	52.66
MJ Clarke	Australia	448	64.00
RT Ponting	Australia	385	48.12
MJ North	Australia	367	52.42
SM Katich	Australia	341	42.62
BJ Haddin	Australia	278	46.33
MEK Hussey	Australia	276	34.50
MJ Prior	England	261	32.62
PD Collingwood	England	250	27.77

Hundreds

Player	Team	Runs	Ground
AJ Strauss	England	161	Lord's
RT Ponting	Australia	150	Cardiff
MJ Clarke	Australia	136	Lord's
MJ North	Australia	125*	Cardiff
SM Katich	Australia	122	Cardiff
BJ Haddin	Australia	121	Cardiff
MEK Hussey	Australia	121	The Oval
IJL Trott	England	119	The Oval
MJ North	Australia	110	Leeds
MJ Clarke	Australia	103*	Birmingham

HIGHEST PARTNERSHIPS

Highest partnerships by runs (100 or more)

Partners	Runs	Wkt	Team	Ground
SM Katich, RT Ponting	239	2nd	Australia	Cardiff
MJ North, BJ Haddin	200	6th	Australia	Cardiff
AJ Strauss, AN Cook	196	1st	England	Lord's
MJ Clarke, BJ Haddin	185	6th	Australia	Lord's
MJ Clarke, MJ North	185	5th	Australia	Birmingham
MJ Clarke, MJ North	152	5th	Australia	Leeds
MJ Clarke, MJ North	143	5th	Australia	Cardiff
KP Pietersen, PD Collingwood	138	4th	England	Cardiff
RT Ponting, MEK Hussey	127	3rd	Australia	The Oval
SR Watson, RT Ponting	119	2nd	Australia	Leeds
AJ Strauss, IJL Trott	118	4th	England	The Oval
SCJ Broad, GP Swann	108	8th	England	Leeds
AJ Strauss, IR Bell	102	2nd	England	The Oval

Highest partnerships by wicket

Wkt	Runs	Partners	Team	Ground
1st	196	AJ Strauss, AN Cook	England	Lord's
2nd	239	SM Katich, RT Ponting	Australia	Cardiff
3rd	127	RT Ponting, MEK Hussey	Australia	The Oval
4th	138	KP Pietersen, PD Collingwood	England	Cardiff
5th	185	MJ Clarke, MJ North	Australia	Birmingham
6th	200	MJ North, BJ Haddin	Australia	Cardiff
7th	70	MJ North, MG Johnson	Australia	Leeds
8th	108	SCJ Broad, GP Swann	England	Leeds
9th	68	JM Anderson, GP Swann	England	Cardiff
10th	47	JM Anderson, G Onions	England	Lord's

BOWLING RECORDS

Leading Wicket Takers (10 or more)

Player	M	Overs	Mdns	Runs	Wkts	Ave
BW Hilfenhaus (Aus)	5	180.5	40	604	22	27.45
PM Siddle (Aus)	5	161.4	24	616	20	30.80
MG Johnson (Aus)	5	162.1	15	651	20	32.55
SCJ Broad (Eng)	5	154.1	25	544	18	30.22
GP Swann (Eng)	5	170.2	30	567	14	40.50
JM Anderson (Eng)	5	158.0	38	542	12	45.16
G Onions (Eng)	3	77.4	11	303	10	30.30
NM Hauritz (Aus)	3	103.2	17	321	10	32.10

Best Innings Analysis (5 wickets or more)

Player	Figs	Team	Ground
SCJ Broad	6-91	England	Leeds
PM Siddle	5-21	Australia	Leeds
SCJ Broad	5-37	England	The Oval
MG Johnson	5-69	Australia	Leeds
JM Anderson	5-80	England	Birmingham
A Flintoff	5-92	England	Lord's

Best Match Analysis (6 wickets or more)

Player	Figs	Team	Ground
GP Swann	8-158	England	The Oval
PM Siddle	6-71	Australia	Leeds
SCJ Broad	6-91	England	Leeds
MG Johnson	6-99	Australia	Leeds
SCJ Broad	6-108	England	The Oval
A Flintoff	6-119	England	Lord's
JM Anderson	6-127	England	Birmingham
NM Hauritz	6-158	Australia	Cardiff

Best Strike Rate (balls per wicket, 10 wickets or more)

Player	Wkts	SR	Team
G Onions	10	46.6	England
PM Siddle	20	48.5	Australia
MG Johnson	20	48.6	Australia
BW Hilfenhaus	22	49.3	Australia
SCJ Broad	18	51.3	England
NM Hauritz	10	62	Australia
GP Swann	14	73	England
JM Anderson	12	79	England

Most Economical Bowlers

Player	Wkts	Econ	Team
NM Hauritz	10	3.1	Australia
A Flintoff	8	3.23	England
GP Swann	14	3.32	England
BW Hilfenhaus	22	3.34	Australia
JM Anderson	12	3.43	England
SCJ Broad	18	3.52	England
PM Siddle	20	3.81	Australia
G Onions	10	3.9	England
MG Johnson	20	4.01	Australia

ENGLAND PLAYERS' TEST CAREER RECORDS

Batting

Player	Span	M	I	NO	Runs	HS	Ave	BF	SR	100	50
JM Anderson	2003–2009	42	56	27	412	34	14.20	1116	36.91	0	0
IR Bell	2004–2009	49	88	9	3144	199	39.79	6294	49.95	8	21
RS Bopara	2007–2009	10	15	0	502	143	33.46	936	53.63	3	0
SCJ Broad	2007–2009	22	31	6	767	76	30.68	1228	62.45	0	5
PD Collingwood	2003–2009	53	93	9	3565	206	42.44	7718	46.19	9	16
AN Cook	2006–2009	48	87	5	3509	160	42.79	7438	47.17	9	20
A Flintoff	1998–2009	78	128	9	3795	167	31.89	6134	61.86	5	26
SJ Harmison	2002–2009	62	84	23	742	49*	12.16	1290	57.51	0	0
G Onions	2009–2009	5	5	2	19	17*	6.33	52	36.53	0	0
MS Panesar	2006–2009	39	51	17	187	26	5.50	635	29.44	0	0
KP Pietersen	2005–2009	54	97	4	4647	226	49.96	7404	62.76	16	15
MJ Prior	2007–2009	23	37	7	1326	131*	44.20	2061	64.33	2	10
RJ Sidebottom	2001–2009	21	29	11	298	31	16.55	880	33.86	0	0
AJ Strauss	2004–2009	67	123	5	5266	177	44.62	10639	49.49	18	17
GP Swann	2008–2009	12	14	4	354	63*	35.40	452	78.31	0	3
IJL Trott	2009–2009	1	2	0	160	119	80.00	274	58.39	1	0

Bowling

Player	Span	M	I	Overs	Maidens	Runs	Wickets	Ave	5wI	10wM
JM Anderson	2003–2009	42	76	1408.5	300	4883	140	34.87	7	0
IR Bell	2004–2009	49	6	18.0	3	76	1	76.00	0	0
RS Bopara	2007–2009	10	7	49.2	7	199	1	199.00	0	0
SCJ Broad	2007–2009	22	37	697.5	134	2290	64	35.78	3	0
PD Collingwood	2003–2009	53	46	254.3	40	846	15	56.40	0	0
AN Cook	2006–2009	48	1	1.0	0	1	0	–	0	0
A Flintoff	1998–2009	78	135	2457.5	502	7303	219	33.34	3	0
SJ Harmison	2002–2009	62	113	2198.4	426	7091	222	31.94	8	1
G Onions	2009–2009	5	9	123.1	20	503	20	25.15	1	0
MS Panesar	2006–2009	39	65	1507.0	308	4331	126	34.37	8	1
KP Pietersen	2005–2009	54	31	122.3	9	518	4	129.50	0	0
MJ Prior	2007–2009	23	–	–	–	–	–	–	–	–
RJ Sidebottom	2001–2009	21	35	771.0	182	2133	77	27.70	5	1
AJ Strauss	2004–2009	67	–	–	–	–	–	–	–	–
GP Swann	2008–2009	12	21	490.1	108	1459	48	30.39	2	0
IJL Trott	2009–2009	1	–	–	–	–	–	–	–	–